CUBA

CONFRONTING THE U.S. EMBARGO

Peter Schwab

St. Martin's Press
New York

CUBA: CONFRONTING THE U.S. EMBARGO

ISBN 0-312-21620-3

Library of Congress Cataloging-in-Publication Data

Schwab, Peter, 1940-
Cuba : confronting the U.S. embargo / Peter Schwab.
p. cm.
Includes bibliographical references and index.
ISBN 0-312-21620-3
1. Economic sanctions, American--Cuba. 2. Embargo. 3. United States--Foreign economic relations--Cuba. 4. Cuba--Foreign economic relations--United States. 5. Cuba--Economic conditions--1990- I. Title.
HF 1500.5.U5S38 1998
337.7291073--dc21 98-44271
CIP

Book design: Acme Art, Inc.
First edition: January, 1999
10 9 8 7 6 5 4 3 2

CONTENTS

Acknowledgments v

Preface vii

ONE

Introduction: The Embargo and Human Rights—
U.S. and Cuban Perspectives 1

TWO

The United States, Cuba, and the Eastern Caribbean 19

THREE

A War against Public Health 53

FOUR

Starving the Cuban People 79

FIVE

The Question of Religion 103

SIX

Political Dissent 133

SEVEN

Conclusion: Cuba's Future and the Embargo 163

Notes 189

Bibliography 205

Index 217

To Michael, Bobby, . . . and Sascha

ACKNOWLEDGMENTS

This book has been a labor of love, with emphasis on the word labor. It required an enormous amount of time, attention, and concentration that exacted a toll on friends and acquaintances. This page is usually used to acknowledge those who have been helpful and supportive with their time, intellectual sustenance, encouragement, and even curiosity. But alongside the people who have been gracious with their assistance, I would like to recognize those who found me absent, who heard me say "no" more often than I enjoyed, and who managed to indulge my recitations about Cuba on the telephone even when they were not always infectious. Their consideration and attentiveness, even in my absence, is noted.

Rather than present an inventory of all those who have contributed to my efforts, I would like to mention those four people who have been especially valuable both personally and professionally, and who, in their own distinctive fashion, have endowed this book. I am proud to have their friendship. First, perhaps foremost, is my Purchase College colleague in political science Zehra F. Arat, who through her enterprise convinced me to present a proposal to St. Martin's Press in the first place. Adamantia Pollis of the Graduate Faculty of the New School for Social Research is one of the formative scholars on the subject of human rights and indisputably the most powerful intellectual presence in my life, and she has consistently been a fount of ideas and a source of inspiration. There has also and always been Albert Fried, one of *the* experts on labor history, and socialism, in the United States, now retired from Purchase College. Our conversations over the years have often resembled seminars as much as discussions and have had a significant impact upon my thinking. Lastly there is Nahama Broner, Research Director of the SAMHA New York City—Link Project at New York University, whose enthusiasm remains infectious.

In Cuba, Edgardo Valdes Lopez and Tony Guardado, of the Ministry of External Relations (MINREX), were especially helpful to me, while Leonel Lopez-Nussa, one of the country's premier painters, and his wife Wanda Lopez-Nussa, a professor of literature at the University of Havana, first guided me in circumnavigating the social and economic aspects of the embargo and the concurrent concerns confronting the people of the island. Pedro Piñeiro, at the Permanent Mission of Cuba to the United Nations, aided me in numerous ways. Those many others in Cuba who graciously granted me their time and afforded me their knowledge also deserve recognition.

Finally, Evelyn F. Cohn, as well as Sandra Levinson and her unique institution, the Center for Cuban Studies, helped me immeasurably and I am deeply appreciative. I would also like to acknowledge the efforts of those at St. Martin's Press, particularly my editor, Karen Wolny, whose ongoing zest for this project has meant a lot to me, and the production manager, Alan Bradshaw, who always responded gently to my queries. Thanks, too, to Kate Lovelady, a superb copy editor, and to Chris Cecot.

What is reflected in this work comprises solely my own views and perspective. No one else is responsible for the ideas presented herein. But without the attention afforded me by those named and those who will remain anonymous this project may very well have been a far more aimless undertaking.

Peter Schwab

PREFACE

In 1783 when John Adams, later the second president of the United States, indicated that Cuba was America's natural extension, the island appeared on America's radar screen and has never left it for long. Four decades later, in 1825, John Quincy Adams, secretary of state under President James Monroe, and the sixth U.S. president, insisted it was a law of nature that Cuba would one day "gravitate only to the North American Union." In 1898 the United States, pursuing the goal articulated by the imperial concept of Manifest Destiny, used the 1823 Monroe Doctrine, which defined the Americas as vital "to our peace and safety," as justification to intrude into Cuba's war against Spain. The United States militarily occupied Cuba from 1898 to1902, and in 1903 it imposed the Platt Amendment, which granted the United States the right of intervention as well as territory at Guántanamo Bay, which it still holds.

In 1906, the United States again occupied the nation, this time for three years, in order to strengthen what it saw as its soft underbelly in the south, determining Cuba's labor rules and thereafter virtually running the country. In the late 1930s and 1940s the mafia turned Cuba into an American gambling casino, and after 1952, when Fulgencio Batista seized power by means of a military revolt (he had earlier served as an elected president from 1940 to 1944), the U.S. government and corporate investors took control of virtually the entire economy while the American organized-crime syndicate dominated much of what remained and helped mutate the country into a brothel for U.S. tourists. For Cubans themselves there was precious little. The United States seemed to believe Cuba existed for American investors and would never just let the country determine its own future.

After January 1, 1959, when the Cuban revolution took power by defeating Batista, the United States fully expected that its overwhelming prerogatives would not be disturbed. A little bit of liberalism was presumed, even welcomed. But the radical direction of the revolution infuriated President Dwight Eisenhower and impelled him to initiate the first fatal step in America's ongoing war with Fidel Castro's Cuba—the initial phase of the embargo that was announced in October 1960. If, as some authorities maintain, an embargo is an act of war, then since that very first act, which prohibited almost all U.S. exports from being transported to Cuba, the United States has vigorously pursued a policy of war against Cuba.

The U.S. - directed invasion of the Bay of Pigs by Cuban exiles on April 17, 1961—which was soundly defeated by the Cuban military—first planned by Eisenhower and carried out by President John F. Kennedy inaugurated the combative feature of U.S. aspirations to once again fully control the future of Cuba. Immediately following the invasion and only one year after he had signed a trade agreement with the Soviet Union, Fidel Castro declared Cuba first a socialist, then a communist state (and proclaimed he would be a Marxist–Leninist until his death), and U.S. decision makers became apoplectic. Multifarious attempts to assassinate Castro were made during the Kennedy administration, energetically pursued by the president's brother Attorney General Robert Kennedy,[1] in an effort to rid Cuba of an American antagonist who was offering an alternative and more sympathetic model of economic direction to the poor and needy of the developing nations of Latin America and the Caribbean. The growing arsenal of economic weapons in the numerous U.S. embargo laws—declared by Executive Order or passed by legislation under virtually every administration from Eisenhower's to Bill Clinton's—were merely additional measures taken in the frustrated hope that Castro could be removed from power one way or the other. Indeed, the effort to unseat Fidel Castro through increased and concerted pressure on Cuba was typified by President Lyndon Johnson on December 2, 1963, when, in his often colorful but obscene style, he raised the issue with Senator William Fulbright, then chairman of the Senate Foreign Relations Committee, by asking him to think about "what we ought to do to push their nuts more than we're doing."[2] Yet Fidel Castro, this charismatic president of a very poor and underdeveloped nation of merely 11 million people, has survived nine U.S.

presidents and their attempts to take him out, and he will, should he continue to survive, soon be sparring with his tenth.

From late 1956 when Castro and his fellow *Fidelistas* broke through to the Sierra Maestra in eastern Cuba to initiate the mountain insurgency, he has been an object of fascination, adulation and hatred. Simone de Beauvoir, as well as Jean-Paul Sartre, C. Wright Mills, Leo Huberman, and Paul M. Sweezy, in their earliest writings on the revolution, spoke for the left and marked Castro as a romantic revolutionary who would lead Cuba, and by implication the newly emerging countries, away from U.S. domination. Even Herbert L. Matthews, correspondent and editorial writer for The *New York Times,* fell under his spell and in numerous articles touted Castro as a redeemer surrendering himself to a larger cause, identifying Castro as the Great Cuban Hope. Castro, recognizing Matthews' sympathies, used him to spread the gospel abroad.

One of the more charismatic leaders of the twentieth century, Castro has utilized his considerable success in driving out a hated dictator to charm the left and sway liberal opinion to his side by successfully standing against military invasion and embargo. The United States, using its extraordinary power to try to destroy this man, has failed and failed again. Each failure has only added to the reputation of and fascination with this almoner working on behalf of his people while standing virtually alone against Big Brother. It helped, of course, that alongside stood the Argentinean Che Guevara, an effective (at least in Cuba) and doctrinaire guerrilla fighter romanticized by the left as adventurous, virtuous, and the very symbol of revolutionary activity. From his emergence Castro was not perceived as an ordinary leader, but one who stood apart, battling what all client states and Third World countries were then battling—the overbearing superpower that would allow no independence from its policies. But Castro was independent; he could not be pushed around by Washington, and he consistently offended it by his impudence and very survival. As Arthur M. Schlesinger Jr. summed it up in the earliest days, in remarks about his own liberal-minded students at Harvard University, "They saw in him, I think, the hipster who in the era of the Organization Man had joyfully defied the system . . . and overturned a government. . . ."[3]

Castro's trips to the United States, mostly to participate in United Nations (UN) meetings, only added to his aura. Standing before the General Assembly he would harangue Washington and its policies and then use his considerable charm in television interviews. Whether in 1959 or in 1995 (when he addressed the United Nations during its fiftieth anniversary celebration ceremonies), his visits drove the press into a frenzy. He was always the center of attention, no matter which other world leaders were around, and the network anchors fell all over themselves to obtain interviews— in 1959 with a young revolutionary, and in 1995 with a communist statesman, one of the world's longest serving heads of state whose tough, hard-nosed approach to the United States made great copy. When Pope John Paul II traveled to Cuba to meet Castro in 1998 the world's attention was drawn to the event; a similar trip two months later to Nigeria was substantially ignored. Clearly, this political leader who for 40 years has stood against the United States in its very own backyard has used his political skills, and his very existence in the face of Washington's desperation, to attract new supporters and captivate old ones.

But it is not merely sympathy for his stand against the United States and its embargo that draws this audience to Castro. He is seen as a leader standing up for the poor, the hungry, the downtrodden, for women's rights, for the very existence of his people, and for those desperate masses in all the regions of the Third World. His ability to articulate their desires through his rhetoric in six or seven hour–long speeches has drawn to his side intellectuals such as the Colombian writer Gabriel García Márquez, a Nobel Prize laureate in literature, one of Latin America's foremost writers and Castro's most widely known foreign "brother." In a region where intellectual leftists carry enormous weight such a relationship only adds to the mystique of this aging revolutionary. Sartre played the same role in the early days of the revolution. Literary figures have always supported Castro, and they have been able to bring to his side generations of young people by drawing a sympathetic portrait of what this man is attempting to accomplish for those without sustenance in the face of constant U.S. harassment. It is, of course, an accurate portrait if one's ideological leanings are to the left or if one empathizes with the poor. For the left, Castro is one of the great leaders of the latter half of the twentieth century offering a vision, a model if you will, of what can be done about the economic and social dilemma confronting the hungry and the destitute within the underdeveloped world.

The right, however, detests him. He is viewed as a pretender who sold his country to the Soviet Union and brought Marxism to within 90 miles of America's shores. Not satisfied to violate the political rights of his people and imprison his opponents, he is seen as having created an economic catastrophe in Cuba by imposing inappropriate and alien economic policies. The right, led by the exile Cuban community in Miami, which lost everything in the revolution and will never forgive Castro that loss, views him as the devil incarnate. Even many liberals feel that their original sympathies have been betrayed. Castro is blamed for bringing the Soviet empire to the underbelly of the United States and thereby playing a role in causing the 1962 Cuban Missile Crisis. Conservatives will never let pass his survival. Seeing the United States and its values as the best hope for humanity, its constant humiliations and defeats at the hands of Castro remain unforgivable.

The economic crisis confronting Cuba since 1991, when the Soviet Union collapsed, is viewed even by many moderates as the handiwork of Castro's failed theories. The lack of food and the semi-paralyzed health care system are blamed purely on Castro's policies and the embargo is seen as quite irrelevant. Castro's concern with the redistribution of Cuba's resources to the whole population, rather than merely to the formerly wealthy elite, is interpreted as a violation of democratic standards, individualism, and capitalism—the economic model seen by many of his antagonists as the only acceptable standard.

Fidel Castro, hero or villain, has been and remains one of the more controversial figures of our time. But whether one stands with him or against him there can be no question that through 40 years of the revolution he has attempted to finally excise America's domination of Cuba and restrain its intrusiveness. Since 1783, Cuba has been coveted; after 1898 and until 1959, Cuba was seen as almost wholly a part of the United States—sovereign, but its to do with what it liked.

Castro's stand continues to draw potent support both on and off the island, but it has also created the bitterest of opponents, internally and exogenously. Since there appears to be almost no middle ground,

Castro has always been at the center of a colossal battle between ideological and political foes, which is why he never seems to go away. And because he is politically astute and talented, exudes charisma, and has had marked successes against the United States, while he still leads Cuba his opponents remain bitter and frustrated, while his supporters, although recognizing his failings and limitations, continue to marvel at his survival and respect his achievement.

Cuba: Confronting the U.S. Embargo details and analyzes the role and impact of the embargo on Cuban politics and society and the response of Fidel Castro—its most stentorian antagonist—Cuba, and its population to overcoming its consequences. Although this 40-year effort to unseat Castro disrupts and harms almost all aspects of life, I will focus on the sectors most affected and of most interest. The book is framed by the issue of human rights from both the U.S. and Cuban perspective—an ideological gulf so large that it underpins the political differences that exist between the two countries and raises the question of how extensively the implementation of the embargo violates the human rights of Cuba and its citizens. Although the country has been ravaged by the embargo, it has fought back, sometimes successfully, often not. The results of the confrontation over human rights are joined in a number of areas. Matters that relate to foreign, domestic, and social policy are all examined.

Cuba's relations with the world at large, and very specifically with the nations of the Eastern Caribbean, have been severely affected by the embargo. The political dynamic among Cuba, the United States, and the international community is observed within the context of the embargo cum blockade along with the political outcome each struggled to reach. Cuba and the Eastern Caribbean serves as a particular case study detailing how the U.S. attempted to isolate Cuba using military and economic instruments and how Fidel Castro responded. Who won and who lost is an important consideration; even more decisive is the nature of the struggle.

The composition of the Cuban health care system and its extraordinary accomplishments are analyzed within the context of what the United States has done to paralyze, even crush, its structure and accompanying technological innovations. The embargo disallows both medicine and food from being exported to the island, so the analysis of the blockade's effects on the availability of food looks into the very human problems that result when an entire nation must confront hunger.

With the meeting of Pope John Paul II and President Castro in Havana in early 1998, the changes in Cuba's religious climate since 1991 came into focus. These changes, related in part to the embargo's impact, are fascinating in and of themselves and vital to understanding why the visit took place at all. The papal journey represented the beginning of the end of the confrontation between the Catholic Church and the Cuban government, and the analysis of religion reviews the more normal relationship that now exists for the Catholic, Jewish, Santería (those descended from African peoples originally brought to Cuba as slaves), and Protestant communities. Other aspects of the meeting between these two political titans are reviewed; they jousted over questions such as human rights, political prisoners, underdevelopment, and the embargo itself, and some have remained irritants in the diplomatic relations between Havana and Vatican City.

This study also includes a discussion on political dissent, within the framework of two very different interpretations of human rights. Opposing political views inside and outside Cuba are looked at, as is the role of the Miami-based Cuban American National Foundation (CANF). In analyzing the views of the dissenters and their organizations the discussion indicates that as long as the United States and the Miami Cuban establishment push for Castro's downfall little movement toward political liberalization can be expected, and indigenous organizations will continue to be harassed.

The final chapter is an exploration of what is likely to happen in and to Cuba when the embargo is slowly lifted or eliminated altogether (one of which will surely happen in time). How will the embargo's demise and the lengthy and controversial rule of Fidel Castro affect future Cuban-American relations? Analyzed too is the possibility of the retention of the embargo in a post-Castro Cuba. The future of Cuba and the United States–Cuba relationship given either of these scenarios is investigated and serves as the conclusion to this book.

ONE

INTRODUCTION: THE EMBARGO AND HUMAN RIGHTS—U.S. AND CUBAN PERSPECTIVES

EVER SINCE THE PRESIDENCY OF JIMMY CARTER, the polemic surrounding human rights has reached a crescendo that tends to overwhelm any rational discourse on the subject. President Carter, who maintained that under his administration human rights practices would help to determine the format of U.S. foreign policy, predicated his interpretation of human rights on the Universal Declaration of Human Rights, which was approved by the United Nations General Assembly in 1948 and has since become the consecrating document for determining whether nations indeed do uphold human rights.[1]

Until 1977, human rights remained a relatively dormant aspect of U.S. foreign policy as America's cold warriors—both liberal and conservative—who accepted the demonology of the Soviet Union and the People's Republic of China enshrined a hard-headed foreign policy and developed "an ideological and bipartisan movement . . . of national purpose against the Communists."[2] Human rights had no place in the foreign policy framework of U.S. exceptionalism in which military might and client-state supporters, whatever their disposition toward human rights, were seen as vital and thus not to be criticized as long as the United States was confronted with, in the words of John F. Kennedy, "the wide dispersal of Soviet–Red Chinese power."[3] From 1934 to 1940 President Franklin D. Roosevelt had thrown his support behind then Colonel Batista allowing him to run Cuba to America's advantage through a series of puppet presidents. Roosevelt prosaically referred to Latin American dictators in the mold of Batista and the Dominican Republic's Rafael Trujillo as "S.O.B.s, but *our* S.O.B.s," a notion strenuously rejected by Carter, whose "semi-pacifism and strong religious convictions—a belief that American Protestant ideals could be exported through . . . respect for human rights" led him to try to lead by "moral example."[4]

But the Western political philosophy of rights upon which the Universal Declaration is based

> provides only one particular interpretation of human rights, and this Western notion may not be successfully applicable to non-Western areas for several reasons: ideological differences whereby economic rights are given priority over individual civil and political rights and cultural differences whereby the philosophic underpinnings defining human nature and the relationship of individuals to others and to society are markedly at variance with Western individualism. Consequently, application in non-Western countries of Western-oriented doctrines such as the Universal Declaration of Human Rights has frequently meant that legal norms whose implementation is contingent upon the state lack the substantive meaning such rights have in the West.[5]

An underlying precept of the Western perspective of human rights, which emphasizes individual and political rights, is that these rights are natural, "prior to and supreme over the sovereignty of the state,"[6] and as such are held to be universally applicable, which infers unquestioning acceptance by all nations; this leads to the rejection out of hand of divergent human rights assumptions based on non-Western ideological values. As John T. Wright explains, the Western concept of human rights based on the philosophical writings of John Locke, Thomas Hobbes, Jean-Jacques Rousseau, and Baron de Montesquieu

> is derived from a view of the human person as possessing inalienable rights anterior to the creation of the state and thus beyond its legitimate reach. No longer absolute, the state is dependent upon the consent of the governed (popular sovereignty) and is itself subject to the law of the land. For the state to act against any individual such actions must be taken in the manner provided by law. Thus human rights in the West are an individualistic conception relying on legal-judicial mechanisms. . . . The notion of natural rights had established a barrier around the individual across which the state might not pass.[7]

Freedom of speech and opinion, the right of peaceful assembly and association, the ability to freely practice one's religion, and ownership of *private* property are among the rights enshrined in the Universal Declaration while economic rights, such as the right to food, which comprise only 4 of its 30 articles, are essentially neglected and the notion of the group, rather than the individual—a notion that is the basis of most Third World cultures—is given short shrift. No concession is made to "the notion of the primacy of the group and the submission of the individual to the group"[8] to insure that the state can meet economic and social needs for the entire society. This "lack of consideration for economic and social rights is one of the major differences between the Western doctrine and other cultural traditions,"[9] and the result of emphasizing political as opposed to economic, social, or cultural rights is that prevention of hunger, ensuring an adequate health care system, and providing shelter and clothing are not seen in the West as *fundamental* rights. Human dignity, and a collective and social cohesion in which "man is not and should not be a competitive, atomized being, but a social being [whose] rights are inextricably interwoven and interdependent with his duties . . . [and] by contrast to civil and political rights, economic, social, and cultural rights are more salient"[10] is neglected in the Universal Declaration.

The American ideology regarding human rights was precisely expressed in 1975 by John Scali, then chief U.S. delegate to the UN, who extolled the position of the United States and rejected the approach taken by the Third World and socialist states, although he sympathized with it. Scali clarified how Third World reality diverges from the Western historical experience and called for a new approach that was ultimately repudiated by the United States:

> The concept of human rights which we share with many other Western nations has evolved over the centuries. It has its roots in the Judeo-Christian emphasis on personal salvation. It has been molded by the historical experience of the British people, from Magna Carta to their present unwritten constitution. The evolving concept of human rights first found logical expression in the works of the 17th and 18th Century philosophers of the Enlightenment. It found practical expression in the events of the American and French Revolutions. Indeed, it is the stirring rhetoric of these two revolutionary periods which continues to best convey our fundamental vision of human rights today.
>
> This Western tradition of human rights centers on the individual and on his need for protection against the society and the state. By freedom we mean personal freedom, the freedom to dissent, to be different, to oppose as well as agree.
>
> Today Americans still tend to accept their own view of man's relationship to society unquestionably and we assume that the rest of the world does too. We sometimes forget that the vast majority of the world's peoples have not been raised in the Western tradition, that they do not automatically share our values and that they, therefore, view human rights issues from a different perspective.
>
> Even our own Western society has produced social thinkers, such as Karl Marx, who have taken a completely different approach to human rights . . . on the need of the masses for protection against the individual, the capitalist exploiter. [Marxism's] collective view of human rights emphasizes the economic as opposed to the political aspects of man's place in society and thus focuses on how material wealth, rather than political power is shared.
>
> No doubt this view of human rights serves as a rationalization, a shield behind which some governments perpetuate their authoritarian regimes. . . . We should realize, however, that this view has a strong appeal throughout the Third World. Personal liberties are fine, is the attitude of many, but you can't eat them. You can't wear

> them, nor will they build a roof over your head. Many Third World leaders feel that the extension of civil liberties must take second place to economic development.
>
> Let us concentrate on securing the widest possible agreement in the United Nations on the proposition that both individual and group rights are vitally important, that neither is incompatible with the other and that the promotion of both is a legitimate pursuit for the international community.[11]

Scali's appraisal, both honest and forthright, establishes the boundaries that clearly separate the Western concept of human rights from that upheld by socialist and Third World nations. But it leaves out important matters that further inflame Third World leaders when it comes to the question of what human rights really mean and why they are so feverishly imposed on the Third World.

Most currently emerging nations were not even independent in 1948 and indeed remained under colonial and rather dictatorial control by those very nations now extolling the virtues of political rights. They remained tied to the Metropole colonial states so that not only were they denied the opportunity to vote on the Universal Declaration, but also, because the United States was in such a dominant position in the UN during that era, alternative cultural values vis-à-vis human rights were hardly even considered as relevant to the discussion. Even those Third World countries that were independent, such as Cuba, were so economically managed and politically repressed by their patrons that they were barely in a position to voice opposition to the wishes and demands of the United States. "The Declaration was ratified while the Cold War was under way and the economy of the United States was in full expansion," and nations that abstained or even voted for the Declaration such as Panama, Brazil, the Philippines, and Saudi Arabia objected to it whole or in part.[12] The Universal Declaration was seen by many nations as simply an additional instrument of cultural imposition and Western imperialism.

Since the Declaration was passed in the General Assembly of the United Nations, which according to its charter may merely make recommendations,[13] "it was not a treaty and was not intended to impose legal obligations."[14] The question of whether or not the Declaration is binding goes beyond the issue of how enforceable a General Assembly vote is. The Statute of the International Court of Justice specifies in Article 38 that customary law can be considered binding when the alleged custom shows "evidence of a general practice accepted as law." If one surveys the states that compose the international community, no general practice regarding human rights is evident, hence "although what is customary law cannot be precisely defined, the principles of human rights do not fall within the domain of customary law and states are not bound by them."[15]

Many Third World nations, and most particularly Cuba, do not reject democracy and human rights, as the United States so flagrantly complains, but as Adamantia Pollis explains,

> the ideal is a participatory democracy in which the multiple elements of the whole—the nation-state—are part of the entire process for determining the well-being and the welfare of the social whole. . . . In the West, it is individuals or special interest groups competing to further their perceived self-interest operating within agreed upon rules of the game that maintains cohesion. In Cuba there is a presumption that interest groups are interdependent and mutually reinforcing within a larger unity. The parameters therefore of each political system differ and both lay claim to democracy.[16]

In the United States, adherence to the principles laid down by the European political philosophers and advanced by Thomas Jefferson and James Madison in the Declaration of Independence and Federalist Paper No.10, and eventually enshrined in the Constitution of the United States created a new conception of popular sovereignty and individual rights, incorporating the sanctity and protection of the rights of private property, as well as preventing the "malady" of the "equal division of property."[17] However, the attempt to impose these ideas on societies culturally, historically, and ideologically at variance with Western norms has, at least since 1977, created an antagonistic construct within which issues of politics and morality are fiercely debated but never really resolved.

Indeed, the very support given by Washington to Third World leaders who blatantly violate the political rights of their citizens calls into question both the honesty and seriousness of the United States when it condemns human rights violations in Cuba. Can a nation that supports Indonesia, has relations with Nigeria, or, as Secretary of State Madeleine Albright emphasized, has "moved well down the road toward building a constructive, strategic partnership" with China,[18] all of which have been accused of illegally imprisoning, torturing, and murdering thousands of their citizens, limiting press freedoms, and disallowing anything remotely resembling free and legitimate elections, really be taken seriously when it accuses Cuba of human rights violations? The double standard indicates that the U.S. position is based less on the issue of human rights and more on its fury in seeing Fidel Castro retaining power in a communist state 90 miles away and in the heart of America's sphere of interest, while being frustrated that its 37-year-long embargo has been unable to alter Cuba's political dynamic. Or as Castro brazenly put it in 1961, "what the imperialists cannot forgive us . . . is that we have made a socialist revolution under the noses of the United States."[19]

"Emotion" may be "the enemy of pragmatism in Cuban relations,"[20] but the language and the rhetoric of the conflict does reflect controversy over the substance of human rights, or community rights vs. individual rights, and despite Scali's 24-year-old appeal to incorporate more nuance into the argument, the polemic shows few signs of being recast.

FIDEL CASTRO'S CUBA AND HUMAN RIGHTS

As early as 1958, while still in the Sierra Maestra, Castro wrote, "I seek absolute sovereignty for the country in the face of all political and economic interference, solidarity with peoples oppressed by dictatorships or assaulted by powerful countries. . . . As the path of all great ideals is strewn with obstacles, my only future aspiration is to continue battling."[21] To that end the 1976 Cuban constitution reiterates Fidel's implicit rebuke to the United States; it condemns imperialism and imperialist intervention and only within that context "guarantees the liberty and full dignity of man, the enjoyment of his rights, the exercise and fulfillment of his duties and the integral development of his personality."[22]

Political rights, however, are constrained in that "None of the freedoms which are recognized for citizens can be exercised contrary . . . to the existence and objectives of the socialist state or contrary to the decision of the Cuban people to build socialism and communism";[23] that is, individual rights cannot be used, or more accurately abused, when their use would lead to the erosion of the goals of the revolution. As Article 52 of the constitution makes clear, "Citizens have freedom of speech and of the press *in keeping with the objectives of socialist society*" (my italics). Political rights must, therefore, not be employed in any way that would further the cause of American "imperialism" or "intervention,"[24] since that would be "contrary to the Revolution."[25] If, as Castro said in 1958, sovereignty is to be maintained in the face of U.S. activity to impugn that independence, then political rights, in terms of what is defined by the state as good for the larger collective whole, the community of Cuba, are always defined within the context of U.S. maneuvers against the island. Individual human rights are not rejected out of hand but are placed within parameters that center on the larger political rights and economic needs of Cuban society. Since the United States is hardly an innocent bystander (and has not been, since prior to the implementation of the first embargo act in 1960), the advocacy of political and civil rights by internal dissidents is often seen by the state as merely a tool through which some seek to advocate a revival of America's imperial tendencies in Cuba.

Despite the limitations placed on individual political rights, clearly the "system appears to have room for slack, even for disagreement."[26] Criticism of the bureaucracy, and even of many domestic policies, is tolerated, as anyone who has attended local meetings of the Municipal Assemblies of People's Power can attest to. Tomás Gutiérrez Alea's Cuban film *Guantanamera,* released internationally in 1997, riotously and caustically ridiculed Cuba's bureaucratic morass. Discussion in homes and at various dinner tables reflecting on the strength or weakness of this or that aspect of Cuban socialism are conventional, though debate is usually narrowly focused. There is clearly a line, which everyone is aware of, that cannot be crossed. The perception by Americans that no one inside the country can criticize Cuba or its policies is false, but the extent of that freedom is severely constrained; the limits were broadly defined by Fidel Castro in 1961 in his oft repeated phrase "Within the Revolution everything; outside the Revolution, nothing."[27] As Cuba's Ambassador Fernando Remirez de Estenoz, the 48-year-old head of the Cuban Interests Section in Washington, reiterated in 1998,

> we have restrictions . . . but it's our own system . . . because it's the first time we have our own system. It's a different country [than the United States] with different traditions, with a different history. And you have to consider the fact that we are facing a hostile condition from the United States.[28]

Economic and social human rights are fundamental in Cuba. The state, according to the Cuban constitution, is obligated to provide the essential elements required by any people for survival (such as medical care and employment), while the population in turn is obligated to accept that "The Republic of Cuba is a socialist state," that the "state organizes, directs *and controls* the economic life of the nation in accordance with the central plan of socioeconomic development,"[29] and that "socialist state property, which is the property of the entire people, becomes irreversibly established over the lands that do not belong to small farmers or to cooperatives formed by the same."[30]

In essence the social contract between the citizenry and the state does not accept the premise of individual rights bestowed by natural law and played out competitively, but, on the contrary, it recognizes the state as being the repository of social and political rights in order to fulfill the economic and social needs of the entire people. In this way, no one class or group of people can take economic advantage of another. Consequently, only "under socialism and communism, when man has been freed from all forms of exploitation—slavery, servitude and capitalism—can full dignity of the human being be attained."[31] The state in Cuba then "is preeminent, claiming that it is and should be the foremost legitimate reference group. The state's power, in turn, is buttressed by traditional attitudes toward group cohesion" in which rights are conceived through the interrelationship of different reference groups, and it is the "nature of that interaction that sets rights."[32]

All Cubans are guaranteed an eight-hour work day, while the state is obligated to provide social security and free health care including the most sophisticated procedures. The opportunity to study at all educational levels free of cost and to secure "comfortable" housing is given to all citizens, while the state has the responsibility to see to it "that no disabled person be left without adequate means of subsistence" and "that no child be left without schooling, food, and clothing." These primary economic and social rights are guaranteed by Article 8 and Chapter VI of the Cuban constitution, which define the obligation of the state to provide human rights and to ensure, and if necessary mediate among, what are referred to as Fundamental Rights, Duties and Guarantees.

Women's rights are accorded special mention in the Cuban constitution, and consequently women make up 27 percent of the National Assembly of People's Power, the national legislature, which places it fifteenth in the world's parliamentary ranking of women in legislative office, while more than 13 percent of the Politburo of the Cuban Communist Party are women. A Women's Commission on Employment prevents discrimination against women in the workplace, and the government subsidizes a host of women's programs including free education, day-care and health care, including contraception and abortion. Women are also guaranteed maternity leaves, equal pay, and are given preference in promotions. The Federation of Cuban Women is granted special status in the constitution and in addition to its role in organizing and representing it has the power to initiate legislation. Largely as a result of the efforts of its leader, Vilma Espín, who has presided over the organization since its inception only one year after the revolution, women constitute 60 percent of medium- and top-level technicians, 46 percent are economically active in industry and agriculture, and 50 percent of the total workforce is made up of women. Of the country's registered student body women make up about half, and all women are provided the opportunity to volunteer for active military service. In effect Cuba has established national machinery to ensure equal rights and equal protection for women.[33] Few nations can genuinely claim a similar commitment to the development of women's economic and social rights.

The human rights guaranteed to the Cuban people speak not to the individual's pursuit of wealth but to certifying that all citizens have the opportunity to contribute to "the good of society and to the satisfaction of individual needs."[34] Individual needs and rights are categorized solely within the context of what is good for the overall society and therefore their meaning is totally different from any Western conception. Individual rights qua the individual are spurned while individual rights *within* the collective are held up as the highest ideal. When the United States and Cuba speak to the concept of individual rights their point of reference is marked by such dissimilitude that not only are they talking past one another but also conceptually they are referring to two totally different doctrines.

The relative value accorded economic/social rights on the one hand and political/civil rights on the other is marked, although not always apparent, in that in Cuba the former have been expanded measurably while the latter are not viewed as either autonomous or individualistic. As Jorge I. Domínguez indicated as early as 1979, the "power of the central government has grown, enabling the government to make impressive redistributions of social and economic resources and to achieve many desirable human rights conditions. Yet there is a trade-off between the growth of centralized power and the liberty and equality of individuals to exercise political power. A single ideology, endorsed by the central governing institutions, prevails."[35] That of course is true, but it is beside the point. For Cuba it is not a question of a trade-off, but, as Fidel Castro pointed out in 1996, of meeting human needs:

> We have talked fundamentally . . . about human settlements in the cities, but we should not forget that the rural areas . . . are more and more abandoned. It is estimated that in Latin America, in a period of just over two decades, 85 percent of the population will amass in the cities. Don't governments care about this? Can the state consider itself excluded from responsibility in the solution of these problems? Is it correct not to consider housing an essential human right? We must proclaim that we do not live in a jungle. . . . Each family

> deserves decent housing, and that should be considered a universal human right. In short, we have the right to live in peace and with honor, to be allowed to work for our peoples, and for the elimination of unjust and criminal economic blockades, not to be exploited, not to be looted, not to be deprecated or treated with repugnant xenophobia.[36]

In the Spring of 1998, the fiftieth anniversary year of the signing of the Universal Declaration of Human Rights, Cuba's foreign minister Roberto Robaina spoke in Geneva before the United Nations Commission on Human Rights. He protested the simplicity of the Universal Declaration in that it refused to account for divergent approaches to human rights. His tone and approach was not meant simply to win political points but to rebut the position of the United States, which had advanced a resolution to censure Cuba for its human rights practices. The resolution specifically demanded that Havana promote and protect human rights and fundamental freedoms and called upon the government to release political prisoners. Robaina pleaded with the delegates to remember that

> nearly two-thirds of mankind were living under the colonial and neo-colonial yokes when the document was adopted. Tens of millions of human beings remained neglected at the periphery of international law. For those, the most traumatic experience was not war itself, but underdevelopment and the alienation forced on them.
>
> Integrality in the concept of the exercise of human rights was disregarded by those who would rather have a simple abstract declaration of the rights of the individual, with no reference whatsoever to the environment for its exercise. These people are the same, and not by chance, who nowadays, from their thrones in the North, are trying to use the Universal Declaration of Human Rights as the holy book of their ideological fundamentalism and as the foundation of their intolerance towards those who think differently.
>
> As the duality and interrelation of the duties and rights of the human being in his social life were ignored, minimal principles of social interrelation, like the respect of human dignity and the need of solidarity among men, were consigned to oblivion.[37]

What the foreign minister did in his curt analysis was to tie the U.S. attempt to force the Universal Declaration of Human Rights upon Cuba to the American embargo by maintaining that the Declaration was merely another instrument used by the United States to castigate Cuba. In effect Robaina viewed the Declaration as simply an adjunct to America's embargo acts. It should not be surprising, therefore, that Cuba sees U.S. support for human rights as a hypocritical policy that lacks seriousness and is infused with contradiction. As Robaina pointed out, "as a result of the conceptual detachment of individual rights from those of human groups and peoples, some of the diplomats who voted for and even proclaimed themselves promoters of the Universal Declaration of Human Rights were defending, at the same time, the survival of . . . colonial empires. It was necessary to wait until 1960 to adopt [a resolution] regarding the grant of independence to colonial countries and peoples."[38]

One month after Robaina made his presentation, the Geneva-based Human Rights Commission voted down the American resolution by a vote of 19 to 16, with 18 members, mostly Latin American nations, abstaining, due certainly to some degree to their fear of running afoul of the United States. Just prior to the April vote Carl Johan Groth of Sweden, the UN Special Rapporteur on Human Rights in Cuba, told the commission that while Castro's government did repress its domestic critics the U.S. embargo was partly to blame, since it caused a "tragic shortage of material goods [and] untold hardships."[39]

The UN Commission on Human Rights, despite the narrowness of the vote, in its own way indicated agreement with Cuba's position that the Universal Declaration of Human Rights could not be divorced from implementation of the U.S. embargo and that Washington's stand against Cuba was certainly not seeped in idealism or purity. Politics was an important factor, and Cuba's approach to human rights was granted a healthy dose of legitimacy by the commission's decision to vote down the U.S.–sponsored resolution. The international community appears to be losing patience with the dogmatic stand taken by the United States, while Cuba's more nuanced posture, though certainly not unassailable, is viewed more sympathetically, particularly in light of the fact that since 1991 Havana has made important overtures to its critics. For example, when Canada's prime minister Jean Chrétien visited Cuba shortly after the UN Commission on Human Rights vote, Fidel Castro, in welcoming him to Havana, paid his respects to Canada and acknowledged that it "has never joined in the longest, the most unfair and brutal blockade in history. Thank you."[40]

THE EMBARGO AND HUMAN RIGHTS

The preamble of the charter of the United Nations refers to the determination of the peoples of the UN to "practice tolerance and live together in peace with one another as good neighbors,"[41] while Article I declares that among the UN's purposes and principles is the development of "friendly relations among nations based on respect for the principle of equal rights and self-determination of peoples. . . ."[42] With perhaps the important exception of President Jimmy Carter, both the Executive Office and the Congress of the United States have not made more than perfunctory attempts to ameliorate the dispute over human rights between the United States and Cuba. Since 1991 particularly, as the Soviet Union vanished from history, Cuba has ceased to be a threat to the national security of the United States, and little reason remains for the lack of tolerance displayed by Washington that has kept Cuba from practicing true self-determination.

Prior to the last decade of the twentieth century the United States had at least a plausible argument in its ruthless determination to isolate Castro, since it was convinced that Cuba, as a dependency and ally of the Soviet Union, posed a threat to America's vital interests. Continuing efforts by Moscow, even after the 1962 Cuban Missile Crisis, to increase its military leverage vis-à-vis the United States, as in 1969 during the presidential administration of Richard Nixon when it initiated but eventually aborted an effort to develop submarine facilities near the coastal city of Cienfuegos,[43] gave Washington ample reason to be concerned.

Through the1980s, Cuba was also seen by U.S. decision makers as a communist nation devoted to aiding the spread of Marxist revolutions, particularly as concerned the Caribbean region, Central America, and Angola and Ethiopia, where some 36,000 Cuban combat troops were stationed and engaged in battles to support their respective governments. Although Cuba had every right to support the nations, especially since the United States was actively and militarily, largely through proxy forces, fighting to overthrow both governments, the cold war at least gave rationale to the American dogma.

But those rationalizations evaporated in 1991, a time when Washington, as the sole remaining super power, could easily have dropped its Great Power hubris and initiated a process of accommodation and negotiation so as to, as the UN Charter stated, "practice tolerance." But it refused to do so. Instead, spotting what it thought was the opportunity to finally dump a much-weakened Castro, in 1992 and then again in 1996 it further tightened the screws of the embargo.

It was in 1960 that a partial embargo was initiated and American exports to the island were prohibited. In 1961 diplomatic relations were severed. By 1962 a virtual total embargo on imports and exports was put in place, while in 1964 provisions regarding the licensing of food and medicine were developed that made it all but impossible for those items to reach Cuba from the United States. In 1992 Congress and the president approved legislation disallowing U.S. subsidiaries abroad from trading with Cuba, while in 1996 the notorious Helms-Burton bill was passed by Congress and signed by President Bill Clinton that imposed the embargo on third-country trade, thus bringing extraterritoriality under the rubric of the embargo. Whether liberal or conservative, Democrat or Republican, most presidents from Eisenhower to Clinton have seen Cuba in the same light and have acted similarly. Castro has to go and the embargo has to be enforced or further expanded despite the fact that in 1998 the Pentagon declared that Cuba was not a threat to the United States.

Although in 1975 Secretary of State Henry Kissinger, serving then under President Gerald Ford, indicated that he was prepared to "move in a new direction"[44] and some expansion in commerce with Cuba was granted to subsidiaries of U.S. firms, the "new direction" was quickly suspended as Cuba continued to deploy troops to Angola.

The sole exception to the parade of presidents who viewed Cuba through the same ideological lens was Jimmy Carter. His secretary of state Cyrus Vance advocated improving relations while Carter supported undertakings toward "ending the embargo on food and medicines . . . saying he would not oppose efforts in Congress to do so."[45] Negotiations between the two states were begun in April 1977, at President Carter's behest, "to raise with the Cubans the possibility of opening interests sections in one another's capitals . . . because even though we had ruled out formal diplomatic relations until the fundamental problems between us had been resolved, we needed direct communications if those problems *were* to be worked out."[46] As Vance noted,

> At the outset of the administration, we had sought to improve relations with Cuba. In my confirmation hearing I signaled our willingness to open a dialogue with Havana. Although it was not our first objective, President Carter and I believed U.S. interests would be served by maintaining diplomatic relations with Cuba. . . .[47]

With agreement having been rapidly reached, on September 1, 1977, a U.S. Interests Section (a low-level diplomatic office that at least allows communication) was opened in the Swiss embassy in Havana while the Cubans opened one in the Czechoslovakian embassy in Washington, with each staffed by a handful of diplomats. According to Wayne S. Smith, who became the second head of the Interests Section in 1979,

> Calling off the cold war with Cuba was intended to signal a more flexible, pragmatic U.S. approach and to make it clear that we no longer intended to respond to all situations in the developing world as though each were a zero-sum game with the Soviets.[48]

Although the interest sections have remained, the attempted opening to Cuba failed. As Cuba sent additional civilian advisors in support of Angola's leftist government, and the U.S. intelligence agencies, congressional opponents of Carter's approach to Cuba, as well as his National Security advisor Zbigniew Brzezinski, who as much as anyone represented the old cold war establishment, falsely claimed the advisors were troops and not civilians, they created such a political hullabaloo that it forced an end to the negotiations with Cuba that might eventually have led to a détente between the two nations. Carter, who was not nearly as concerned about Cuba's actions as were his cold war opponents, nonetheless acceded to the pressure. Cuba then moved to deploy combat troops to buttress Ethiopia's Marxist government, which absolutely doomed the newly budding relationship.[49] When Ronald Reagan, who defeated Carter in the 1980 presidential election, took office the following January the traditional harsh line toward Cuba was reinstated and has remained in place.

What Carter's abortive attempt at achieving a *modus vivendi* with Cuba demonstrated was that accommodation was entirely feasible and that the problem was not so much with the Cubans as it was with the traditional U.S. foreign policy establishment and the powerful cold warriors in Congress who were not about to accept what they viewed as an inconsonant policy so out of sync with what can only be termed their obtuse perspective.

Carter's diplomatic foray did highlight the contradiction of the embargo, which has as its stated goal the expansion of political rights in Cuba. It has failed for almost four decades. Carter's policies also showed that the United States could work with Castro. During the negotiations U.S. representatives were given access to Americans who had been held in Cuban prisons, some of whom had been incarcerated almost since the beginning of the revolution; 3,600 political prisoners were released; "visas were granted to selected Cuban citizens for visits to the United States; [and] a bilateral agreement on maritime boundaries and fishing rights was concluded."[50] As Carter moderated U.S. policy, so too did Castro modify Cuba's position.

The real goal of many of the embargo's supporters is not the achievement of better relations with Cuba that might lead to increased political rights for its citizens, but the overthrow of Fidel Castro. In profiling the inconsistency of America's embargo war against Cuba, Carter developed for all who cared to notice perspective as to the reasons why the embargo has been a conspicuous failure: Written in the lofty language of trying to move Cuba toward democracy, its real purposes are treacherous and violent and have nothing at all to do with achieving that goal. Its unstated but obvious effort is the violation of the human rights of Cubans by trying to destroy and eliminate the only leader in contemporary times who has tried to stand up for the Cuban people. As Fidel so dramatically put it in 1998, "No state should pretend to have the right to starve another people to death. That is turning a nation into a ghetto and imposing on it a new version of the Holocaust."[51]

It is to his everlasting credit that President Carter tried to break the mold. His overall failure gave insight to the power of the forces arrayed against Castro in the United States and to the real lack of interest of those individuals, groups, and agencies in advancing human rights. The human rights argument is obviously fallacious and exposes the hypocrisy and deceptive nature of the U.S. embargo.

Despite the fact that Carter emphasized the aspects of human rights that fall outside the parameters of Cuba's experiences, his endeavor to improve U.S./Cuban relations by trying to reduce the severity of the embargo was a wholesome challenge to the mores of the cold war. And although he was labeled a naif for his failed efforts by traditional cold war advocates,[52] his struggle to alter preconceived notions took courage and pluck. Insofar as human rights and Cuba is concerned, the fetidness of the cold war, as typified by the embargo, continues in the United States.

TWO

THE UNITED STATES, CUBA, AND THE EASTERN CARIBBEAN

IN ITS CONTINUING EFFORT TO ISOLATE CUBA from the international community and to reassert its hegemony in the Caribbean region, the United States under President Ronald Reagan quietly but steadily developed its military interests in the Eastern Caribbean.[1] While the press and the public have been fascinated by recent events in Nicaragua, Panama, Haiti and Cuba, they have largely ignored U.S. activity in the West Indies that have turned these tourist havens into centers of military intrigue. Indeed, since 1981 many of the region's eight micro-states and ten colonial territories have become U.S. clients representing U.S. military and economic policy. To confront the ideological challenge of Cuba the Eastern Caribbean governments have been turned into "full scale proxies of the United States."[2]

In the past two decades the United States has militarized the region and incorporated virtually all the independent states of the Eastern Caribbean into a maritime police force. Collective security networks have been established to guard against Cuba's influence ushering in what has been called a "second cold-war period in the Caribbean."[3] Even with the demise of the Soviet Union and the subsequent cultivation of improved relations with Cuba, there continues to be a particularly noticeable conservatism in the region stemming from the insertion of U.S. military aid and the growing trend of international capitalism.[4] As James Mitchell, prime minister of St. Vincent and the Grenadines, acknowledged in 1996, "We've surrendered our sovereignty. . . .We've given the U.S. all the cooperation in the world."[5]

Dominica, Antigua and Barbuda, St. Kitts-Nevis, Barbados, St. Lucia, St. Vincent and the Grenadines, and Grenada are elements of Cuban containment providing small military bases, military support, or armed forces that serve U.S. interests (Trinidad and Tobago, though closely tied to the United States does not officially participate in the region's militarization). In return, beginning in the 1980s the United States sharply increased military aid to these countries and economic support to their conservative governments and political parties. While incorporating the area into an anti-Cuban cold war by developing surrogate states, the United States also influenced the internal political dynamics of the region, shifting them to the right.

U.S. foreign policy in the Caribbean has historically been predicated on the Monroe Doctrine,[6] on the fact that more than 50 percent of oil imports are shipped through the region, and on Castro's Cuba—seen first as a Moscow-directed subversive state, and after 1991 as a menace of its own. In 1979, however, the United States viewed itself as under siege in the Caribbean. The Sandinista triumph in Nicaragua and Maurice Bishop's coup in Grenada threw the United States into something of a frenzy. President Reagan saw Soviet-Cuban power projected into the region and vowed to "isolate or liquidate"[7] leftist forces; he supported intrusion in the internal affairs of Caribbean states to insure the survival of conservative governments in the face of the perceived growing Cuban threat. U.S. intervention in the Caribbean region was shifted in 1981 to the Eastern Caribbean with a single-minded determination to contain the virus of the Cuban revolution. As Thomas O. Enders, assistant secretary of state for inter-American affairs during the Reagan administration, explained in 1984, "It has been and remains a principal objective of the Government of Cuba to stimulate and support the overthrow of non-Communist governments in the Western Hemisphere and to replace them with

Marxist-Leninist regimes acceptable to Cuba. Cuban success would be contrary to the national interests of the United States."[8]

U.S. STRATEGY

In 1985 General John R. Galvin, commander-in-chief of the U.S. Southern Command, testified before the House of Representatives Subcommittee on Military Construction on the U.S. military buildup in the Caribbean. He maintained that U.S. policy was predicated on "an enormous amount of effort being done by the International Marxist-Leninists to do things there. . . . The threat is an inpouring of the kind of pressure that is very destabilizing."[9] Galvin's thesis was supported by Deputy Assistant Secretary of Defense for Inter-American Affairs Nestor D. Sanchez, when he affirmed that "U.S. interests in Central America and the Caribbean are based upon hard economic, geographic and political realities. It has been our policy to support . . . institutional reform where needed. The military construction program for the region is an essential element of this overall policy."[10] In nonbureaucratic parlance, "the United States saw Cuba as the head of a strategy to weaken U.S. influence and jeopardize declared U.S. security interests in the region."[11] In his grandiose effort to nullify Cuba's influence in the Eastern Caribbean, to in effect "embargo" it from its neighbors and deny it political or economic support, Reagan initiated a confrontational approach leading to a militaristic stand in pursuit of U.S. ambitions. A newly developed vigilant containment of Cuba and communism from the perspective of a conservative cold-war tendency virtually guaranteed that the United States would pursue a far more proactive approach to the Caribbean in order to keep Cuba from generating any further support. The policy was to be carried out predominately by the armed forces of the Caribbean who would protect U.S. economic and security interests; in return, the United States would shore up conservative local elites by providing military and economic funding. The United States would contain Cuba, Nicaragua, and Grenada while working to overthrow the governments of those countries, thus preventing the fall of any further dominos. Containment was to be energetically pursued.

THE MILITARIZATION OF THE EASTERN CARIBBEAN

Between 1980 and 1986 annual U.S. military aid to the states of the Eastern Caribbean jumped from $200,000 to $20 million. Total military assistance during those years reached a whopping $85 million with most of the monies being used to support the Eastern Caribbean Regional Security System (RSS)—a newly developed American-sponsored regional security pact—and to construct U.S. military bases. The RSS Mutual Assistance Pact was signed in October 1982 by Barbados, Antigua and Barbuda, Dominica, St. Lucia, and St. Vincent and the Grenadines. St. Kitts-Nevis joined in 1983 and Grenada became a member in 1985, two years after the U.S. invasion of Grenada that overthrew its Revolutionary Military Council. Headquartered in Bridgetown, Barbados, the RSS also has a branch office in Antigua, which is used for intelligence activities. Special Service Units (SSUs) were established by the RSS to provide military backbone and are composed of elements of local police forces under the control of the respective member states. The United States has furnished the SSUs with military supplies, naval coast guard vessels, vehicles, weapons, and communication equipment. The RSS activates the SSUs when it is agreed there is an individual or collective threat to the national security of its members. To put muscle into the enforcement process in 1982, the United States allocated an additional $5 million in foreign military sales credits to Barbados for its defense force and coast guard to be used in support of the RSS.

The RSS has not taken a conservative approach to its task but has used as its model the aggressive actions taken by Barbados in defending the region's status quo. In 1979, prior to the creation of the RSS, Barbados sent its shore patrol to Dominica and St. Vincent and the Grenadines, successfully putting down attempted coups in both states. It took action again in 1981 when the government of Dominica under Prime Minister Eugenia Charles asked for help in battling antigovernment insurgents; France also dispatched troops from Martinique to assist the Barbadians in quelling the revolt in Dominica.[12]

The SSUs participated in the invasion when the United States invaded Grenada on October 25, 1983, and overthrew the Marxist-leaning Revolutionary Military Council, led by Deputy Prime Minister

Bernard Coard and General Hudson Austin, commander of the army, which only six days earlier had murdered Prime Minister Maurice Bishop, head of the leftist People's Revolutionary Government. In fact, in March of that year President Reagan set forth the framework of the invasion to come when he maintained that "on the small island of Grenada, the Cubans . . . are in the process of building an airfield. . . . The Soviet-Cuban militarization of Grenada can only be seen as Soviet power projected into the region."[13] Using the dubious rationale that the airport would serve as a Cuban, perhaps even a Soviet, military base, Reagan and Dominica's Eugenia Charles developed the strategy to move in and overthrow the government of Grenada. The RSS was invoked and served to frame the invasion within a regional security operation. In the case of Grenada, and later Nicaragua, containment was augmented to incorporate the rationale of liberation.

Member states of the RSS have periodically conducted war games in concert with the United States and Great Britain. In 1985 both countries, along with Jamaica and the countries of the RSS, conducted joint naval exercises—under the name Exotic Palm—in St. Lucia. In Soufrière, in the southern portion of Dominica, whose "location midway between the French islands of Guadeloupe and Martinique, and about twenty miles from each, has given the island an unusual strategic importance,"[14] the same countries engaged in war games to "develop counter-insurgency operations where friendly RSS forces . . . attempt to contain hostile forces who enter the country. . . ."[15] Six hundred military personnel participated in these May 1987 exercises code-named Lava Flow. Upward Key 87, a two-week training program for SSUs conducted by the United States in Antigua and Barbuda, was held in 1986.

The regional security system of the Eastern Caribbean serves as the instrument of the reassertion of U.S. hegemony within the context of the ideological challenge of Cuba. This security network is "expected to play the central role in keeping [Eastern Caribbean] societies together . . . [and] serve[s] as the bulwark of the status quo and as the protector of U.S. political and economic interests."[16] The islands of the Eastern Caribbean, meccas of Western tourism, now share their sun, sand, and reefs with the military bases scattered throughout the region. Yet the tiny installations and the anti-Cuban militarization remain concealed from the paradise-seeking and predominately "white tourists, with skins rosied and bronzed by sunshine."[17]

Antigua and Barbuda is known for its premier status as a tourist resort, but it has become, along with Jamaica, Barbados, and Dominica, an influential surrogate of the United States. Former Prime Minister Vere C. Bird, in the 1980s, and his son Prime Minister Lester Bird, in the late 1990s, basically sold their nation to the United States. U.S. citizens purchase vast tracts of property, build condominiums, and flock to the resort hotels that line the pink sandy beaches offering paradise at more than $500 per day.[18] Almost bordering V. C. Bird International Airport, where the tourists disembark, are U.S. air force, army, and naval bases. According to testimony before the House Subcommittee on Military Construction, "the continued U.S. presence in the Eastern Caribbean is the primary reason for this investment."[19]

And it is quite an investment. In February 1985 Antigua and Barbuda permitted the United States to turn its oceanographic research institute, in existence since the 1960s, into a naval facility, making available to the United States "Rights of access, rights of way and easements being used in Antigua."[20] Construction costs for the facility were estimated at more than $8 million. Scores of U.S. naval personnel are assigned to the base; facilities exist for the training of regional naval forces and for the planning of military exercises with neighboring islands. The U.S. air force and army bases in Antigua and Barbuda are, together with Grantley Adams International Airport in Barbados, the major staging and launching sites for any U.S. military action in the region; indeed the airport was the take-off point for the invasion of Grenada. The U.S. role in the Eastern Caribbean, fueled by the fear of Caribbean nationalism and Cuban communism, is supplemented by its presence in the northern tier of the Caribbean, by the presence of its NATO allies—France, the Netherlands, and Great Britain—and by the extremely pro-U.S. governments in Jamaica, Dominica, Antigua and Barbuda, Grenada, and St. Lucia. Military bases in Guantánamo, Cuba; the Panama Canal (which the United States will turn over to local authorities in 2000); and Roosevelt Roads, Puerto Rico; as well as the geographical location of the U.S. Virgin Islands give increased leverage to America's expansive strategy in the Lesser Antilles. The entire regional defense network is organized under the umbrella of the U.S. Forces Southern Command, which operates out of Miami, Florida.

The British crown colony of Bermuda (where the United States also has a military base); the British Virgin Islands; the French Antilles (which include Martinique and Guadeloupe); and the Dutch possessions of Aruba, Bonaire, Curacao, and St. Maarten add to the weight of Western influence that permeates the Caribbean. France periodically acts to quash communist activity in its *dèpartements,* as it did in 1985, a time of increased Western military activity, when it rushed troops to Guadeloupe after a rash of bombings and political murders in Pointe-à-Pitre, the capital city.

In the 1980s, an era of marked military activity, the United States was not content merely to develop bases and alliances. The election victories of Eugenia Charles in Dominica, Edward Seaga in Jamaica, Vere C. Bird in Antigua and Barbuda, and John Compton in St. Lucia shifted the political balance sharply to the right. According to Edward J. Greene, "That this phenomenon . . . coincided with similar tendencies in Washington's foreign policy appears to be significant."[21] The political ideology of these leaders was symbolized by Prime Minister Bird, who proclaimed in 1983 that "a bigger and more active . . . U.S. presence to safeguard democracy . . . in this region is necessary. . . . We cannot afford to have another Cuba or another Grenada."[22] Indeed, it was Prime Minister Charles who urged the creation of the RSS—the pact was signed in Dominica's capital Roseau—and who vigorously urged the United States to invade Grenada and topple its government.

The United States maintains a proactive role in the Eastern Caribbean and has not been shy about displaying force to its clients when it comes to elections. In July 1984 the battleship Iowa anchored off the coast of Martinique during elections in St. Vincent and the Grenadines, elections subsequently won by James Mitchell and his pro-American New Democratic Party. Still prime minister 12 years later, Mitchell admitted to having surrendered the sovereignty of St. Vincent and the Grenadines to the United States.[23] In 1996 the refrain was identical in Grenada. In relation to the issue of drug smuggling, Prime Minister Keith Mitchell insisted on accepting a detachment of U.S. marines to build a base for the Grenada coast guard on the island of Petit Martinique. Arguing that the base was essential for Grenada's security, Mitchell dismissed accusations that national sovereignty was being compromised and said "I only wish we could have gotten other bases built [by the U.S.], so that we can protect the people . . . and the integrity of our country."[24] The contradiction of giving away pieces of their countries to the United States is defined by this group of leaders as vital to their "integrity," as proclaimed by Mitchell. The irony of his statement borders on the absurd. But Washington's desire to support the political parties representing conservative and right-wing ideologies in the Eastern Caribbean is complemented by its activity in seeing to it that they remain in power.

The fortresslike U.S. embassy in Antigua and Barbuda's capital, St. John's; the U.S. mission established in Grenada after the 1983 invasion; the tiny U.S. diplomatic offices in Dominica, St. Vincent and the Grenadines, St. Lucia, and St. Kitts-Nevis; the posting of U.S. security teams in Bridgetown and St. John's; and the training programs conducted for SSU units in Panama's Canal Zone and at Fort Bragg, North Carolina, indicate that the United States has placed itself in a position to state its views directly and immediately so as to sway the region's political and military actors. And the anti-Cuban policies of the United States have been embraced by the region's leadership. Charles Maynard, Dominica's Minister of Tourism (and in 1987, when I interviewed him, also Minister of Agriculture, Trade and Industry), said that "Grenada taught us [to oppose] an entrenched dictatorial government that can't be removed." The same sentiment was echoed by one of the officials in his ministry: "we're afraid of a Cuban invasion; thank God for the [U.S.] bases."[25] One authority on the Caribbean notes that American influence in Antigua and Barbuda has turned its culture on its head, while Prime Minister James Mitchell of St. Vincent and the Grenadines—one of America's staunchest regional clients—"has himself become caught up in [T]he center-right political orthodoxy . . . of resorts, condos and marinas."[26]

ST. LUCIA AND IRAN-CONTRA

A dramatic illustration of the demands placed upon the leaders of the Eastern Caribbean by the United States and their extraordinary willingness to accommodate Washington's imperious commands is St. Lucia's connection to the Reagan administration's arms-for-hostage deal with Iran and its shipment of U.S. arms to antigovernment rebels in Angola while Cuba was militarily supporting Angola's leftist government. In 1987 St. Lucia's capital, Castries, was aswirl with newspaper reports debating Prime Minister John Compton's knowledge of the Iran-Contra/Angola affair. No matter the extent of Compton's knowledge (and it is doubtful St. Lucia's support could have been gained without it) the Reagan administration clearly felt that its political and military ties to St. Lucia, via the RSS, gave it the right to insist that the country participate in secret and illegal arms shipments. Apparently, the decision makers in Castries had no choice but to say yes.

Although St. Lucia's connection to Iran-Contra/Angola was reported on throughout the Caribbean it remains relatively unknown in the United States. There were four elements to St. Lucia's participation. (1) St. Lucia Airway's sole Boeing 707 jet and its C-130 cargoes flew at least eight missions in 1986 from Kelly Air Force Base in Texas, via Castries, to Zaire (now once again the Congo) packed with small arms and antiaircraft and antitank missiles for the forces of the National Union for the Total Independence of Angola (UNITA), the U.S./apartheid South African – backed guerilla group fighting to overthrow the leftist Angolan government aided and supported by Cuba; (2) A number of flights were made in 1986 from St Lucia to the Middle East to deliver U.S. arms to the Iranians; (3) St. Lucia's airport facilities were used in the transshipment of U.S. arms; (4) White House National Security Adviser Robert McFarlane, on his secret visit to Tehran, traveled most of the way on St. Lucia Airways so as to avoid detection.

Prime Minister Compton's response to the revelations was to deny absolutely any knowledge of the sordid business. He refused to admit or deny whether there was an investigation of the matter, while the United States rejected the Foreign Ministry's demand for official clarification. The political opposition asserted that Compton had to know, that he had mortgaged St. Lucia to the United States, and that Washington had used St. Lucia "to make sure that our black brothers in Africa kill each other."[27]

In the face of all the military activity going on in the Eastern Caribbean at the time it seems impossible that Compton could have remained unaware of what was transpiring. His conservative credentials and his close association with U.S. policy in the region indicate that he had been seduced to accept the hegemony of the United States. In any case St. Lucia certainly played out its client status in this matter. Compton, with the wholehearted support of the United States, remained in office until 1996.[28]

THE AMERICAN DOGMA

Since the end of World War II the United States prescribed the dogma that, in the words of President Harry Truman, "the whole world should adopt the American system. The American system could survive in America only if it became a world system." [29] In pursuit of that policy Truman announced the Truman Doctrine of 1947 in which he sternly admonished the American people "that it must be the policy of the United States to support free peoples who are resisting attempted subjugation by armed minorities or by outside pressures."[30] The containment theory and the domino theory were developed by the speech, which defined American policy for the next half-century.

With the United States emerging as the only Western superpower, it moved to supplant newly marginalized countries such as Great Britain and France as their empires were dismembered and their colonies freed. The United States filled the vacuum left by the departure of the colonizers so as to prevent the spread of communism and radical nationalism, which would threaten American interests. The Soviet Union, emerging as the Eastern superpower after World War II, represented just such a threatening and alien communist ideology. The Cold War evolved. The Truman Doctrine provided the framework for the United States to pursue a policy of intervention. For, as Truman argued, only the United States could provide the military, economic, and financial support to help other nations resist subjugation by communist forces.

As British power and influence waned in the Eastern Caribbean, the United States moved in via the rubric of the Monroe Doctrine and the Truman Doctrine.[31] When in the 1970s and the early 1980s the contemporary sovereign countries of the Eastern Caribbean attained independence from Great Britain, the United States acted to apply its containment program, underpinned by its belief in the domino theory, to those countries within the region. Grenada was seen as a communist state influenced by Cuba, which was considered to have immense political leverage over its leadership, and because it was located in the southern tier of the Eastern Caribbean, Washington responded swiftly, blockading the Cuba/Grenada axis so as to disallow Grenada and Cuba any political or economic connection to the other islands in the Eastern Caribbean. The United States, under the Reagan administration, drew a *cordon sanitaire* around the Leeward and Windward Islands. It replaced Great Britain as the dominant power in the region and placed the Eastern Caribbean under America's containment umbrella so as to disallow any further dominos from toppling into the Cuban sphere of influence. The Truman Doctrine had now moved into the Eastern Caribbean.

The military aspect of the Truman Doctrine, though the most vital, was merely stage one. As Truman had indicated in his speech, economic leverage had to be integrated into the overall policy. Ronald Reagan moved rapidly to supplement his armaments policy with an economic program that would lock the Eastern Caribbean into the framework of American capitalism. Cuba was to be economically blockaded and isolated from its neighbors.

THE ECONOMIES OF THE EASTERN CARIBBEAN

The economies of the states of the Eastern Caribbean are closely bound to the United States. It was because of its evolving ties to its northern neighbor that in the 1970s the Commonwealth Caribbean broke its link with the pound sterling and aligned its currencies with the U.S. dollar. The economies of the Leeward and Windward Islands have been in a steady state of decline since the 1970s. Virtually all the Eastern Caribbean islands have minute populations (Anguilla, which remains a British colony, has just 7000; Dominica, 71,000; Barbados, 263,000; St. Kitts-Nevis, 40,000; Antigua and Barbuda, 66,000; Grenada, 92,000; St. Lucia, 144,000; and St. Vincent and the Grenadines,113,000) producing agricultural crops such as sugar cane, bananas, coconuts, and cotton, goods whose export prices are so low that the islands are constantly in financial straits. During 1983, for example,

> The Caribbean countries without exception continued to show evidence of deep-seated structural problems, as indicated by large account payments deficits, increasing external debt, widespread fiscal deficits and structural unemployment.[32]

In 1992/93 the economic stagnation remained unchanged. The merchandise balance of payments deficit for the nations of the Eastern Caribbean was quite remarkable:

Balance of Payments—1992 and 1993 (in millions of U.S. dollars)[33]

	EXPORTS	IMPORTS
Dominica (1993)	48.3	-98.8
Antigua and Barbuda (1992)	54.7	-260.9
Grenada (1992)	23.2	-113.6
St. Kitts-Nevis (1992)	31.9	-92.2
St. Lucia (1992)	122.8	-275.4
St. Vincent and the Grenadines (1992)	77.5	-118.6
Barbados (1993)	152.4	-511.3

Source: *UN Statistical Yearbook 1993*, 1995: 746-750.

In 1996, agricultural production declined markedly because of hurricane destruction in the area. Dominica's sugar harvest declined by 95 percent while St. Lucia's income from banana exports was down substantially. Grenada's nutmeg, fruit, and vegetable earnings also suffered.

Although tourism is an appreciable economic factor everywhere in the Caribbean, it tends to be a variable resource due to the ebb and flow of politics (Grenada, Jamaica, Haiti), devastating hurricanes (Dominica, St. Kitts-Nevis, the U.S. Virgin Islands), extreme poverty (Haiti), high cost (Antigua and Barbuda), and the effect at any given time of the U.S. economy on American travelers. However, since 70 percent of each dollar earned in foreign exchange via tourism must be spent on imports to meet the demands of tourists, the leakage factor of dollars lost is extremely high. Additionally, all-inclusive resorts (in which foreign exchange does not benefit the people of the country at all since virtually everything is imported and money is spent largely within the resorts) are growing in popularity, while the cruise-ship industry is absorbing more and more travelers. Benefits to the general population from tourism are, as a result, rather meager,[34] so the tourist industry can not be counted on to provide the indigenous population with a consistent and dependable inflow of funds.

In 1993, Grenada had only 94,000 tourists who brought in receipts of U.S. $45 million. For Antigua and Barbuda the figure was 240,000 tourists and U.S. $372 million; St. Lucia,177,000 and U.S.$221 million; Barbados, 396,000 and U.S. $1.304 billion. In comparison, Cuba, the largest island nation of the Greater Antilles, had 544,000 tourists and receipts of U.S.$720 million.[35] In 1996 earnings from tourism in the Eastern Caribbean fell by more than 30 percent due to hurricane destruction and the damage from the 1995/96 eruption of Montserrat's Soufrière Hill volcano. Anguilla's receipts dropped 22.4 percent, while the decline in Antigua and Barbuda was 9.5 percent. A further eruption of Soufrière in 1997 destroyed two-thirds of Montserrat. Tourism does not bring the economic benefits that foreign tourists assume.

The countries of the region also suffer from extraordinary emigration, which on the one hand serves as an outlet for economies under severe pressure but on the other hand depletes them of some of their most talented and skilled citizens. St. Kitts-Nevis lost 17,572 of its citizens from 1960 to 1970, and another 5,000 from 1983 to 1996.[36] Few countries can economically afford to lose almost 40 percent of their population and expect to prosper.

In economic terms, Eastern Caribbean states remain at the mercy of the United States. They depend on Washington to provide economic policies that will help them survive. Their ability to develop policies, foreign and domestic, that differ from the expectations of the United States is limited by their poverty, economic dependency, and geographic location. As they are dominated militarily by their northern neighbor, so too are they constrained economically. They have little choice but to adhere to the demands of the U.S., which disallows them from developing relations with Cuba that would in any way be seen to threaten the national interests of the United States. Some of the presidential initiatives regarding trade and aid policies that have insured the dependency of the economies of South America, Central America, and the Caribbean include Roosevelt's Good Neighbor Policy, Truman's Point Four Program, and President Kennedy's Alliance for Progress. Reagan's Caribbean Basin Initiative (CBI) of 1982/83 was meant to assure that such control would be maintained and extended to the Eastern Caribbean.

THE CARIBBEAN BASIN INITIATIVE

U.S. economic policy in the Caribbean goes hand in hand with its military goals. According to Ken I. Boodhoo, "These include the maintenance of a stable climate for its foreign investment and its exports and the perpetuation of its influence and control over the region's economy, thus assuring itself reliable and continuous supplies. To achieve these goals, Washington has tried to minimize leftist . . . influence and has been quite willing to provide substantial economic and especially security assistance to anticommunist, pro-U.S. governments. . . ."[37] Reagan's Caribbean Basin Initiative (CBI) permitted duty-free treatment of most products imported from the Caribbean, granted $350 million for emergency economic and military support, and increased tax incentives for U.S. investors. CBI heightened expectations among Caribbean leaders regarding U.S. financial aid but it was less than it appeared to be and eventually generated disappointment and unhappiness among the leadership and populations. However, given the strategic power imbalance between the United States and the Eastern Caribbean there was nothing local leaders could do but accept Washington's new program. The great contradiction within patron/client relationships is that the client may not approve of a program but still must agree to and abide by its terms. In fact, CBI would aid the United States and its investors far more than it would assist recipients.

CBI called for duty-free treatment of Caribbean products, but pressure from unions in the United States led to the exclusion from the pact of textiles, apparel, footwear, and petroleum, while sugar quotas were reduced drastically. In addition, between 1981 and 1987 the sugar quota for the Dominican Republic was cut from 493,000 tons to 160,000 tons, while that of St. Kitts-Nevis was reduced from 16,000 tons to 7,500 tons causing half the country's workforce to be laid off. Since almost 90 percent of all other Caribbean exports already entered U.S. markets duty-free, CBI turned out to be of little value to the Caribbean community. As Dominica's Minister of Agriculture, Trade and Industry, Charles Maynard, explained while expressing his disappointment with CBI's limited impact on apparel and textiles, "job creation is very important. The best for this is the development of our garment industry, which could wipe out unemployment. But we are not helped in this by CBI. Though it has helped create some jobs in our grapefruit and cosmetics industry CBI provides more jobs for consultants in the United States."[38]

Other CBI initiatives turned out to be similarly disappointing. Of the supplementary emergency assistance of $350 million, itself a small amount spread over 25 countries and territories, 75 percent went to El Salvador, Costa Rica, and Honduras. Thus the micro-states of the Eastern Caribbean were essentially shut out, even though their poverty levels are such that the extra funding would have been extremely helpful.[39] Finally, the tax incentives offered by CBI, which emphasized the importance of the private sector, did not markedly increase the volume of U.S. investment in the region.

Economic aid outside the parameters of CBI was also relatively feeble considering the need and the number of countries within the Eastern Caribbean. In the financial year 1984/85, U.S. Development Assistance funds to the area came to $30 million, with an additional $25 million allocated from Economic Supplementary Funds.[40] Although the amount of economic aid increased throughout the Reagan years,[41] the rhetoric from the U.S. president, particularly since the Grenadian invasion and occupation, led leaders and peoples of the Caribbean to expect far more monies than they finally were allocated. As the North American Congress on Latin America (NACLA) commented,

> The paradox of the CBI was that the conservative Eastern Caribbean figures most ideologically predisposed to the program's free-market principles had no way of taking advantage of them. The CBI seemed to them more like a symbolic good conduct medal than a tangible source of prosperity. They also recognized that the CBI crudely proposed to divide and rule.[42]

The politics of CBI was evident in the allocation of funds. With El Salvador and Honduras receiving the preponderance of U.S. dollars the message was clear: If your country was very right-wing, or battling communist or leftist insurgents alongside the United States there was money to be obtained. Since a similar theme was played out in U.S. funding of militaries it is little wonder that the governments of the Eastern Caribbean moved so far to the right.[43] They were, of course, caught in a political bind, having to accept the terms of the program even though there were few benefits to it. As monies flowed to virulent anticommunist regimes it seemed that if you moved right more CBI money would flow in your direction. But in reality that was not the case. Ideological conservatism was required irrespective of CBI, and because the micro-states of the Eastern Caribbean were in no position to exert any political leverage on Washington they were forced to accept CBI despite its lack of consequence for them, and they were required also to participate in the military regional alliance sponsored by the United States. They were merely clients of the United States expected to do its bidding and to support its vital interests, which meant subsuming their own interests. In return, the conservative leadership would gain the financial and military support to remain in power. Although ruling elites may have benefited monetarily and politically, it was at the cost of virtually relinquishing the sovereignty of their nation-states. The Eastern Caribbean had become a minor player in advancing U.S. national security interests, yet the United States tightened its grip on the region throughout the 1980s and into the 1990s. Any political actor seen to be independent or nationalist, or otherwise dangerous to U.S. interests, would suffer the consequences. The Eastern Caribbean leadership certainly must have watched with interest what happened to the Nicaraguan Sandinistas in 1990, who, after years of military pressure by the United States, through its military proxy the contras, were defeated in American-pressured free elections; to the antigovernment rebels in El Salvador, who were defeated in 1989/90 after battling a government supported and financed by the United States; and to Panama's General Manuel Noriega, who was overthrown in 1989 when the United States invaded the country with 24,000 troops.

Presidents Reagan and Bush completed the decade of the 1980s by cleansing the Caribbean region of opponents, including Panama's Noriega and Bishop, Nicaragua's Daniel Ortega, and El Salvador's Farabundo Martí National Liberation Front (FMLN). Bishop was murdered just prior to the U.S. invasion, his successors captured and jailed by the invaders. Noriega, captured during the invasion, sits in a federal prison in the United States; Ortega, while still a political player, has been marginalized and made powerless.

The political, economic, and military crusade in the Caribbean conducted by Reagan and Bush was extraordinarily successful. There can be no doubt whatsoever that the Caribbean is securely within America's sphere of influence. Cuba's allies in the region, the nationalist or socialist political organizations and leadership, were stripped of their power by the virulent actions of the United States. Once again Cuba found itself isolated. The United States had contained Cuba, liberated Nicaragua and Grenada, and destroyed Havana's ideological allies and sympathizers in El Salvador, and in so doing it had blockaded Cuba politically. The lesson was absorbed by the Eastern Caribbean leadership. Washington was not to be taken lightly and there would be harsh, perhaps deadly consequences to developing anything more than a nominal connection to Cuba. Fidel Castro had been regionally embargoed.

The Reagan and Bush administrations furnished the United States with a rock-solid grip on the sovereign states of the Eastern Caribbean by supporting a steadfast and reliable conservative indigenous leadership. The military occupancy by the United States became more obvious, while its economic promises were extravagant. Still, despite CBI the agricultural sector of the Eastern Caribbean economies remained stagnant, unemployment and underemployment hovered at over 35 percent (and employment was often only seasonal), decent housing remained out of the reach of most, and manufacturing and industry were constrained by the small size of the domestic market. As the United Nations indicated at the time, the region continued to experience "little real growth [and] hardly any real per capita gains."[44]

THE AMERICANIZATION OF THE WEST INDIES

Although the economic, political, and military policy of the United States through the1980s was certainly an overwhelming success in the Eastern Caribbean, the benefits to the states of the region were limited. The West Indies had been militarized by the United States to an extent grossly out of proportion to the size of the mini-states; economies continued to languish; the explosion of U.S. tourism overwhelmed the local cultures, making people feel like aliens in their own land;[45] and the ruling elites had more in common with their American benefactors than with their own populations.

Any traveler to the islands of the Caribbean in the 1980s could not help but notice the overwhelming impact of U.S. culture on the region. From music to food to architecture, the American way of life was in command. U.S. multinationals opened fast-food restaurants; American, British, French, Dutch and Israeli firms built high-rise hotels that destroyed the ambiance of the towns and villages surrounding the capital cities. Condominiums facing the Caribbean Sea were constructed by and for Westerners, and entire villages were razed in the process. The Miami Beach–like Paradise Island in the Bahamas and the Caribbean island of Cozumel, Mexico, were developed solely and explicitly for American tourists. An entirely new, artificial culture was created to appeal to these largely American tourists—a culture neither indigenous nor Western, but a crass combination designed to give visitors an exotic but nonthreatening experience. From Guadeloupe to Barbados, from the Cayman Islands to St. Maarten, the Americans came en masse and with them hamburgers, pizza, and many gambling casinos. In my own travels to almost all the islands of the West Indies, it appeared remarkable that in each, no matter the colonial heritage, almost every aspect of the urban culture seemed to be made over and turned inside out for the North American visitor. Colonial convention and indigenous cultural values were both radically transformed. Should the United States have its way all these countries would mirror Puerto Rico, Aruba, or even St. Maarten, in which it is almost impossible to find any remaining vestiges of a formerly rich culture. Even in Belize, the American director Francis Ford Coppola built Blancaneaux Lodge and "taught his Bilizean cooks how to make pizza and pasta (perhaps with sun-dried tomatoes flown in to the lodge's own airstrip). At this point . . . tourism is subverted into surrealism."[46] With travelers rarely venturing away from the beaches fronting the major hotels, there was no recognition of the villages and townships, and the people in the interior did not benefit very much from the influx of dollars. These islands remained Third World countries, not the paradises they might appear to the American lying on the beach enjoying a rum punch. Neither economic growth nor any substantial increase in per capita income was occurring. Despite CBI and tourism, the region was stagnating, and the people of the region had to be wondering, as their economic life continued to decline, when the payoff would come. The Americanization and Westernization of the West Indies had increased dramatically in the 1980s (prior to that point traveling to the Indies had been largely for the very rich) but it would become even more intense in the 1990s, while the indices of the local economy would deteriorate even further. As the decade turned vast changes were taking place in the Soviet Union that would reverberate throughout the world and drastically affect Cuba and the Eastern Caribbean.

THE COLLAPSE OF THE SOVIET UNION AND ITS AFTERMATH

In 1991 the Cold War came to an abrupt conclusion as the Soviet Union imploded. The United States stood as the sole remaining superpower, its power unchallenged. In the Third World nations swiftly came to realize that their status as proxies for the United States in its struggle with the Soviet Union was now meaningless. Former Soviet clients were abandoned, left without a patron to support their ideological struggles. America's military, political, and financial prowess invested it with an extraordinary power and authority that it had never before held. Political relations between the United States and its Third World clients and opponents would undergo a dramatic change. America's allies in the so-called emerging countries found that their importance to the national security of the United States in terms of spheres of influence and balance of power was gone. They were no longer seen as vital to America's defense. Many opponents of the United States, once supported by Moscow, were now on their own financially and militarily and found themselves under extraordinary pressure.

This was certainly true of Cuba, which had to discontinue its cause in Ethiopia, where it had 16,000 troops stationed since 1977 to support the Marxist government of Mengistu Haile Mariam, as well as in Angola, where Cuba had 20,000 troops stationed since 1975 in support of the Popular Movement for the Liberation of Angola (MPLA), which in 1976 had become the governing party. Presidents Jimmy Carter and Ronald Reagan countered Cuban and Soviet influence, and by 1991 Cuban troops had been evacuated from both countries; Mengistu's regime was toppled and negotiations leading to an electoral compromise ensued in Angola.

It was a new era in which the rules of the game were unknown; the United States, however, moved to establish new international parameters. This was as true in the Caribbean Community (Caricom) as elsewhere, and the nations of the Eastern Caribbean found themselves in deep economic trouble as the United States sharply cut the *economic* aid that had been flowing to the region. With Cuba dramatically weakened by the end of Soviet support, and now on its own economically, the United States, in concentrating its attention on China, the new state of Russia, and the newly independent countries that made up the old Soviet Union, deserted the Eastern Caribbean states.

THE CRISIS IN CUBA

The demise of the Soviet Union had staggering repercussions to Cuba. The economy went into a tailspin and Cuba entered what President Fidel Castro called in 1990, as the USSR was already tightly restricting its aid, a "Special Period in the Time of Peace." According to Avi Chomsky and Alfredo Prieto between 1989 and 1992 "Cuba lost 70 percent of its import capacity; imports declined from over $8 billion annually to under $2½ billion per year, a drastic decline that no Caribbean country could withstand without grave social and political consequences."[47] Gillian Gunn commented that "The fall in oil supplies was the most critical result of the Soviet bloc's breakdown for Cuba. Shipments fell from 13.3 million tons in 1989 to . . . an estimated 4 million tons in 1993. . . . By late 1992 Cuba's trade with the former socialist bloc had fallen to 7 percent of its 1989 level."[48] In 1993 Cuba's most important export, sugar, drew one half the subsidized price it once received from the Soviet Union.[49]

As late as 1995, during the first of my research visits to Cuba, the combined effects of the Soviet collapse and the continued imposition of the U.S. embargo were still obvious. Many children and adults appeared malnourished, and mothers with their children prowled the avenues of Havana desperately begging for money to buy rice, bread, and potatoes. Only children under seven could acquire milk through a ration card. There were rumors of famine in the east. Few cars were being driven because of the shortage and the exorbitant cost of gasoline, while most of the population moved about on "Flying Pigeons"—bicycles imported from the People's Republic of China. A common sight in the cities was two or three people on a bicycle with one carrying a number of shopping bags. The most trivial supplies, including toilet paper and soap, were unavailable or too costly to purchase. From Pinar del Río in the west, to Havana, to Santiago de Cuba in the east existence was desperate. It was particularly acute since throughout the Castro years Cubans had never experienced such an economic catastrophe and were clearly in shock. I vividly remember one evening during the summer of 1995 when I was invited to dinner at the home of a professor of French literature at the University of Havana and her husband, who is a well regarded painter. To save money the lights were off, and candles were substituted. With repeated apologies for such a sparse meal, cheese sandwiches were served. The only extravagance was a bottle of Pepsi Cola (bottled in Venezuela) for their American guest, which cost the equivalent of 1/14th of her monthly university salary. Although both blamed Cuba's troubles on the U.S. blockade, they were clearly embarrassed by the starkness of their new lives.

Another grim aspect of that remarkable time was the huge increase in prostitution. Young women, many of once relatively prosperous families, took to lounging near the major hotels, particularly in Havana, to attract foreign sex partners and acquire access to the U.S. dollars needed to buy food. These desperate women were horrified by the situation they found themselves in, but they did what they had to do to help their families survive. It was a time of the survival of the fittest, or certainly of the most inventive,[50] as the country confronted a virtual state of siege.

At this time, Castro began the process of opening the country to new foreign investment, particularly from Europe, Canada, and Spanish America (especially Mexico), in order to mitigate the economic turmoil sweeping Cuba. He also took steps toward liberalizing the economy and creating greater religious space for the population. But although Cuba had diplomatic relations with most countries in the region, there had not been much economic connection, and Dominica, Antigua and Barbuda, St. Kitts-Nevis, Barbados, St. Lucia, St. Vincent and the Grenadines, Grenada, and the territories of the Leeward and Windward Islands could offer Cuba little relief economically. On the one hand, few of the countries had a consumer market of any size, and most agricultural produce was exported to Europe, the United States, or Trinidad and Tobago. On the other hand, Cuba, with its lack of hard currency and economic turbulence, offered little of economic value to the Caribbean countries. Additionally, all the countries of the Eastern Caribbean remained in the grip of the United States, and even though economic aid from America would soon be sharply curtailed, the regional security pact, the RSS, would remain in effect. The United States was still the patron and the Eastern Caribbean the client. Now that the United States appeared to have Cuba on the ropes, it would not approve any warming of relations between Cuba and the RSS countries. The new American president, Bill Clinton, who took office in 1993, had every reason to expect that Fidel Castro's presidency would not survive much longer. Cuba was staggering economically, its foreign policy was in tatters, its military had lost its main supplier, and Castro himself indicated by his "special period" speech that Cuba was in crisis. The right-wing Cuban American National Foundation in Miami (which had provided Clinton with the votes of Miami-based Cuban exiles) was pressuring him to stand fast on Cuba claiming that Castro would soon fall, a view echoed by the new conservative and Republican–controlled Congress. The blockade of Cuba outside and within the Eastern Caribbean would continue. Either Castro would relent to American pressure, or Cuba would continue to be isolated, and thereby weakened further. For the only existing superpower this was not the time to soften its stance.

DISAPPOINTMENT IN THE EASTERN CARIBBEAN

On October 23, 1992, just three months before he left office, George Bush expanded the Cuban embargo by signing the Cuban Democracy Act (CDA), which closed U. S. ports to all foreign vessels carrying goods to or from Cuba (for 180-days) after docking in a Cuban port.[51] Promoted by Congressman Robert Torricelli (D-NJ), the ban extended to third-country vessels transporting produce in which Cuba had any "interest." The message to the nations of the world, including those in the Caribbean, was clear: Trade with Cuba by corporations or countries was discouraged. For the Eastern Caribbean community, whose trade with Cuba was limited in any case, the prohibition meant that commerce with Cuba would poison their vital commercial relations with the United States.

Since the states of the Eastern Caribbean were no longer seen as important as they were during the cold war, the Clinton White House and the Republican Congress, led by Speaker of the House Newt

Gingrich and Senate Majority Leader Robert Dole, sharply cut Washington's economic aid to the region. By 1996 American economic assistance dropped 90 percent—from $225 million to $26 million.[52] The Reagan Caribbean Basin Initiative, although still in existence, was functionally moribund. More bad news for the region was to come.

The United States next moved to prod the World Trade Organization (WTO) to eliminate the trade preferences that Caribbean bananas have in Europe, in response to arguments from American banana growers and exporters in the United States that the preference unfairly restricted access to Europe by American firms. Since bananas are "to [the Caribbean] what cars are to Detroit,"[53] elimination of the preferences would devastate independent banana growers in these micro-states and cripple the banana industry. Clinton, however, refused to budge. He also rejected calls to integrate the Caricom states into the North American Free Trade Association (NAFTA), which presently includes Mexico, Canada, and the United States. In August 1996 Clinton signed legislation eliminating the federal tax incentives that had encouraged low-interest loans to the region, although one year later, in an effort to smooth relations with furious Caribbean allies, he agreed to lower tariffs on Caribbean textiles and leather goods.

Neither the U.S. Congress, in a conservative mood to cut back aid programs—and in this case, as in others, the effort is led by Jesse Helms, the Republican Chairman of the Senate Foreign Relations Committee—nor President Clinton, who has made the hallmark of his presidency the balancing of the federal budget, are willing to compromise with Eastern Caribbean leaders. After all, without the Soviet Union, and with Cuba severely weakened, there is no one else for them to turn to. Even Keith Mitchell, the prime minister of Grenada and one of Washington's supporters, was impelled to cry out: "What is the message being sent? It is that our friends are abandoning us, that the rug is being pulled from under us, that we are being told we must sink or float on our own."[54] Jamaica's prime minister, P. J. Patterson, the 1997 chairman of Caricom, said it a bit more diplomatically: "In the closest of families, difficulties are bound to arise from time to time in their relationships."[55]

The U.S. economic aid has been reduced even in the face of increased cocaine and heroin trafficking within and around the Caribbean countries, since the continuing cooperation between the Caribbean Community and the United States in antidrug efforts is encompassed by the RSS military pact, and bilateral military antidrug enforcement agreements. Although he is a democrat, Clinton's first concern is with domestic fiscal responsibility, making him an ally of the conservatives in Congress, and it is the nations of the Eastern Caribbean who suffer for it.

GRENADA'S RESPONSE

Two weeks before the 1997 Barbados summit meeting between President Clinton and the leadership of the Caribbean Community, Grenada's prime minister traveled to Havana for a meeting with Fidel Castro. It was the first such visit by a Grenadian leader since 1983. Fourteen years after the U.S. invasion of his country, Prime Minister Keith Mitchell displayed his unhappiness with Washington's attitude toward the Eastern Caribbean. In an attempt to overcome the effects of America's reduction in economic aid Mitchell signed a series of agreements in Havana. Cuba agreed to help train Grenadian health care practitioners, to assist in constructing a new national stadium, and to provide technical aid to Grenadian industry and agriculture. Scholarships for students to study in Cuba were also provided. Although the Cuban aid was minimal, and certainly not threatening to the United States, the trip and the agreement were most probably meant to convey a message to Washington to pay more attention to Grenada in light of its faltering economy. Officials in the United States did not respond negatively to the trip, presumably because Cuba was no longer seen as a threat to the region. But, just in case Mitchell's message was overlooked, shortly after his return to Grenada from Cuba, he spoke quite frankly about its purposes.

> Our traditional friends have indicated that the days of grant aid and soft loans and so on are gone. We have to be able to strike strategic relationships with those who are willing to help us in charting a course of serious development. I believe in getting all the available

> help you can in the building of your country, so long as it is done on your terms and does not interfere with your independence and sovereignty.
>
> When we look back at the relationship with Cuba, I think most Grenadians of all ages and groups will agree that overall, the role and presence they played in Grenada was positive. We never thanked them officially for their support, so when the opportunity was presented to me to pay a special thanks, I thought I should correct that wrong.[56]

In one respect, Mitchell was on firm ground in making the trip, as he had good relations with the United States. Only one year earlier he had signed an agreement with the United States allowing it to send the U.S. marines to construct a military base for the Grenada coast guard, both to aid the United States in its drug interdiction efforts and to enhance Grenada's own national security. The minimal aid granted by Cuba would be helpful to Grenada but was so minor economically that, for Mitchell, its primary purpose was to send a message to Washington. If the communication was received, it was all but ignored; two weeks later at the Barbados summit Clinton refused to bow to any of Caricom's demands. Still, Mitchell's public display of appreciation to Castro for his help during the Bishop years took some courage, particularly since he had always been so supportive of U.S. military strategy, and it added credibility to his stature as a leader ready to speak out against Clinton's policies. As The *New York Times* stated, Mitchell's trip (not to mention his words of thanks) "sent shock waves from one end of the Caribbean to the other."[57]

THE BACKLASH AGAINST U.S. POLICY

By 1998, the Caribbean leadership had begun to follow Prime Minister Mitchell's lead. Prime ministers Patterson of Barbados and James Mitchell of St. Vincent and the Grenadines traveled to Cuba on official visits in 1997. Jamaica received 20 Cuban teachers in early 1998 who were to spend two years teaching, and the country signed trade agreements with Cuba. Trade between Cuba and Caricom increased from $5 million to $50 million from 1990 to 1998, and it is expected to grow even further. Cuba, which is not a member of Caricom, was officially invited to attend its 1998 summit meeting held in St. Lucia, a move that was not opposed by President Clinton, and its application to join the 34-member Association of Caribbean States, which had included every country in the Caribbean with the exception of the United States and Cuba, was accepted. The goal of the Association is to create a Caribbean free-trade area in the twenty-first century. Clearly, the Caribbean Community was following the lead of Mexico, which is presently Cuba's biggest booster and its largest foreign investor.

But the states of the region, particularly the Eastern Caribbean countries with membership in the Regional Security System, have been quite careful in insuring they do not alienate the United States. Caribbean leaders discussed developing closer relations with Cuba with President Clinton at the Barbados summit meeting, at which time they acknowledged "that they would not take any steps that might invite American reprisals."[58] Opposed as they are to the economic embargo and particularly resentful of the U.S. cutbacks in their own countries, they agreed as a group "that in accordance with our sovereign rights we have the capacity to determine with whom we trade and on what terms." In fact, Keith Mitchell invited Castro to Grenada in the summer of 1998 to officially applaud Cuba for "its contribution in the construction of the Point Salines International Airport. . . . We must give credit where credit is due."[59]

The response by the United States was mixed. Clinton rebuffed summit demands for a liberalized trade policy between the United States and the Caribbean and indicated that he opposed expanding membership in the various regional groupings in the Caribbean to include Cuba. In 1997 a Cuban-American Republican congressman from Miami introduced legislation that would prohibit trade benefits to and the expansion of trade with any Caribbean country advocating Cuba's entry into Caricom or any other regional association, legislation that did not pass and that former president Jimmy Carter called "total stupidity."[60] Even so, on the one hand the United States had already so drastically reduced aid to the region that the leaders of the Caribbean clearly felt they had little to lose by expanding their trade with Cuba. On the other hand, President Clinton, by agreeing to lower tariffs on some Caribbean goods, suggested that he could accept the limited amelioration of Caricom relations with Cuba that had taken place *thus far.*

Cuba has taken political advantage of the resentment among Caribbean states caused by the decline in U.S. aid and the reduction in trade. Beginning in 1992 Cuba opened its economy to "entertain . . . virtually any investment proposal."[61] By 1996, according to the U.S.-Cuba Trade and Economic Council, foreign investment in Cuba reached $5 billion,[62] much of it from Mexico and Spain. During the same year more than 45 nations signed 340 association agreements for investments in 34 areas of Cuba's economy, while more than 650 companies had a presence on the island and by 1998 had committed $6.5 billion to future investment. By the year 2000 tourism is expected to double from the 1.2 million visitors in 1997 who spent $1.6 billion.[63] To generate good-will, Cuba has sent medical workers and teachers to numerous Third World countries in Africa and the Caribbean to work for two- or three-year periods. Fidel Castro continues to speak to the frustration of the leaders and peoples of the Third World, appealing to their declining influence in an American-dominated world. As he proclaimed in Istanbul, Turkey in 1996, "Discouragement is spreading in the Third World countries. They're losing faith. . . . [W]hat's left for us, the forgotten of the earth?"[64] With Cuba far more open to foreign trade and investment than at any time since the 1959 revolution, there is now greater opportunity for the Caribbean countries to increase their trade with Cuba. But the expansion will have to be limited and not threatening to U.S. national interests, as the micro-states of the Eastern Caribbean in particular are unwilling to push the United States, one of their largest trading partners and provider of their security, into taking "reprisals" against them.

QUARANTINE IN THE EASTERN CARIBBEAN: SUCCESS OR FAILURE?

The 1992 CDA not only restricted ships docking in Cuba from coming to the United States for half a year, but it also prohibited U.S. subsidiaries abroad from trading with Cuba, which primarily affected trade in food and medicine. On March 12, 1996, President Clinton signed the Cuban Liberty and Democratic Solidarity Act, better known as the Helms-Burton Act, which extended the embargo. It gave U.S. citizens and Cuban exiles who had become citizens since 1959 the right to sue non-American companies doing business in Cuba and deriving benefit from property worth at least $50,000 confiscated from Americans without compensation after the Cuban revolution. It also permitted the government the right to deny U.S. visas to foreign businesspeople who derived benefit from confiscated property in Cuba. Access to the U.S. sugar quota was denied to countries that did not certify that they were not importing Cuban sugar that could find its way to the U.S. Helms-Burton basically invested extraterritorial application to the U.S. embargo in trade with Cuba by creating a legal framework to force other nations to abide by it.[65] In effect it created a world-wide blockade and developed "the notion that the United States can foist its foreign policy objectives on other nations through the threat and actual imposition of trade sanctions."[66] Indeed, the United States prohibitions evident in the CDA (as well as in Helms-Burton) "have brought the United States into sharp conflict with virtually the entire international community, including its closest allies."[67]

By 1997 life in Cuba had improved dramatically, and everyday existence had become less tense and onerous for the population as foreign investors took advantage of Cuba's new and more open investment policy and poured billions more into the economy.[68] However, the U.S. laws expanding the embargo to the status of a blockade clearly had a chilling effect on the countries of the Eastern Caribbean. Canada, Europe, and Mexico were contesting the United States in the WTO, but members of the U.S. Congress were introducing still more bills to prohibit trade between Cuba and any Caribbean nations who had the audacity to try to integrate Cuba into the regional associations putting the small states of the Eastern Caribbean in an impossible situation. As indicated at the 1997 summit in Barbados these nations are frightened of confronting the United States over Cuba. Sure, their leaders may travel to Havana, and some minimal trade agreements have been signed with Cuba, but these states are too small to take on the United States without inviting the "reprisals" they all fear. Indeed, at Barbados they said as much. The

United States is a large trading partner. It is responsible for their security through the aegis of the RSS through which the United States has military personnel and bases scattered throughout the area. The patron is able to keep close watch over its clients, who are in no economic or geographical position to really challenge and confront it. They are able to accomplish little. Indeed, Cuba was even barred from attending the Chile-based Summit of the Americas held in April 1998.

Direct air travel between Cuba and the islands of the Eastern Caribbean is slight. Most Caribbean travelers fly into Cuba via Nassau in the Bahamas, Jamaica, the Dominican Republic, or either Cancún or Mexico City in Mexico. The United States increasingly is attempting to restrict shipping through the expansion of its embargo legislation. Through cutbacks in banana imports, restrictions on sugar imports, and a panoply of reductions in economic aid, the United States continues to insure the Caribbean nations' poverty, thus keeping them dependent. Cuba, as poor and undeveloped as it is, cannot provide what is needed. Barbados, St. Lucia, St. Vincent and the Grenadines, St. Kitts-Nevis, Dominica, Grenada, and Antigua and Barbuda need the United States and the assistance it provides, reduced as it may be, and their leaders have become dependent on the United States for political security. The United States has a solid grasp on the sovereign states of the Eastern Caribbean and functionally retains a veto over the policies its leaders may wish to pursue. Despite the rhetoric in Washington it is not Cuban interference, or even its potential tampering with the internal affairs of the Eastern Caribbean states, that is of concern. It is the conduct of the United States that is intrusive and limiting of national sovereignty. While the United States has failed to live up to its own promises it has supported a dependent conservative leadership in the Caribbean, one that shares America's capitalist value system and ideology. Such leaders are not about to break with the United States over the issue of Cuba, even though they may oppose the U.S. embargo. The conservative leadership of the Eastern Caribbean knows where the power lies—and it resides in Washington, not Havana.

From the promulgation of the Monroe Doctrine in 1823, to its continued implementation at the dawn of the new millennium, the United States has invaded and occupied countless numbers of countries throughout the region. When President Lyndon Johnson sent U.S. forces to invade the Dominican Republic in 1965, he maintained, "we don't propose to sit here in our rocking chair with our hands folded and let the Communists set up any government in the Western Hemisphere."[69] The invasions of Grenada and Panama under Presidents Reagan and Bush were followed by the 1994 invasion of Haiti by President Clinton to restore Jean-Bertrand Aristide to office and thus curtail the flow of Haitian refugees to the United States. Military action, responding to the excuse of the moment, has always been undertaken to ensure U.S. security imperatives irrespective of its effect on the peoples of the Caribbean. Economic sanctions and reduction in economic aid should really be considered economic attacks, as they are almost as violent as military invasions in regard to the ensuing chaos they inflict on the targeted country or countries. Sanctions, which are always imposed on the basis of U.S. national security, "impose severe economic penalties in order to coerce the target country to alter its policies."[70] Reduction in aid, in the case of the Eastern Caribbean, reflects the recognition of the United States that the countries are so securely incorporated into its sphere of influence that economic aid can be severely curtailed without ramifications that would impact foreign policy interests. Policy remains the same and presidents, whether democrat or republican, conservative or liberal, will impose it when necessary. Reagan, Bush, and Clinton expanded the parameters of the Cuban embargo, and all three persisted in reducing trade benefits to the Eastern Caribbean to profit the United States, despite the rhetoric of Reagan's Caribbean Basin Initiative.

The Council on Foreign Relations, the conservative think tank founded in 1921 by U.S. corporate leaders to help define and coordinate foreign policy, sponsored the publication of *Arms and Politics in Latin America* in 1961 so as to help revitalize U.S. policy in light of the "especially troublesome" issues arising in Latin America and the Caribbean in the 1950s.[71] The book advanced the position that the region was threatened by communism and that the security of the United States, its strategic areas and lines of communication, could be guaranteed only by increasing military assistance, as "the weapons received improve the recipient government's ability to cope with internal disorder."[72] To that end the

United States augmented its traditional policy in the Caribbean and began the process of expanding military aid and, only when necessary, providing additional economic assistance to shore up conservative Caribbean governments who would be able to maintain themselves and/or their conservative political parties in power, thus ensuring that more nationalistic political movements would be shut out. The policy advocated by the Council on Foreign Relations was indeed incorporated by the United States and has proven to be a marked success in the Eastern Caribbean. The conservative governments and political parties in Dominica, Barbados, St. Kitts-Nevis, Antigua and Barbuda, St. Vincent and the Grenadines, St. Lucia, and Grenada retain their hold on power while opposition radical movements, whose success was at least a possibility in the 1970s and early 1980s, have been largely suppressed.

The policy of the United States to politically quarantine Cuba within the Eastern Caribbean must be acknowledged as having been considerably successful, although its primary goal of removing Castro from power, or as Jesse Helms inelegantly put it just prior to Helms-Burton being signed into law, "adios, Fidel,"[73] has failed. As the political scientist H. Michael Erisman has argued,

> As far as Havana is concerned, the U.S. redefinition of security threats in the Caribbean (that is, migration and drugs) can be seen as a mechanism that provides Washington with a rationale, bolstered by its charges of human rights violations and antidemocratic values, to maintain its Cold War hostility toward Cuba. Such a new justification became necessary, of course, when it could no longer be argued that Havana had close ties to the Soviet bloc that represented a political-military threat to the Caribbean region and to U.S. security interests therein. This reconstituted belligerence takes the form of intensified economic warfare against Cuba, as exemplified by the [CDA] and Helms-Burton laws. The goals of this newly rationalized policy are straight out of the Cold War: to destroy Cuba's government and to eradicate the revolution.[74]

Fidel Castro and the Cuban Communist Party remain in power in Havana, but Cuba's connection to the states of the Eastern Caribbean remains so negligible as to be of little concern to the United States. On this front the United States has incontestably been victorious.

THREE

A WAR AGAINST PUBLIC HEALTH

SINCE THE ONSET OF THE CUBAN REVOLUTION IN 1959, Americans have been mesmerized by the continuing conflict between Fidel Castro's Cuba and the United States government, particularly as it concerns foreign policy. Yet, the ongoing war has affected Cuba's domestic policy in far more wrenching ways, though largely unknown to a U.S. audience. When Castro marched into Havana in the first days of January 1959 he was met with "the thunderous applause of an overwhelming number of his compatriots,"[1] while Americans looked on with admiration. But the Eisenhower administration regarded these young, radical revolutionaries with a wary eye, as "the United States could not tolerate a revolution it was unable to influence or control immediately south of Key West, Florida."[2] As acceptance turned to disenchantment and then outright hostility, decisionmakers in Washington initiated policies that were predicated on removing Castro from the scene.

Five days after first meeting Fidel Castro in April 1959 Vice President Richard M. Nixon drafted a memo to former Secretary of State John Foster Dulles in which he indicated that Castro "is either incredibly naive about Communism or under Communist discipline . . . but because he has the power to lead . . . we have no choice but at least to try to orient him in the right direction."[3] Reorientation failed, and as relations between Havana and Washington deteriorated the first embargo act was initiated by President Dwight D. Eisenhower, who stated flatly in his memoirs that "something would have to be done" about Castro.[4] On October 19, 1960, the Eisenhower administration announced the prohibition of American exports to Cuba "except for nonsubsidized foodstuffs, medicines, and medical supplies."[5] On February 3, 1962, President John F. Kennedy imposed a total embargo against trade with Cuba, exempting only "certain" medical supplies, while in May of 1964 the U.S. Commerce Department, under President Lyndon B. Johnson, initiated a policy of denying requests for the export of *all* medicine and medical supplies to Cuba. With the passage of the 1992 CDA, the United States restricted its subsidiaries abroad from trading with Cuba, thereby denying "access to much needed foods and medicines because 70 percent of this trade is in food and medicines."[6] The 1996 Helms-Burton Act imposed even harsher limitations on the imports of medicine to Cuba by imposing sanctions on third countries trading with Cuba. An unqualified blockade of medicine and medical equipment had been achieved.

Presently, Cuba is the only nation in the world denied medicine as part of a U.S. embargo. With the application of extraterritoriality it is "abundantly clear that economic sanctions are, at their core, a war against public health."[7] Indeed, because the embargo prohibits products that contain any U.S. component or material from being exported to Cuba from third countries, including products based on U.S. design and technology, and because most major new drugs are developed by U.S. pharmaceutical companies, Cuba has access to only a small percentage of the new medicines available on the world market.[8] The embargo, as it affects medicine, scientific technology, textbooks, and periodicals, is a virtual worldwide blockade vigorously enforced by the United States. The minutiae of enforcement, according to the *New England Journal of Medicine*, "are all encompassing. The interdicted trade includes visits by medical delegations and the mailing of medical journals. . . ."[9]

The economic and domestic crisis that affects Cuba is particularly striking in the field of health care, which has been dramatically crippled by the U.S. embargo. While the United States attempts to destroy Cuba's public health organization in order to turn a desperate Cuban population against Fidel Castro, Cuba has confronted this aspect of the blockade head-on. To comprehend what the embargo has meant in the field of health care it is important to analyze the structure of the Cuban health care system while examining what the United States is doing to destroy it. This will clarify Cuba's extraordinary accomplishments in the development of medicines through biotechnology and pharmacology, and it will also explain the political and economic impediments Cuba must deal with to continue providing a public health care program. There is little question that this aspect of the blockade is a fearful and awesome violation of the human rights of the Cuban people that, as Miguel Barnet, the prominent Cuban novelist and folklorist, indicated to me in Havana in a 1997 interview, may very well come back to haunt the United States.[10]

A blockade that affects the health and, thus, the very lives of Cubans is not nearly as obvious and dramatic as a Bay of Pigs invasion or a Cuban Missile Crisis, but its results are as dire, perhaps even more so, because like real tragedy it is ongoing. It is practically an act of war, but it "doesn't yield vivid television images [of] pilots zoom[ing] off the flight deck of the carrier Independence,"[11] which would attract the attention of the citizenry. Beyond the anti-Cuban rhetoric emanating from Washington exists a brutal and vicious campaign that the U.S. population is scarcely cognizant of. This popular ignorance is precisely what Washington desires. Americans may be susceptible to anticommunist bombast, but they are a moral people who would, if they knew the details, be repulsed by the effects of a crusade against health care by which no Cuban is untouched and almost all are harmed. The struggle to combat this aspect of the U.S. embargo has arguably represented Cuba's finest hour, bringing with it both success and hardship.

HUMAN RIGHTS AND HEALTH CARE

Prior to 1959, Cuba was characterized by profound inequalities between Havana and the rest of the country. The health care sector was concentrated within the capital where 26 percent of the population resided. The Batista dictatorship all but ignored the rural population and directed only slightly more attention to other urban areas. Fully 60 percent of physicians and 80 percent of hospital beds were in Havana, "while four out of five rural workers . . . had no access to health care."[12] Rural populations were plagued by poverty, undernourishment, intestinal parasites, and such a complete lack of medical facilities that in 1958 there was but one single hospital in rural Cuba. In the countryside Cubans were "living in unbelievably stagnant, miserable, and desperate conditions," while Havana was prospering.[13] As Jean-Paul Sartre put it, "The system had pronounced sentence on itself. The population of the poverty-stricken had *quadrupled* in 50 years."[14] Other observers echoed Sartre's remarks: "With the lack of proper water and sewage systems . . . with the almost total absence of teaching of the fundamentals of good hygiene, with medical care for the rural masses often unobtainable, it is easy to understand why health conditions in Cuba have been deplorably bad."[15] C. Wright Mills, in his book reflecting the mood of Cuba at the time of the revolution, commented, "wasn't there after all something good about the old order? The question is—Good for whom? The answer is, good for this sort of man."[16] In Batista's time, monies were squandered on the military, the few in the upper and middle classes, and American investors—Cuba's poor suffered neglect and oppression, particularly as regards the abysmal lack of health care.

At the time, Cuba was practically the property of the United States, which bore extensive responsibility for the economic condition of the country. The largest nickel plant was owned by the United States; of the 174 sugar plantations 52 were controlled by Europeans, while 67 were American-owned, as were 9 of 10 of the largest sugar estates. Standard Oil, Republic Steel, U.S. Rubber, the King Ranch, and Pan American Land and Oil Royalty Company were among the corporations owning huge tracts of land or major enterprises, transferring their profits abroad while "most of the people ha[d] only the bare necessities of life."[17] The completeness of the ownership and the public crowing about it was historic. As former U.S. Ambassador Earl E. T. Smith remarked in 1960, "let me explain to you that the United States, until the advent of Castro, was so overwhelmingly influential in Cuba that . . . the American Ambassador was the second most important man in Cuba; sometimes even more important than the President."[18]

If the word "revolution" means anything, it refers to fundamental change in the political, social, and economic systems of society, a complete uprooting of the old social order and pre-revolutionary ideology. It was Castro's "magnificent obsession from the beginning . . . to do away with human, social, and economic underdevelopment."[19] Indicating as much in his "History Will Absolve Me" speech in October 1953, made while defending himself in court for the July 26, 1953, attack on the Moncada army barracks, Castro proclaimed the revolutionary struggle was for the "unredeemed masses to whom . . . nothing is given except deceit and betrayal; those who yearn for a more dignified and just fatherland; who are out of work . . . who live in miserable huts . . . and go hungry . . . and whose existence would move anyone without a heart of stone to compassion."[20]

After January 1959, Fidel Castro revolutionized the Cuban health care system, turning it on its head. Henceforth, there would be a cleansing of the old order, which had failed to accommodate the rural poor into the structure of society. A new framework would be enacted in which social rights would be emphasized, the health care system would be transformed, and Cuba's poor would be liberated from the tyranny of a neglectful health care system. The revolution in human rights had come to health care.

The Western perspective of human rights, based on the notion of atomized individuals possessed of certain inalienable rights in nature and emphasizing political and civil rights as opposed to social and economic rights, is embodied in the Universal Declaration of Human Rights. Although adopted unanimously by a vote of 48 for with 8 abstentions, most Third World and all socialist states have never considered the Universal Declaration binding. They have argued (1) that since it was not passed by the UN Security Council it remains merely a recommendation of intent; (2) that the conception of human rights founded on natural rights doctrines does not at all square with the concept of rights adhered to by them which is based on the well-being of the collectivity and not on the individual qua individual. In essence,

> the Universal Declaration of Human Rights is a document whose underlying values are democratic and libertarian. . . . These political values, distinct from economic rights or communal rights, can be traced directly to the experiences of France, England, and the United States. The Declaration is predicated on the assumption that Western values are paramount and ought to be extended to the non-Western world.[21]

In the Third World, which includes Cuba,

> An interrelated and interdependent set of factors account for the limited viability and applicability of the Western concepts of human rights. . . . Broadly speaking these factors can be divided into two categories: the cultural patterns and the development goals of new states, including the ideological framework within which they were formulated. Traditional cultures did not view the individual as autonomous and possessed of rights above and prior to society. Whatever the specific social relations, the individual was conceived as an integral part of a greater whole, of a 'group' within which one had a defined role and status.[22]

Freedom from starvation, the right for *all* to enjoy the benefits of an economy, and freedom from exploitation by colonial and imperialistic powers became the articulated goals of Third World countries. "Individual political rights, so revered in the West, at most take second place . . . to the priority of economic rights."[23] For Cuba, so extraordinarily dominated by the United States, "political and civil rights appeared as tools of the ruling class for maintaining themselves in power. . . . The conditions requisite for the internalization of concepts of individual human rights as defined by the West [were totally lacking]. Cuba's historical experience—cultural patterns, dependence on the West either as a colony or semi-colony . . . its continued underdevelopment—did not augur well for the emergence of a Western conception of human rights."[24]

The Cuban revolution rejected the political/civil rights philosophy so lauded in the West. A commitment to economic/social rights became the hallmark of the new government. The Western concept of rights had historically implicated Cuba in poverty, oppression, intolerance, and class bias, and it had caused its economy to be dependent upon and controlled by the United States. According to Adamantia Pollis, "The doctrines articulated by the modern political philosophers and the classical economists" regarding political and civil human rights "were not solely philosophic speculations . . . but concurrently an explanation of and a rationale for the development of industrial capitalist states."[25] In rejecting capitalism as the foundation for Cuba's economy Fidel Castro denied the validity of the Western concept of human rights, since the one was directly tied to the other. As a socialist state Cuba opted for an alternate perspective, one that emphasized the betterment of the nation as a whole, based on the notion that "civil and political rights cannot prevail if socioeconomic rights are ignored."[26] The state, eventually the Communist Party, would be the repository of collective values determining the "good" of the community, replacing and enlarging upon the tribe, religion, or ethnic group that had played that role in prior historical epochs.

The Third World and socialist conception of rights is of "rights with. Rights are not individual attributes. . . . They derive from relational situations with other persons. . . . Such a conception of rights is congruent with the notion of self not as an autonomous individual but as an integral part of the group; the individual has identity and a self only in terms of his or her relations with others in the reference group."[27] In this context, individual human rights become subservient.

Castro, operating within the framework of group rights, group needs, and group responsibilities, prioritized economic rights and social benefits. Health care would be refashioned, refocused, and redistributed to the entire population. It would not be developed for the individual who could afford to buy his or her way into the system, but as an entitlement, a human right, not fabricated through the concept of natural law but granted by the state. In the West, freedom of speech is an inherent right, though not absolute, while health care is a privilege; in Cuba, health care would be a state-granted right, while speech would be considered within the context of what was "good" for the larger community. The colossal polemic between Cuba and the United States over the meaning and interpretation of human rights on one level comes down to whether health care is a right or a privilege or whether individual civil freedoms are more central to the functioning of society. When Fidel Castro took power there was really never any doubt on which side of the divide he would stand. Health care was to be a right that all Cubans would have access to. And the history of the United States in Cuba from at least 1898 on gave it little legitimacy to invoke and impress a principle that had heretofore been used to oppress the people of Cuba.

COMPREHENSIVE HEALTH CARE

In 1959, Cuba created a universal, comprehensive, and free health care system both remarkable and successful, one "uniformly considered the preeminent model in the Third World."[28] Article 49 of the 1976 constitution provides that the state will guarantee that "Everybody has the right to health protection and care—by providing free medical and hospital care by means of the installations of the rural medical service network, polyclinics, hospitals and preventive and specialized treatment centers."[29] In developing a social policy that provides health care for all its citizens while at the same time organizing a pharmaceutical and biotechnology industry that is as resourceful as it is inspiring Cuba has made advances in medicine admired throughout the world. As even *The Economist,* which has taken a strident anti-Castro position, had to admit in 1996, "Cuban medicine is disciplined and innovative. . . . Cuban research establishments have made breakthroughs in vaccines, immunology and biotechnology."[30]

Cuba has become a powerhouse of medical innovation. In this small country of only 11 million people there are 284 hospitals, 440 polyclinics, 11 national research institutes, 4 dental schools, and 28 medical colleges, while with some 60,000 doctors and more than 5,000 researchers, "the national average ratio of physicians to total population is one doctor for every 180 people, and this does not count . . . nurses [72,000], physical therapists, medical technicians and medical researchers."[31] According to the *American Association for World Health,* "96% of the Cuban population was attended by physician-and-nurse teams living in the neighborhood they served, each assigned the care of approximately 150 families."[32] The priority of health care is indicated by the 1995 national budget, in which the third highest allocation of expenditures is given over to health care, following social security and education.[33] All Cuban physicians must complete a nine-year medical program with formidable medical standards and an additional three years of study for specialization.

Under the authority of the Ministry of Public Health free medical and health care is provided through a network of doctors, polyclinics, family doctor-and-nurse teams, and hospitals supplemented by the pharmaceutical and biotechnology industry. Women, under Article 43 of the constitution, have been given priority in medical care, as have children, and preventive-care programs such as the National Maternal-Child Program, the Family Doctor Program, the National Immunization Program, and the Early Detection Program for Breast and Cervical Cancer give resonance to that commitment. Life expectancy, infant mortality, and maternal mortality are comparable to Western nations and superior to that of almost all countries in Latin America.[34]

Urban and rural neighborhoods each have polyclinics that serve 30,000-40,000 people, which are supplemented by the neighborhood doctor-and-nurse teams. The community-based centers emphasize preventive and primary care and reach 95 percent of the population. Particularly in rural areas it is through these polyclinics that 98 percent of all children have been vaccinated against 12 major diseases including meningitis-B and hepatitis-B, polio, typhoid fever, and diphtheria The National Immunization Program was established in 1962, and the extensive inoculation of children and pregnant women has been credited with cutting the "infant mortality rate in Cuba [to] roughly half that in Washington, D.C."[35] The vaccines are provided to the clinics, doctors, and hospitals by the biotechnology industry and are distributed free of charge. Prescriptions for drugs and antibiotics are filled at state pharmacies (when the medicines are available) at no cost to the patient.

The polyclinics are integrated with maternity homes and the National Maternal-Child Program through which "90% of pregnant women receive prenatal care beginning in the first trimester."[36] According to Dr. Michele Frank, health editor of *Cuba Update* and a researcher with the *American Association for World Health*, the maternity homes offer residence to high-risk cases and also offer meals and vitamin supplements to outpatients to increase birth weights.[37] Family planning programs and contraceptives are provided by the polyclinics. Since 99 percent of births occur in hospitals it is clear that pregnant women are observed and taken care of to an extraordinary degree. Dr. Michele Frank and Gail Reed declare that "This fact has been credited with helping to reduce infant mortality . . . , which in 1996 stood at 7.9 per 1,000 live births, or the lowest rate in Latin America."[38] Cuba has recognized and acted upon the knowledge that most "of the major health risks for women are the direct consequences of pregnancy, such as uterine prolapse and obstetric fistulae. Others . . . are often exacerbated by pregnancy."[39] Day care centers and free abortion are also part of the network of services available. The rate of literacy in Cuba, 96.2 percent,[40] facillitates communication, so that the rural and urban polyclinics are easily able to gain access to and develop a positive relationship with the population.

For more serious cases and for treatment of the chronically ill, municipal hospitals exist in all cities. Of the 284 hospitals, 82 offer general services, 26 pediatric, 16 maternity, 19 OB-GYN, 30 surgical, 38 specialized, 64 rural, and 9 some mixture of the above. Many of the hospitals are really quite old, having been constructed prior to the revolution, and do not have the up-to-date facilities that are often required. Thus, these hospitals, such as Hospital Calixto Garcia, in Vedado, Havana, service patients whose illnesses are too complex for the clinics, but who do not require the services of the more modern hospitals. These antediluvian hospitals are usually made up of merely one building, or a series of low-rise structures each associated with a different specialty, but with only a limited number of beds available. In observing many of the older hospitals, which prior to the revolution may have been buildings serving other purposes, I often found that the beds were in large, poorly maintained rooms, with no separation between them. Waiting rooms usually were overflowing with patients, while treatment rooms had little medical stock and were barren of technology. In both old and new facilities specialists in the major fields were usually available, although they often did not have the resources to deal capably with their patients. Whatever services are available are provided free of charge, but, in the older hospitals certainly, the availability of medicines is sorely lacking as a result of the U.S. embargo.

The more modern and recently constructed hospitals, such as the Hospital Clinic Quirurgico "Hermanos Ameijeiras" in Central Havana—which had been partially constructed by Batista to house the National Bank but was completed by Castro as the largest hospital in Havana—offer services and treatment in the fields of bacteriology, microbiology, gastroenterology, optomology, dermatology, neurology, oncology, pathology, and trauma, among others. Clean, modern, often high-rise structures, these newer hospitals have a large number of beds that offer private and semiprivate facilities not found in the older hospitals. The technology available, including computer-driven equipment, is also newer. The National Oncology Institute and Hermanos Ameijeiras hospital have the two mammography units available in Havana (there are also 15 mobile units serving Havana and the other provinces). The newer hospitals, such as the Celia Sánchez Manduley Rehabilitation Center for Asthmatic Children, which opened in 1985, offer more specialized services and therefore the patient-to-doctor ratio is more reasonable than in the hospitals that provide multiple services. In visiting the various hospitals it was apparent that the newer ones were far less chaotic and far more organized. However, the organization can end at the hospital doors if one is not picked up by a private car, as patients are "released into the sweltering chaos of the hospital gates, where people on stretchers wait for hours for a gasping public service jitney."[41] Still, into these newer hospitals, and a few of the older ones, "modern techniques were introduced in virtually all 54 fields of medicine practiced in the country. This included . . . the first nuclear magnetic resonance equipment in Latin America, and an organ transplant program."[42]

Cuba has also developed an extensive mental health network for both adults and children. Mental health clinics are largely in urban areas and are often found in hospitals. Tension and mental disease have increased markedly due to the effects of the embargo, and psychiatrists and psychologists report that they are overwhelmed because "the more modern, better psychiatric medications produced in the U.S. are not available."[43] Health workers are also overburdened by the increase in patients and the complexities of the illnesses tied directly to physical deprivation. Since the latter can not be resolved until the embargo is lifted, or at least modified, treatment is often marginal at best, and most often unsuccessful. The stress accompanying the embargo is particularly striking among pregnant women and children, many of whom are often hungry, distraught, and angry with their parents for not being able to provide adequate amounts of food.

HIV/AIDS

HIV-positive cases were originally identified in 1986, three years after the Ministry of Public Health established the National AIDS Prevention and Management Commission to create a task force to track the disease. In 1985 the government allocated $2 million to develop a National AIDS Prevention and Control Program, through which 42 diagnostic centers were erected throughout the country. From 1986 to1996 1,200 HIV-positive cases were identified, of which 847 were men and 353 women, and which included 520 who were gay or bisexual.[44] According to the Ministry of Public Health 50 percent of the cases were transmitted through gay or bisexual activity while 43 percent resulted from heterosexual behavior. Of the HIV-positive cases 440 turned into full-blown AIDS, and 292 people died.[45]

Early on, the Cuban government established a policy of isolating AIDS patients in sanatoriums located in apartment houses or homes in rural areas. Although patients were permitted to return home on weekends, they usually did not due to the fear surrounding the disease. The sanatoriums essentially excised patients from the community; they were not given the medical support structure necessary, and some observers who saw them from the inside seemed shocked by their condition. After an outcry from the international AIDS community the policy was altered. In 1993 the Ministry of Public Health approved new guidelines under which AIDS patients would undergo initial diagnosis in upgraded and more substantially financed sanatoria for six months to determine treatment and to undergo psychological, social, and medical counseling. After doctors had determined the extent of their illness, patients deemed eligible would return home, be reintegrated into the community, and receive outpatient care. By 1996, 192 of those patients who had not developed full-blown AIDS were enrolled in the outpatient program.

The Havana-based Pedro Kourí Institute for Tropical Medicine "is the national reference center for clinical management of HIV-AIDS and provides hospitalization for AIDS cases when necessary and for those whose AIDS-related illness requires more complex services than those offered by sanatorium infirmaries."[46] Through the Havana Sanatorium and the National Center for AIDS Education, public lectures and other AIDS-related educational activities are conducted as outreach to affected families, the general public, and high school and university students. A National Blood Bank has been created, while research on the development of a vaccine has been under way for years at the Centro de Ingeniería Genética y Biotecnología (CIGB), with testing on humans presently ongoing.

As is clear from the statistics Cuba has kept the number of HIV-positive and full-blown AIDS cases low. The state has made a concerted effort to restrain the growth rate of the disease and, through its enterprise, has undertaken to test periodically and regularly adolescents and adults for the AIDS virus. But the effects of the ongoing embargo are particularly insidious as regards HIV/AIDS, since the United States holds pertinaciously to its present course of action. Because it is denied necessary medicines, Cuba's success in holding down the number of AIDS cases is due in large part to the emphasis placed on prevention.

PRIVATE HOSPITALS

As well as its extensive public hospital system Cuba has also developed a number of private hospitals providing specialized services, mostly for foreigners. For example, the Centro Internacional de Retinosis Pigmentaria Camilo Cienfuegos, a small hospital in Vedado, Havana, treats retinitis pigmentosa, glaucoma, and other eye diseases. The Center for Placental Histotherapy treats skin diseases, while the International Center for Neurological Restoration is one of the world's leading centers for the treatment of Parkinson's disease. People travel from all over the world to avail themselves of Cuban medical care. Other private hospitals provide treatment for cancer, open-heart surgery, and kidney transplants.

At the Camilo Cienfuegos hospital over 2,500 foreign patients from more than 38 countries have received treatment, while some 5,000 Cubans have been treated free of charge. Since the cost to foreign patients is not cheap, while the services provided are extraordinary, fees for services brought Servimed, Cuba's foreign health agency, $24 million in 1995.[47] No private services are available for U.S. citizens since a license from the U.S. Treasury Department is required for travel to Cuba and is not granted for such purposes. Dr. Michele Frank and Gail Reed reveal that "As a result, 78 people . . . have had to come to Cuba in defiance of U.S. law in order to receive treatment for retinitis pigmentosa, a treatment without which they would have gone blind. In this case, the U.S. embargo on Cuba forced people from the United States to choose between U.S. law and their health [since no treatment is available in the United States]."[48]

The private hospital infrastructure is generally superb since the hard currency paid by foreign patients is used to support this network of institutions. In fact the buildings often look like private clinics for the wealthy, reminiscent of the expensive town-houses on the Upper East Side of New York City, and the clinics are able to obtain almost everything they need in the way of supplies. Inside, everything from the private room furnishings to the spotlessness to the availability and diversity of medicine is eye-popping. They are first class enterprises. Even their location is usually in the wealthier part of Havana. Of the fees, 70 percent remain with the hospitals while 30 percent is turned over to the Ministry of Public Health to supplement its budget. Yet, even these private hospitals must often deal directly, or through the public health ministry, with Canada, Europe, Asia, South America, Mexico, and Israel to locate countries or enterprises willing to break the embargo so that medical supplies can be accumulated. The academic administrator of Centro Camilo Cienfuegos told me during a January 1997 interview that the hospital must often engage in such surreptitious purchasing despite the added expense. Public hospitals don't have that ability, but the private hospitals have the dollars to do so.

Clearly, a two-tiered class-based medical system exists to some degree. Foreigners can obtain the best fee-for-service procedures and rarely entertain deficiencies in obtaining medical care. Although Cubans can sometimes use the services in the private hospitals, often they can not and similar care, though available free for Cubans in public hospitals, can not be obtained because of the cost involved for Cuba in defying the embargo. Medicine, medical supplies, and technology are too often inaccessible.

BIOTECHNOLOGY AND PHARMACOLOGY

Cuba's primary research facilities are located in Havana, the most prominent being the Centro de Ingeniería Genética y Biotecnología, which was organized in 1986. Located on the outskirts of Havana and employing more than 800 people, this multi-building complex has developed a large quantity of medical products for Cubans while also exporting its innovative medical technology abroad. Two tertiary institutes exist outside Havana that concentrate on agricultural research and veterinary medicine. Exports of diagnostic equipment and pharmaceuticals are the sixth largest currency earner in U.S. dollars for Cuba, generating $120 million in 1995.[49] According to historian William Smaldone:

> These operations are world class and have been very successful in providing Cuba with human and animal medicines and in competing in foreign markets. The employees of the institutes tend to be young and highly motivated. The scientists we spoke with often worked fifteen hour days for very low salaries and lived on site. They saw their work as a privilege and laughed when we asked them if they were tempted to defect during their trips abroad.[50]

Most of the medical personnel I interviewed in 1997 said they remain in their positions because they are proud to be participants in what amounts to a reformation in health care. They are committed—most Cuban doctors are paid the equivalent of $14 per month in pesos; many volunteer for one-, two-, or three-year service programs that Third World countries contract out to Cuba. These nations request their services because of the international reputation Cuban health care has attained. To date some 23,000 Cuban health workers have participated in more than 40 countries, largely in Africa or the Caribbean, in such places as Grenada, Algeria, Angola, Ethiopia, Jamaica, South Africa, and Yemen.

CIGB contains multiple divisions, the most notable being vaccine development, immunotechnology, animal and plant biotechnology, and the production of recombinant molecules. Among their most noted work, researchers at CIGB have developed a recombinant vaccine against hepatitis-B or serum hepatitis, which is caused by a DNA virus. Cuba is also presently the sole producer of a vaccine against the bacteria that cause meningitis-B. The use of this vaccine in Cuba has reduced the incidence of the disease by 93 percent. Because "no vaccine against serogroup B menigococcal disease is currently licensed in the United States," the embargo prevents U.S. citizens from having access to this innovation, an instance of the embargo's effects being reversed.[51] While the highly renowned Cuban Institute of Hematology uses molecular biology in the treatment of leukemia and lymphomas, CIGB developed a process to extract interferon from leukocytes to treat such cases. A microsurgical approach to cure retinitis pigmentosa, a genetic disorder that causes a degeneration of the retina and leads to tunnel vision or total blindness and that affects one out of every 4,000 people worldwide, has been developed, with an 80 percent success rate. This process draws scores of foreign patients yearly for treatment that they would not otherwise be able to obtain. Alpha interferon is used to halt or delay the progression of AIDS and has extended the lives of many with the disease. Vitiligo, the loss of skin pigmentation, which was regarded heretofore as untreatable, is successfully being treated by newly developed substances that evolved from research at the Placental Histotherapy Center. The remission rate in severe cases is some 80 percent. The Cuban Institute of Cardiovascular Surgery created a special line of electro-cardiographic diagnostic equipment that is marketed internationally. Scientists at CIGB have also emphasized improving the food supply, which directly affects the health of the population. Researchers have "equipped sugarcane with bacterial genes that confer pest-resistance [and] developed a monoclonal antibody to detect tristeza, a lethal virus that threatens to devastate the Caribbean citrus industry."[52]

The medical technology developed by Cuban researchers certainly far exceeds that spawned in other Third World countries and, in many cases, matches, even sometimes surpasses, developments in the west. Breakthroughs have been made and the results are impressive, to say the least. The significance of Cuba's initiatives in this area is matched by its public health care system and the attention devoted to the primary health of its citizens. Impressive too is the fact that the United States, in violation of any human rights standard, is doing what it can to spoil, indeed even destroy the medical advances made by Cuba, and that whatever success is achieved is accomplished despite the deadly effects of the Cuban embargo cum blockade.

Because of the blockade the Cuban health care system exists within a framework of political and social contradiction. It is one of the jewels of the revolution, perhaps the most sparkling one, yet it is handicapped by the fierceness of the embargo and the fury of U.S. enforcement. While developing innovative medicines and techniques for delivery of services, the Ministry of Public Health and Cuban hospitals must literally shop around the world and pay exorbitant rates to obtain, often secretly, supplies that are available but inaccessible 90 miles away. In 1991 Ricardo Alarcón, presently President of the Cuban National Assembly of People's Power and a member of the Politburo, argued that the "U.S. embargo has caused Cuba substantial material losses. Total prohibition of Cuba's acquisition of foodstuffs, medicine and medical supplies and equipment of United States origin . . . has caused and still causes appreciable additional harm to the Cuban people."[53] The *American Journal of Public Health* goes further: "By reducing access to medicines and medical supplies from other countries and preventing their purchase from U.S. firms the embargo contributes to [the] rise in morbidity and mortality."[54] The United States, as concerns health care, has literally gone to war against Cuba. And since the embargo against Cuba is the longest embargo in history, lasting 37 years so far, the U.S. war against public health in Cuba has been unrelenting. It is curious that a nation that claims to be upholding human rights values would set those values aside to harm, not merely a government, but an entire people. The issue is not merely when the siege will end but what the destructiveness has already accomplished.

THE U.S. WAR AGAINST PUBLIC HEALTH

Prior to the passage of the March 12, 1996, Helms-Burton Act U.S. citizens who traveled to Cuba with an appropriate license from the Department of the Treasury were permitted to deliver untold amounts of medical supplies, but only to a single individual or family and only if the travel was by the daily U.S. chartered flight from Miami. Since the 1963 Trading with the Enemy Act requires a license from the U.S. Treasury Department even to donate medicine to Cuba, and the CDA only authorizes donations to nongovernmental organizations *provided* the donor can guarantee by on-site inspection within Cuba that the exported item is used for the purpose intended (which, since it involves Cuban sovereignty and extended periods of follow-through, is usually impossible), these Miami-to-Havana flights were a gateway through which large amounts of medicine and food found their way to Cuba. The charters were abruptly canceled by President Clinton in connection with Helms-Burton and were not re-authorized by him until March 20, 1998, at the behest of Pope John Paul II, who had earlier that year met with Fidel Castro in Havana and condemned the embargo.

Flying to Havana from Miami is a sad and telling experience; the process seems to have been concocted by some Washington bureaucrat who wanted to make travel to Cuba difficult and frustrating. Departure gates are not posted; you have to know ahead of time which foreign airline counter is being used for that day's single departure. The gate is usually far away from the turmoil of Miami International Airport so as to avoid attracting attention. The airline itself, although a U.S. charter, is often a plane with Haitian markings but flown by American pilots. From the check-in counter snakes an amazingly long line of people, mostly Cuban-Americans from Miami on their way to visit relatives they have perhaps not seen in years. Each passenger carries assorted boxes of medicine and food so heavy they can barely be lifted, which are tightly wrapped by airport officials so as to avoid being tampered with. It takes about four hours for the check in to be completed, by which time everyone has been thoroughly harassed and exhausted. Then come numerous security and passport checks. Since there is no assigned seating a mad scramble ensues on the plane to find an appropriate place. The entire process is an ordeal that Washington must have enjoyed inventing. (On arrival in Havana, you take your bags, which are not opened, quickly go through passport control, and within minutes leave the airport.) But the plane is a flight of rescue since medicines brought to Cuba in such bulk can not be transported privately in any other fashion, other than, in accord with the 1998 Executive Order, by licensed Catholic relief agencies on special and rare charter flights. On my flight, in 1995, which was my first into Cuba and my last from Miami, I was the single non–Cuban-American and the only one not weighed down by medical packages. On arriving in Havana that year, I discovered the importance of these flights, why Helms-Burton, perversely, did away with them, and why the Pope sought and attained their reinstatement. There was no medicine anywhere to be found. The pharmacies were empty. Upon entering the large and once-bountiful Drogería Johnson on the once-fashionable Calle Obispo, an expansive Batista-era drug store almost entirely fashioned of expensive wood, one could find no medicine at all—no Band-Aids, no vitamins, no aspirin; nothing. The shelves were entirely bare, except for the occasional empty and dusty medicine jar that looked decades old. While I was there, a couple entered the store, requested that a prescription be filled, and were told it was impossible. That was and remains Cuba in the "Special Period in the Time of Peace."

Ever since 1989-1991, when the Soviet bloc unraveled and Cuban subsidies ended, the U.S. embargo on medicines and medical technology traveled the road from obstacle to crisis. Whereas earlier it led to only some dislocation because Cuba's East European allies saw to it that embargoed medicine found its way into Cuba, after 1991 the embargo bit severely. With a 60 percent decline in the gross domestic product of Cuba within one year, probably one of the steepest in history in a non-war circumstance, the economy was in shambles, and there was precious little hard currency to buy anything with. "Up to 1989, the embargo placed conditions on the 15 percent of Cuba's international trade which fell outside the socialist market; after 1991, the embargo had a restrictive influence on more than 90 percent of that trade."[55] As the crisis arrived the United States and its embargo struck hard and unfalteringly. Cubans would immediately learn what scarcity in the field of health meant.

In examining the practice of medicine in various hospitals and polyclinics, and in interviewing medical personnel, it is clear that although the precise effects of the U.S. embargo vis-a-vis health care and medical research may be little known elsewhere they are exceedingly apparent in Cuba.

Because most antibiotics are produced under U.S. patents they can not be exported to Cuba under terms of the embargo. Of the more than 300 major drugs on the market since 1970 nearly 50 percent were of U.S. origin and thus effectively blocked from shipment to Cuba. Additionally, the various embargo acts disallow Cuba from using the U.S. dollar in international trade, costing the country additional money for exchanging currencies. U.S. regulations also disallow the re-export of U.S. products from a third country, while products even developed through the use of U.S. technology or design can not be sold to Cuba. Any domestic corporation, foreign enterprise, or third country found doing so can be slapped with U.S. sanctions, while companies that "traffic" in nationalized property in Cuba (that is, use its facilities) may find their executives prohibited from entry into the United States and can be sued in U.S. courts. Indeed, in 1996 President Clinton barred major executives from Canada's Sherritt International Corporation, a mining conglomerate, from entering the United States for just such "trafficking." Third-party countries can also be denied aid for trading with Cuba on credit, while the U.S. has effectively blocked any help from reaching Cuba via the World Bank or the International Monetary Fund (IMF), largely cutting Cuba off from foreign loans. In 1998 the United Nations Development Program did grant Cuba $1.15 million in aid, but monies allocated to Cuba by the UN are usually quite paltry. Extra shipping costs incurred by having to purchase supplies from far away and mark-ups resulting from both legal and illegal trade added up to some $9 million between 1994 and 1997.[56]

Waterborne diseases are prevalent in Cuba because of prohibitions against the sending of equipment to replace parts for water pumping stations purchased decades ago. Chlorination equipment and replacement parts are so laborious to obtain that an increase in the incidence of intestinal infections occurs sporadically. Chlorination installation operations are half what they were prior to 1991.

Items related to nutrition and sanitary conditions are in short supply. There is always a severe shortage of soap and toilet paper, and milk is rationed, with the only steady supply going to children under seven; basic foodstuffs are in short supply. The 1997 *American Association for World Health* report indicates that foreign shippers, hesitant to run afoul of the United States, often refuse to transport goods that Cuba has already purchased.

As far as women's health is concerned the effect has been drastic. Since most chemotherapy drugs are of American origin these life-saving medications often remain unavailable. American X-ray film for mammography units, which remains the best in the world, is embargoed, and the units are often without supply. Drugs used in protocols for breast cancer are not always sufficient, causing delayed treatment, increases in death rates, and great anxiety among patients and their families. Anticancer agents developed locally by the biotechnology industry are also affected as U.S. licenses have been denied for some of the ingredients necessary for production. With more than 25,000 cases of cancer diagnosed yearly, and therapies and medication restricted because of the embargo, hospital stays have increased, as have life-threatening situations. Radiation therapy is also influenced as the best quality equipment is manufactured in the United States. Low birth weights among newborns as a result of mothers' poor nutrition have become a major concern.

Dr. Michele Frank and Gail Reed assert that "Limiting Cuban AIDS patients' access to medicines is the most critical result of the U.S. embargo."[57] No AIDS medications approved in the United States are consistently available in Cuba, and as the U.S. manufactures some 70 percent of the available medications the ramifications are critical. Although some purchases of AZT and interferon are made in Europe, the cost is excessive and the supplies rare. Because of licensing prohibitions, Cuban families of AIDS patients residing in the United States are severely restricted in their ability to visit their relatives. Another by-product of the embargo is an increase in sexually transmitted diseases caused by the lack of condoms. Although Cuba requires 125 million per year only some 23 million were available in 1995, and those purchased, predominately in India, cost three times as much as they would in the United States. The safety of the blood supply is also threatened as American reagents for laboratory work have been cut off while the lack of fuel curtails air-conditioning and disrupts refrigeration.

In late 1995, America's largest pharmaceutical corporation, Merck, announced it would never do business again with Castro's Cuba after it suffered U.S. sanctions and a fine for providing medical information, and only information, to Cuba. Examples of technologies banned because they were partially developed by a U.S. firm or contain U.S. components include

> A sale by the Japanese company Toshiba of medical equipment used to detect cardiovascular diseases and blood analysis laboratory equipment from the Swedish firm LKB. U.S. Commerce officials also forbade the Argentine supplier Medix from shipping spare parts needed by Cuban hospitals to maintain U.S.-made dialysis machines and ophthalmologic sonar equipment already in use throughout the island.[58]

According to the U.S.-based Disarm Education Fund Cuban Medical Project, which raises money to donate medicine to Cuba, "Over 75 percent of the world's insulin supply is made in Puerto Rico. . . . But because of the U.S. blockade Cuba must spend scarce foreign currency to purchase insulin half-way around the world, at four times the price available right next door!"[59] Licensing of U.S. medical doctors to even donate services to Cuba is highly restricted, as are the donated medicines themselves. In fact, "The U.S. denied travel licenses to a group of ophthalmological surgeons to operate on dozens of Cuban patients in a professional exchange between Project Orbis and Cuban teams at the Pando Ferrer Ophthalmological Hospital in Havana."[60]

U.S. sanctions, according to the *New England Journal of Medicine,* were the immediate cause of an epidemic of 50,000 cases of malnutrition-induced optic and peripheral neuropathy between 1991 and 1993, and the Ministry of Public Health had to initiate a crash program of importing multiple-vitamin supplementation for the Cuban people.[61] To add insult to injury, in 1994 the U.S. Commerce Department denied an export license for X–ray replacement parts costing less than $175.[62] For Washington nothing is too petty when it comes to lacerating the Cuban people through the instrument of the embargo. Because gasoline is in such short supply, and travel is expensive and difficult, medical patients in the interior often find that they cannot travel to hospitals in which services are performed. Even mobile hospital vans and ambulances are affected by the embargo because of a lack of fuel oil and spare parts.

U.S. medical journals, periodicals, and texts, required by the various Cuban medical schools and necessary to keep up-to-date, are disallowed, costing Cuba inordinate amounts of additional hard currency to acquire the materials elsewhere (if they are attained at all) at inflated prices. In browsing through various university and medical libraries in Cuba what leaps out from the stacks and card-catalogues is the dearth of books and periodicals published in the United States after 1976. There are almost none.

In the effort to deprive Cuba of access to U.S. dollars Americans are disallowed from benefiting from Cuban medical innovations and technology either in the United States or in Cuba. Those who violate the Cuban Assets Control Regulations may incur penalties of up to ten years in prison and $1,000,000 in corporate and $250,000 in individual fines.[63] Licensed travel is sharply restricted, while the travel agents who handle arrangements in the United States must themselves receive government authorization. Only certain categories of travelers may be licensed—those traveling for research, religious, educational, or informational activities or persons visiting sick relatives (journalists, government officials, and travelers visiting relatives in extreme humanitarian need once yearly do not require a license). Requests for permission to travel made to the Department of the Treasury are often denied without explanation. The goal of such constraints is to isolate Cuba economically while depriving it of U.S. dollars. If granted approval, visitors may spend only $100 per day on travel, accommodations, and goods personally used by the traveler; records of such expenses may be requested by the Treasury Department. Despite the fact that about 17,000 Americans travel illegally to Cuba every year—mostly younger people looking for a good time—the penalties can be harsh, although youthful travelers, usually back-packers without much money, are not normally pestered by U.S. customs agents unless contraband Cuban cigars are being carried.[64] Approximately 70,000 legally licensed U.S. citizens traveled to Cuba in 1998.

Because Cuba is a poor country with a severe shortage of hard currency and is hobbled by agricultural shortfalls, the embargo's ramifications on the health care system are enormous. In sum, according to the *American Journal of Public Health,* "the embargo has contributed to the deterioration in the quality of health care and has exacerbated undernutrition by raising the cost of medical supplies . . . to the island. . . . The medical system is still able to provide near universal coverage and to ensure the continuance of low mortality of those under 65 years of age even in the face of rising health threats. Yet despite the highly efficient use of health goods, these goods can no longer be stretched to meet the needs of the entire population."[65]

That Fidel Castro, the Communist Party, and Cuban government authorities continue to pour precious funds into health care certainly indicates the importance that sector has within society. In 1959 Castro affirmed a commitment to providing a comprehensive health care system in which everyone would benefit, regardless of their economic standing. That promise has been kept. Despite the evident contradiction of having developed an extraordinary health care model while being bedeviled by the United States, which has successfully destroyed much of its effectiveness, the Cuban people and Cuba's many medical practitioners can be proud of what has been accomplished through perseverance and engagement. The behavior of United States, on the other hand, has been disgraceful.

THE QUESTION OF IDEOLOGY

Article 25 of the Universal Declaration of Human Rights states clearly that "Everyone has the right to a standard of living adequate for the health and well-being of himself and his family, including . . . medical care and necessary social services."[66] Articles 12 and 10 of the 1976

United Nations International Covenant of Economic, Social and Cultural Rights (which the United States has not ratified) "recognize the right of everyone to the enjoyment of the highest attainable standard of physical and mental health" and that "special protection should be accorded to mothers during a reasonable period before and after childbirth."[67] The Republic of Cuba has attempted to adhere to these international covenants, while the United States, one of the formidable advocates of the Universal Declaration of Human Rights, promulgated by the United Nations Commission of Human Rights chaired by Eleanor Roosevelt, has taken every opportunity to subvert these statutes when it comes to health care in Cuba. Human rights has become a "tool of international power politics . . . because the ideological function fulfilled by the drive for fundamental human rights rests precisely from their being detached from the concrete life experiences and circumstances of individuals living in the world's various societies."[68]

At a time when the United States embraces governments in Peru, Serbia, Indonesia, Liberia, Kenya, the Congo, and China, among others, nations in which the civil and political human rights of populations continue to be suppressed, people are imprisoned, or murdered for their beliefs, and which usually offer little in the way of economic benefits (but where capitalism is often praised as an economic model), it is ironic that the United States continues its oppressive and illegal ways in Cuba. What the United States continues to make apparent is that its "human rights policies have tended to promote the Western conception of rights as superior to indigenous third world ideologies and as more salient than socioeconomic realities."[69] Presidential administrations from Eisenhower to Clinton have steadfastly adhered to an archaic policy that places ideology and frustration with Castro's incredible survival skills, ahead of vital national security interests and adherence to its own position on human rights, which proclaims the right to life. Violating the human rights of the Cuban population "carries within it implicit assumptions which represent the unspoken givens of cultures and societies in historical time."[70] Since Washington has supported many governments that violate the political rights of their people far more extensively than does the government of Cuba without guaranteeing any economic or social rights, its Cuban policy is not based solely on Cuba's violations of political rights. Ideology, economics, and domestic political considerations are the relevant variables, and America's activities, which zero in on the very health and survival of Cubans, can not be said to have very much to do with human rights.

Fidel Castro will soon be fencing with his tenth U.S. president; his struggle with the first nine has not only been about the violation of human rights in Cuba but, at least in the later years, has also had much to do with ideological differences, particularly Castro's rejection of the entire capitalist notion. Health care and Cuba's human rights position are caught up in ideology and the hubris of the sole existing superpower, which believes it can exert its authority unconditionally since there is no countervailing power to constrain it. "Western nations, do not consider the right to food, clothing, and shelter as fundamental,"[71] and since Cuba, a weak and underdeveloped communist nation, is not China, politically and geopolitically commanding and now a promoter of capitalism and a huge U.S. trading partner, the United States remains quite prepared to demolish a health care system that is a first world enterprise in the Third World, and that has attained the status of being the ultimate model of what health care ought to be for and in emerging nations.

In late 1959 Che Guevara insisted "that the common bond shared by Cuba with the newly independent former colonial states was the drama of freedom from economic exploitation. He argued that revolutionary Cuba, personified by Fidel Castro, was a model for change not only in Latin America but in Asia and Africa as well."[72] For the United States, the ferocious onslaught against health care continues to be a consummate effort to tarnish the model that, at least in health care, is Cuba.

FOUR

STARVING THE CUBAN PEOPLE

THE MOST EXPLOSIVE IMPACT OF THE U.S. EMBARGO, even worse than that on public health, is the effect on food and hunger. In 1991, when Cuba encountered what has been termed a "second embargo"—the elimination of virtually all trade with the former Soviet bloc—the country faced a crisis that few nations would be able to surmount. With 85 percent of its trade directed to its former socialist allies and 93 percent of that trade vanishing almost overnight, Cuba entered a period of economic disintegration. Between 1991 and 1994 the economy contracted by between 35 and 50 percent, while its import capability for food, fuel, fertilizers, and pesticides plunged by more than 60 percent. Key foodstuff imports by Cuba prior to the collapse of the Soviet Union included 100 percent of its wheat, 50 percent of its rice, 38 percent of its milk and dairy, 99 percent of its beans, 44 percent of its fish, 33 percent of its poultry, 21 percent of its meat, 94 percent of its oil and lard, and 64 percent of its butter. Of the population's total calories in diet 57 percent came from imported food items.[1] The country also lost 98 percent of its petroleum supplies. In 1991 economic aid from the Soviet Union to Cuba totaled $1 billion, $3 billion less than one year earlier; by 1992 President Boris Yeltsin proclaimed an end to all economic assistance. Already by 1986 it was estimated that Cuba's Soviet bloc debt stood at $22 billion.[2] In a grand understatement, agriculturalists Peter Rosset and Medea Benjamin indicated that "when trade collapsed with the socialist bloc, the degree to which Cuba exhibited an essentially monocrop agriculture [in sugar] proved to be a major weakness."[3]

Although the situation appeared as dire as could be imagined it would only get worse. The United States, recognizing the frightful economic plight that Cuba was now in, proceeded to tighten the noose in a "final push" to eliminate Fidel Castro; it helped to create such overwhelming distress via the weapon of starvation that the population would direct its fury against him, leading, the theory went, to his being toppled from power. In bureaucratic language cold and foreboding a study published by the Institute for International Economics calculated that

> sanctions are supposed to impose economic penalties in order to coerce the target country to alter its policies; if the sanctions impose no costs, they are unlikely to change foreign behavior. In short, the level of costs importantly determines the success or failure of a sanctions episode. The 'success' of an economic sanctions episode—as viewed from the perspective of the sender country—has two parts; the extent to which the policy outcome sought by the sender country was in fact achieved, and the contribution made by the sanctions . . . to a positive outcome.[4]

The "positive outcome" desired was to force Castro out or, inconceivably, to pressure him to rescind his socialist belief system and move toward a "democratic" and electoral system based on Western values. The "contribution," of course, was starvation. The result was that the United States presumed to provoke the most extraordinary food crisis the Cuban nation had ever faced. The irony is that rather than driving Castro from power it only helped to eventually solidify his authority. Cuba reeling was what Washington witnessed; Cuba sans Castro was what it desired and it rapidly moved to try to make that a reality.

In 1992, President George Bush signed into law the Cuban Democracy Act (CDA), an act of incredible meanness and vindictiveness, but one that was also supported by President-elect Bill Clinton. Both men had campaigned strenuously in Miami for the Cuban-American vote, promising to stiffen resistance to Castro, and this act was the fulfillment of campaign pledges made. As Bush said at the signing ceremony, the leaders of the Cuban-American community were the "key forces behind this" act. Another force was its primary sponsor, New Jersey Democratic Congressman Robert Torricelli, who, though usually liberal on foreign policy issues, represented a sizeable Cuban-American community from which he received extensive campaign contributions because of his anti-Castro stand. In 1996 Torricelli, heavily supported by his Cuban-American constituents, was elected to a Republican-controlled United States Senate, having defeated his Republican opponent Richard Zimmer by ten percentage points.

The CDA, under Section 1707, reiterated the embargo on the sale of food (initiated in 1960 and reinforced in 1962 and 1964), which could now only be lifted if (in a phrase that smacked of true chutzpah) a "Transitional Cuban Government" was prepared to conduct "free and fair elections for a new government" and publicly committed itself to respect "internationally recognized human rights" (i.e. the Western perspective based on the Universal Declaration of Human Rights). Under Section 1706, the CDA intensified the embargo on exports of food to Cuba by prohibiting vessels that entered Cuban ports from loading or unloading any freight in the United States for a period of six months after departure from Cuba, and prohibiting ships in which Cuba has any "interest" from entering a U.S. port. It also restricted U.S. subsidiaries abroad from trading with Cuba, which curtailed Cuban food imports even more dramatically since most such trade was in food and medicine. The issue of extraterritoriality was approached, not only in Section 1706 but also in Section 1704 in which the president was authorized to withhold foreign aid to any country providing assistance to Cuba "on terms more favorable than that generally available in the applicable market."[5] The Cuban Democracy Act was seen by the U.S. Congress and President Bush as the instrument that would result in the denouement of the Castro era, finally achieving the "outcome sought by the sender country," as "the evident inability of Cuba's economy to survive current trends, provide[d] the United States . . . with an unprecedented opportunity. . . ."[6]

The necessity for the CDA, from the perspective of the conservatives in Washington and their allies in Miami, is evident in one striking trade figure for the years 1988-1992. Although it was assumed that the catastrophe of 1991 could not be overcome, exports by U.S. subsidiaries of "grain, wheat and other consumables to Cuba increased nearly tenfold," even though "the island was battered full-force by economic crisis. . . ."[7] Thus, to eliminate one of the few avenues through which food imports could still be garnered and to assert U.S. authority to get third-party countries to withhold exports, the CDA was passed by Congress, signed by the president, supported by the incoming president, and imposed on Cuba.

Prior to the passage of the CDA, the Cuban American Committee Research and Education Fund complained that "We understand that Congressman Torricelli has been heavily lobbied by the extreme sector of the Cuban American community. But most of the community is increasingly concerned for the well-being of their relatives on the island. The bill does nothing more than increase the suffering of Cubans on both sides of the straits of Florida."[8] Perhaps, but the elemental distress would be in Cuba, and it is the United States—the country U.S. Secretary of State Madeleine Albright referred to as the "indispensable nation" that "stand[s] tall" and sees "further into the future"[9] but, as one observer wrote, whose "moralism and exceptionalism only make it harder to accept . . . self restraint"[10]—that must be held fully accountable for the hunger, malnutrition, and, as some Cubans insist, famine that would afflict the island of Cuba.

CHAOS IN CUBA

In 1959 the National Agrarian Reform Institute (INRA) was created to incorporate the more than 40 percent of the land that had been ordered nationalized into cooperatives, and eventually state farms. Although compensation of 20-year bonds at 4½-percent interest was offered (and rejected by most American companies and Cuban landowners as inadequate), by 1960 more than 2.5 million acres of sugarcane plantations and cattle ranches had been confiscated, including the estates of the largest American corporations. By 1962 the state controlled 63 percent of all cultivated land; by the late 1980s it was above 80 percent. "The implementation of the agrarian reform program . . . laid to rest, finally, that dream of a sturdy, independent peasantry. Though many small farmers were permitted to keep their lands, their activities were severely circumscribed. As in all other matters [Castro] was firmly convinced that he knew more about agriculture than the farmers did."[11] The development of INRA was the first solid evidence that Cuba was developing into the planned economy that two years later would be officially designated as socialist. In agriculture at least the planned economy was proving to be a failure.

Up through 1970, when, by a monumental effort, Cuba harvested 8.5 million metric tons of sugar, 1.5 million metric tons short of its goal, production never reached the expected quotas. But from that point to the end of the decade "the Cuban economy enjoyed a period of unprecedented economic growth. Decentralization of economic management and rationalization of the planning process . . . combined to improve the efficiency of the economy."[12] But the reliance on "King Sugar," whereby 60 percent of the land is dedicated to sugarcane, monopolizing the country's most fertile soil, negates any capability for diversification, disallows large-scale investment in sustainable organic/traditional forms of agriculture, and along with low commodity prices and declining harvests, can devastate the economy. By 1993 the sugar harvest stood at some 4 million metric tons,[13] while in 1995 output of Cuba's main cash export fell to merely 3.3 million metric tons. As prices declined, "the Cuban economy's expansion declined with them."[14]

The collapse of the Soviet Union in 1991 could not have come at a more inopportune time. With small harvests, low commodity prices, and the Soviet Union having been purchasing Cuban sugar at a subsidized price of 5.4 times above the open market world price,[15] Cuba was in a fragile position, truly perhaps even a political turning point. Though it quadrupled its nickel exports, largely to Canada, increased delivery of medicines abroad, and received monies from foreign patients making use of its extraordinary rehabilitation clinics,

Cuba could not stem the looming economic mess. By 1994 Cuba's real Gross Domestic Product (GDP) annual growth rate had declined by more than 50 percent from the 1985 level—from 1.6 percent to 0.7 percent.[16] As Castro admitted, "For decades our plans were based on the existence of a socialist camp, on the existence of several socialist countries in eastern Europe, in addition to the Soviet Union, with whom we signed agreements and established extensive economic relations. We have no security as to what trade will be like . . . and we have complete uncertainty for the period 1991-95."[17] The crisis was full-blown by 1991, the period Castro had designated one year earlier as the "Special Period in the Time of Peace." Cuba's almost nonviable agricultural sector and the elimination of all Soviet aid and most trade indicated that the U.S. embargo would be more devastating than it ever had been in the past.

Beginning in 1991, the people of Cuba had to confront a situation perhaps more frightening than anything they had ever faced. Although some would insist that the 1962 Cuban Missile Crisis should receive that distinction, for Cubans at that time there was little they could do, and it did not affect their everyday existence, so life went on more or less as usual, interrupted only by the intermittent radio speeches of Castro vehemently denouncing the United States for its aggressive activities. The fall of the Soviet Union was materially of an entirely different order.

Food disappeared. Meat was no longer available, and even fish vanished from the table of those far from the sea as transportation of foodstuffs, as well as everything else, became impossible because of the lack of fuel and spare parts. "Food shortages emerged . . . ; all basic products were returned to the ration system, and supplies of many became highly unstable."[18] Bread faded from the diet as fuel shortages intermittently halted production, while imports of wheat were sharply curtailed as exporters encountered roadblocks in transportation because of the embargo. When bread was available, Cubans were rationed one roll per day. Caloric intake dropped from 2,800 a day per person in 1989 to 1,863 in 1993, a reduction of some 33 percent, and government-provided lunches at workplaces and schools furnished 300 of those calories. Protein intake plummeted 40 percent.[19] In the ten-year span from 1985 to1995 the food production index sank 34 percent.[20] The decline in agricultural production was exaggerated by a decline of 80 percent in the availability of pesticides and fertilizers due to reduced imports. Anemia made its appearance as iron deficiencies in diet occurred. Nutritional deficiencies increased notably among pregnant women, while low birth weights among newborn children registered a remarkable rise.

Importing food products became time consuming, difficult, and often impossible as a result of the CDA, which of course was the very purpose of the legislation.

> Just weeks after the CDA was enacted a New Zealand milk producer canceled a long-standing contract to sell Cuba 1500 metric tons of powdered milk. . . . An Italian supplier could not find a tanker for some 9,000 metric tons of soy cooking oil. Some 17,000 metric tons of rice sat at sea while the Chinese supplier re-negotiated higher freight terms with the shipper, who cited risks under the newly-enacted CDA as the reason for increasing his rates.[21]

Prior to 1990, Cuba imported 23,000 tons of powdered milk and other dairy products from East Germany and the Soviet Union; that supply was eliminated in 1991. Milk was then removed from the ration card throughout Cuba and only children under seven were guaranteed a daily supply of one quart; pregnant women were given qualified access to milk, the ration being 45 ounces monthly from the third to the ninth month.[22] Indeed, even in 1995 the Cuban government was considering whether to reduce the number of children guaranteed milk by capping the age at three-and-a-half; a policy change that was eventually rejected.[23] Even chicken and eggs were in short supply since almost all starter chicks and chicken feed had been imported. Through rationing the government insured that everybody would have access to minimal amounts, tiny as the ration might appear, and in Havana the yearly per person ration was 1¾ pounds of chicken and 119 eggs. Other yearly rations in 1995 were 24 pounds of fish, 3 pounds of corn meal, 24 pounds of dried beans, 4 pounds of poultry pate, 6 pounds of spaghetti, 72 pounds of rice, 60 quarts of soy yogurt for children between 7 and 13, 2½ pounds of sausage, and 72 pounds of sugar.[24]

Cigarettes and cigars were also on ration but were often traded for other items by nonsmokers.

The writer Tom Miller reported that in the first year of the disaster, "everywhere I went, whomever I spoke with, the talk drifted to the underground price of this item or that product. . . . At the Socialism or Death bakery . . . only one type of bread."[25] The black market or underground economy "enjoyed a spectacular growth, especially in tandem with the apparently inexorable [illegal] dollarization of the economy through the burgeoning tourist sector and remittances from family members in Miami."[26] Another observer wrote of that period that prostitutes "lined the curbs of the road along the sea, and the insistent *jineteros,* hustlers, . . . sidled up to you whenever you took a walk, offering to buy illegal American dollars or sell cheap sex, or Cohiba cigars, or stolen boxes of the energy-enhancing drug PPG."[27]

In 1995, the food crisis remained stark. The people I spoke with at that time were clearly frightened. Senator Jesse Helms and his anti-Castro crusade was on everyone's lips. What was he going to do? What new legislation did he have in mind? Helms was clearly a presence in Cuba, in ways that certainly would have satisfied him. Even in 1997, pop art caricature graffiti representing Helms as evil or comical was painted on walls lining Havana's La Rampa thoroughfare.

Food *was* on everyone's mind, even in 1995, and when I was invited to Cuban homes for lunch or dinner, cheese sandwiches, sometimes only a small piece of fish, and potatoes were the essential fare. Electricity blackouts and brownouts were prevalent, lasting at times for hours, while few cars were on the road. Highways, modern and well paved in almost all cases, were eerily deserted, with only the occasional tour bus roaring by, while bicyclists and walkers were fixtures on these roads that traversed the island from west to east. On the street, mothers with infants begged for milk or some food, while men, many clearly once of the middle strata of society, were forced to hawk their one or two cigars for a few pesos or dollars.

The few restaurants were bereft of customers, while long lines appeared at stores whenever there was a rumor that this food or that item of clothing would be sold. State agricultural markets had little produce, only the occasional grapefruit, head of lettuce, or other fruits or vegetables. Most Cubans survived on one meal a day. As one American reporter indicated, "In today's Cuba, it was everyday irony. At the heart of tobacco country, there is nothing to smoke. Amid canefields that stretch out of sight, there is no sugar for coffee. Or coffee. At the state store in Santa Damiana, shelves were empty but for a cluster of jars: They contained colored plastic buttons. 'There are no shoes' explained a tobacco picker. 'There is nothing. Maybe two eggs a month, maybe one. No cooking oil. No soap for five months.'"[28]

Outside of hotels I saw no toilet paper; books and newspapers could only be published in limited number because of the acute paper shortage. What gasoline there was could only be purchased with U.S. dollars (the use of which had been legalized in July 1993). 35-and 40-year-old Studebakers, Pontiacs, Hudsons, and Chevrolets sat idly in the streets. Society seemed to be torn asunder as students and professionals became taxi drivers, waiters, bellhops, chambermaids, and tour guides to gain access to dollars. Prostitution appeared as a major problem, as formerly secure mothers and daughters were forced into the streets to bring desperately needed dollars home. Salaries were cut to the equivalent of about $14 per month, and food, even on the ration card, was in short or non-existent supply. The struggle for survival was on.

The farther away from Havana the more desperate the situation. With fewer tourists, there were fewer available dollars. In the two sizable cities in the west, Pinar del Río and Viñales, young children and adults roamed the streets begging for food. Outside Havana, sometimes even on the outskirts of the city, donkey- or horse-drawn carts were the prevalent means of transportation aside from bicycles, ancient city buses belching carbon monoxide, and walking. Desperation was everywhere, and more than a few Cubans spoke of famine far to the east. Others denied it, but no one was really certain.

The United States, through the CDA, had clearly sabotaged the Cuban economy. As bad as the economy would have been after the fall of the Soviet Union, the destructive piece of legislation insured that Cuba would descend to the depths of deprivation. Typically, however, by 1995, when the very worst had passed, most people I spoke with and interviewed did not blame Fidel Castro or the Communist Party for the miserable state of affairs. Most assumed it was not Castro's fault. Anger was directed at the U.S.-supported Radio Martí—a Cuban-American enterprise broadcasting propaganda from the United States to Cuba—and to Jorge Mas Canosa, then the head of the Cuban American National Foundation, the leading Miami-based anti-Castro political organization. Castro had turned the crisis to his advantage, again displaying his incredible political shrewdness and survival skills by casting himself as a nationalist—not a communist—standing against the onslaught of the United States. As he said in a radio and television broadcast in 1995:

> Cuba lies at the very gates of a powerful and expansionist nation which has never ceased to extend its frontiers. . . . Few countries in the world have had to face a more colossal challenge and risk than that met by Cuba. Our people, in spite of abruptly losing 70 percent of their imported goods and all military cooperation . . . went ahead to defend, at all costs, their independence, their exceptional social conquests, their glorious history, their ideals, their revolution and the fruit of the blood shed by their children within and outside Cuba.[29]

Even Pico Iyer, in his fine novel on Cuba during this time, *Cuba and the Night,* spoke through his protagonist of Castro's skill in turning the crisis to his advantage: "But who else could help him the way the U.S. government has? They're his best ally—trying to put bombs in his cigars, invading Girón [the Bay of Pigs] and Grenada, so he can always tell the people that all the problems are because of the embargo and he's standing up against Goliath."[30]

Aside from the human toll, by 1993 Carlos Lage, Cuba's vice president and the man in charge of directing its economic reforms, estimated that losses to Cuba due to the blockade totaled $40 billion, which did not "take into consideration all losses, such as lost investments or investments under less favorable terms."[31] Cuba's foreign minister Roberto Robaina, in a 1993 letter to the secretary-general of the United Nations, maintained that the $40 billion was "the approximate equivalent of twenty times the country's current account revenue for 1992. Its effects have been present in practically all sectors of the economy, and have had an accumulative effect over more than 30 years. . . ." [32] In a speech to the WTO in Geneva in May 1998 Castro claimed the embargo had cost Cuba close to $60 billion.

The toll on social existence remains remarkable as values are twisted to deal with America's exsanguination policy. Breadwinners are forced to practically pimp themselves economically to Western tourists, having to give up solid professions in the process. Family life is disrupted and distorted. Mental health is affected as adults develop psychological problems because they are unable to fulfill responsibilities that heretofore were experienced as intrinsic to their self-worth and fulfillment. Children experience anger toward parents for being unable to furnish food and other essentials. Workers can't work, parents can't provide, children's needs can't be met, and, most ironically, since 1993 the U.S. dollar, the currency of the enemy, has become far more important and far more necessary to survival than the Cuban peso.

A startling dislocation of values have occurred in the hotels visited by tourists. Whether in the grand Hotel Nacional that overlooks the Malecón, the circular boulevard astride the Caribbean Sea; the Hotel Inglaterra, opposite Parque Central; or the Habana Libre—better known to some as the former Hilton Hotel in its pre-nationalized life—or any hotel for that matter, the amount of food available is disconcerting. Enormous quantities of ham, cheese, bread, yogurt, milk, coffee, and fruits are available for breakfast at a cost of about $15, an entire month's salary for the average Cuban employee. In the evening, assorted meats can be ordered that most Cubans won't see in a year, if ever. Cuban waiters, bellhops, chambermaids, desk clerks, and kitchen employees must pander to their guests knowing the food served is unavailable to Cubans. Seventy percent of each dollar earned in foreign exchange must be spent on imports for tourists,[33] and despite the fact that the workers are aware of the importance tourism holds for Cuba, the bitterness, often expressed in talk of a "dual standard," is only slightly less than venomous. Security guards stand at the entrance to all the major tourist hotels, not for political reasons, but to prevent Cubans who are unaccompanied by a foreign traveler from gaining access to the hotel. In the resort area of Varadero, Cuba's ultimate tourist paradise, it is, says author Polly Pattullo, not only lack of "access to beaches that has caused dismay among local people.

There, the re-emerging tourist industry has practiced a virtual economic and social apartheid, barring Cubans from restaurants, bars, nightclubs, hotels, and 'dollar shops' unless accompanied and paid for by foreigners. 'It's disgusting. We are second-class citizens in our own country. And for what? The US dollar, the symbol of our old imperialist enemy,' one Cuban cabaret dancer told a journalist."[34]

Hunger, malnutrition, the essential destruction of life and values are what Senator Jesse Helms, Senator Robert Torricelli, and presidents George Bush and Bill Clinton, as well as the entire United States Congress, have bequeathed Cuba. And while Cuba's own agricultural policies are not blameless, most of the damage, as well as its extent and duration, is a responsibility whose burden falls squarely on the shoulders of the United States. If "Aristotelian prudence" is "the supreme virtue in this world under the visited moon,"[35] as Raymond Aron, the prominent French theoretician and political sociologist once argued, then such virtue, as relates to the embargo on Cuba, is certainly lacking among United States decisionmakers, particularly in light of the fact that through the decade of the 1990s Cuba has hardly been a strategic threat to the United States.

RIOT ON THE MALECÓN

By the summer of 1994 many Cubans, exasperated by the scarcity of food and the unavailability of medicine, turned their anger outward toward the government. In July, thousands of young people began ransacking stores, throwing stones at the police, and hijacking government tugboats to flee to southern Florida. The Cuban navy, which had initially tried to halt the exodus by ramming the boats, killing many people, was ordered to allow the refugees who had been congregating on the Malecón waterfront to leave unmolested after a huge riot took place on August 5. Castro directed his fury at the United States, accusing it of fomenting the demonstrations through the embargo, and he suggested the rioters were free to leave. More than 32,000 Cubans fled to Florida on makeshift rafts, inner tubes, and boats. Opportunistically, Castro claimed Cuba had gotten rid of "oppositionists" and "parasites," "the enemies of the Revolution [who] try to play the game of the imperialists."[36]

Castro had clearly placed the United States in a tender political position, as Florida governor Lawton Chiles declared a state of emergency and demanded that the exodus be halted because of the crisis it was causing in Florida. Even the Miami Cuban community remained neutral (although publicly supportive) to the new refugees, for they, like the 1980 Mariel boat people, came from a lower socioeconomic class than the 1959 refugees who controlled the anti-Castro political organizations in Miami. Demanding that Castro be overthrown was one thing; having working-class or even unemployed Cubans flooding Miami, not for political but for economic reasons, was of an entirely different order.

In a strange bit of irony on August 19, 1994, President Clinton ordered the U.S. Coast Guard to intercept fleeing Cubans; they were brought to the U.S. military base at Guantánamo, placed in detention, and eventually, after languishing often for months in primitive conditions, allowed entrance to different geographic locations in the United States. Then, on September 9, after eight days of negotiations, Washington and Havana signed an agreement whereby the United States would detain all future illegal entrants and return them to Cuba, while Havana pledged to halt the flow of refugees, and both agreed that 20,000 new Cuban immigrants per year would legally be admitted to the United States. In essence the pact ended the policy in effect since 1959 that fleeing Cubans would automatically be given entrée to the United States and then provided with subsidies to make their integration into American life easier. Within days the illegal departures stopped.

Again, Fidel Castro, by unleashing the protesters and causing political chaos in Miami, turned the crisis to his own advantage and cleverly outwitted Washington by ending the opportunity of unfettered access to the United States. Henceforth such rioting would be an exercise in futility, the pact with the United States thereby reducing the probability if its being repeated. A year later the storm had passed, even though it was clear "that the rioting had shaken the government badly."[37]

CASTRO RESPONDS TO THE FOOD CRISIS

Even before the 1994 Havana riots, the government understood that it had to acknowledge the food crisis in some resolute manner. For the Cuban people there was a sense of urgency as the cruelty of the embargo struck at the heart of their livelihood and of their existence. Exanimated by the exceedingly tough measures of the U.S. embargo, the population was virtually pleading with Castro to extricate them from the dire situation. In 1993 the Cuban government moved into action by taking a series of measures that would open up the economy and restore some measure of hope to Cuba's people. The embargo was forcing Castro to create an economic mix of socialism and capitalism, despite his proclamation to the contrary that "this does not imply a return to capitalism."[38]

In July 1993, Cubans were permitted to possess dollars, which allowed them to purchase goods in the dollar stores that to that point had offered hard-to-find products primarily to tourists. Given the dollar remittances many Cubans receive from their relatives in Miami, which can legally total $300 every three months, (when they are not intermittently halted due to the vagaries in relations between Cuba and the United States) an entirely new and legal market was opened up. In October 1995 Cuba permitted its citizens to buy and sell foreign currencies on the open market for the first time in decades, which put an end to what had been to that point a flourishing black market enterprise.

A few months later, in September 1993, self-employment was authorized for 130 activities, eventually expanded to 154. By 1995 more than 200,000 people out of a total workforce of some 3.5 million had registered as privately employed restaurateurs, taxi drivers, electricians, plumbers, automobile repairmen, and so on. A few Cubans in urban centers, under government license, opened private restaurants in their homes, known popularly as *paladares*, offering inexpensive four- or five-course meals to both tourists and Cubans for a relatively small amount of money; the food is homemade, far superior, and more abundant than what is found in traditional establishments. *Paladares* have a 12-seat maximum, and the price of a meal is usually between five and eight dollars. Advertising of these private establishments was also sanctioned.

As a direct result of the crisis of 1994 agricultural and artisans' markets were legally authorized in October. State marketers, upon fulfillment of their commitment to the state, and private farmers were permitted to grow vegetables and fruits to supplement their own diet and to be sold in 130 newly created private food markets, or *agros*, nationwide, some of which are run by former soldiers and enlisted men,[39] many of whom returned to Cuba after the country's military activity abroad was curtailed by 1990. Although the produce is more expensive than in the state markets, the food is plentiful and the cost reasonable. By 1996-97 chicken, pork, plantains, potatoes, and a wide variety of vegetables were readily available and markets were packed with people negotiating for and buying goods. Within the markets, restaurants were opened, and a meal of pork, vegetables, salad, fruit juice, and coffee could be purchased for U.S. 75¢. By 1998, according to Remirez de Estenoz, only 34 percent of cultivated land remained under full government control. Markets had blossomed throughout most cities and had expanded beyond food to include shoes, pots and pans, trinkets, and arts and crafts. The plazas all around Havana became bustling centers where original art could be purchased (as in any flea market some was good, much abominable), while art galleries sold the paintings of more prominent Cuban artists. A free market in manufactured and consumer goods was also permitted in 1994. These measures were exceedingly well received by Cuba's consumers.

The country also opened itself up to foreign investment and tourism. In September 1995 the Cuban National Assembly of People's Power passed legislation allowing foreign investors access to all economic sectors except defense, health care, and education, and to fully own their own businesses in Cuba with the right to transfer capital abroad. Foreign investors along with Cuban citizens were also permitted to open bank accounts, paying interest at market rates, using dollars or other foreign currency. By the eve of the twenty-first century, foreigners had invested more than $7 billion in the country, while tourists were spending close to $3 billion annually. Mexico, Spain, and Canada were among more than 50 countries investing in Cuba totally free of American competition. By 1998 Cuba had clearly climbed out of the economic hole of 1993, as close to 400 foreign-Cuban associations invested billions in tourism, nickel mining, transportation, and other sectors, many of the new enterprises being under foreign majority ownership. Indeed, in March 1998 more than 50 United States business executives traveled to Havana to explore ways they could eventually participate in the expanding trade and investment opportunities. The very presence of executives from Texaco, Mobil Oil, Caterpillar, Bristol-Myers Squibb, and Continental Grain, among others, in Havana was a push for change in U.S. policy so Americans could take advantage of the economic possibilities existing in Cuba. William Lane, Caterpillar's Washington director for governmental affairs and director of USA Engage, a group of more than 600 U.S. companies, maintained publicly that the visit was an effort to raise the issue of the embargo.

With large numbers of privately employed Cubans benefiting from the newly installed market incentives, those Cubans not directly enjoying the fruits of these elements of capitalism began to complain about the dual class system that was evolving. The government was quick to respond to these complaints, as they reflected Castro's own perspective. As he said in October 1997, "We have no reason to create millionaires, to create enormous inequalities."[40]

Although taxes on each *palader* were originally set at 400 nonconvertible pesos (22 pesos = 1 dollar) and $300 monthly in 1993 (when the exchange rate was much higher), by August 4,1994, the Ministry of Finance and Prices announced a new graduated and progressive tax rate based on annual net profits for all private businesses, which it began to fully implement in 1996. For example, net profits of 6,001 non-convertible pesos (the exchange rate on convertible pesos is 1 peso for 1 dollar) were to be taxed at a 15 percent annual rate, while net profits between 48,001 and 60,000 pesos were taxed at a 40 percent rate. Net profits in excess of 60,000 pesos saw a 50 percent levy. On foreign currency income the first $2,400 net was taxed at 10 percent per year while the rate was 50 percent for net earnings over $60,000.[41] Though many complained about the excessive burden of the new tax, given Cuba's overall socialist policies income redistribution was considered only equitable by the powers that be. Additionally, the state wanted to limit the financial prowess of this new entrepreneurial element in society so as to reaffirm socialism rather than capitalism. Raúl Castro, Fidel's brother, defense minister and deputy general secretary of the Communist Party, and apparently a major supporter of economic reform in 1993, also worried about ideological purity in 1997, stating it was vital to "keep the revolution immune from ideological viruses."[42]

The reform policies set in motion by Fidel and Raúl Castro and overseen by Vice President Carlos Lage[43] have not been received with unanimous acclaim, even within the Communist Party hierarchy. Raúl Valdés Vivó, director of the Communist Party school for cadres and author of a prominent book supporting Ethiopia's 1974 Marxist revolution, warned that Cuba's new private entrepreneurs were "nothing more than 'piranhas' capable in a minimum time of devouring a horse [one of Castro's nicknames] down to its bones."[44] Other doctrinaire party members have also bemoaned the admixture of socialism and capitalism but have been overruled by Fidel, though he remains queasy about the reforms that he has often said are only as a necessary vice in this "Special Period." Indeed, in 1996 he criticized the very reforms he had been forced to undertake when he condemned "the birth of a new class. The more powerful it becomes, the greater will be its influence on society and the greater its challenge to socialism."[45]

But the reforms have been very successful. By 1995, according to the Central Intelligence Agency, exports increased for the first time in 6 years, rising 20 percent to $1.6 billion, while imports rose 21 percent to almost $2.4 billion or 30 percent of the 1989 level.[46] The Cuban Ministry of Economy and Planning reported that by the first quarter of 1996 the gross domestic product grew by 9.6 percent, supported by a production growth rate of over 20 percent in the agricultural sector, a rise of 10 percent in the industrial sector, and 30 percent growth in construction. Sugar production increased to 4.5 million metric tons, a growth rate of 33 percent from the same period the previous year. There was also a 38 percent increase in tourism, while tobacco and nickel production jumped 16 percent and 31 percent respectively. As the Ministry proclaimed, "the Cuban economy has experienced a clear recovery process [while] the rehabilitation process of the domestic financial situation continued . . . as a greater financial balance has become evident."[47] According to the United Nations, in 1996-97 Cuban "authorities continued to pursue the dual macroeconomic and structural adjustment program. . . . The purpose of the economic and institutional reforms has been to design a new model for integration into world trade . . . seeking to raise production levels without sacrificing basic social services."[48]

By 1997 the evidence was clearly to be seen even on the daily level of social existence and the impact of the changes was striking. Ninety-four percent of the population had access to electricity. There were many more cars on the road, as people had the money to obtain spare parts for their decaying and extinct automobiles. Gasoline was more readily available than at any time since 1991, and more people had the money to buy it. Cubans were eating better, with a greater variety and abundance of food at their disposal. Even the majority who used ration cards were benefiting from the improved economy. People dressed better, some even wearing American running shoes. More restaurants were open, including an all-night American-style cafeteria inside the Habana Libre Hotel. Bars, clubs, cafes, and local restaurants were filled with young Cubans obviously enjoying themselves, while seats at performances of the National Opera Company and the world-famous National Ballet of Cuba, selling at ten dollars each, were filled close to capacity. Local entertainment groups putting on variety shows were performing in Havana and Santiago de Cuba and the seats were sold out. Young lovers strolled the streets oblivious to everything and everyone, while parents with their children waited patiently to gain entrance to Havana's Coppelia Ice Cream Park, which serves some of the best and most exotic ice cream in the world. By 1998 life had returned to a normality devoid at least of the fright that existed as the decade began. Although the countryside did not participate in the economic revival to the degree the urban centers did, life there too had improved as farmers could now sell some of their produce in the newly dollarized economy of the cities. As Wayne S. Smith, head of the U.S. Interests Section in Havana under President Jimmy Carter, indicated with true prescience as early as 1995: "I'd say without any hesitation that Castro will make it. Investment is pouring in, and the United States is getting aced out. He's not going away. The pressure is off."[49] Three years later Smith's predication is still valid.

All the improvements, however, do not indicate that life is good in the sense that an overall satisfaction exists. Life in Cuba remains strenuous, with many necessities lacking. In 1998, for example, more than half of Havana's 560,000 houses and apartments were in need of repair while more than 60,000 were torn down. It is still a terribly poor country easily qualifying for Third World status. In rural areas, from which 30,000 depart for the cities yearly, life can be especially harsh and grueling, while in urban centers too many people live on the cusp of existence. But the economic changes that have taken place since 1991 *have* led to stark improvements in the lives of many Cubans. The reforms have worked to make life easier and to remove the most frightful aspects of the U.S. embargo on food. Yet the overall embargo and specifically the CDA has devastated Cuba.

The 1996 Helms-Burton Act has continued to impose additional hardship on the Cuban people. Because of U.S. pressure, in 1997 the Mexican conglomerate Grupo Domos, once Cuba's largest foreign investor, relinquished its investment in Cuba's telephone company, while executives of the Israeli-owned citrus company BM Group in 1997 and Canada's Sherritt International Corporation in 1996 were barred from entering the United States.

Passed in the wake of Cuba's decision to shoot down two civilian planes over the Straits of Florida (killing the pilots, who had belonged to the fierce anti-Castro Miami-based Brothers to the Rescue and who previously had "illegally entered Cuban airspace, flying over Havana both times,"[50] clearly terrorizing the population), Helms-Burton attempted to do what the Cuban Democracy Act could not—overthrow Fidel Castro by once again increasing the intensity of the embargo. It too failed in its endeavor. In December 1996, in an effort to assuage the fears of foreign investors, a new Cuban law went into effect declaring invalid any claim made under Helms-Burton, and stating that any U.S. citizen making such claims would be excluded from any future property settlement.[51] As Ricardo Alarcón maintained before the United Nations' General Assembly in 1997: "No one can take away from us Cubans our houses, our lands, our factories, our schools, our hospitals. No one shall despoil us of our properties or our rights. . . . Cuba is not and shall never be a colonial possession of the United States."[52]

The embargo seems to be conducted much as the Vietnam War was. For the United States nothing seemed to work in that war. Neither air power nor ground troops were effective. Vietnam was physically devastated but Ho Chi Minh's insurgency could not be stopped. Yet, according to Secretary of Defense Robert McNamara, he and President Johnson opted to pursue a more-of-the-same policy because, not wanting to admit failure of their overall strategy and unwilling to consider another strategic approach, they didn't know what else to do.[53] The same holds true for the embargo. It has not caused the removal of Fidel Castro, its primary purpose, but it has basically helped to destroy Cuba's health care system and exacerbate the troubles of an already marginal economy and caused extraordinary food shortages. Still, failure of a 40-year policy has not led to its reconsideration. In Cuba as in Vietnam an unsuccessful U.S. policy never went through the rigorous evaluation that might have brought forth other policy alternatives. In both cases, the United States failed in achieving its primary goal; in both cases a Third World leader successfully staved off the United States; but in both cases the targeted country was pillaged.

THE FAILURE OF HUMAN RIGHTS

The primacy of political rights as articulated in the Universal Declaration of Human Rights is evident when one considers that of the 30 Articles therein, merely 4 speak to the issue of economic rights while only 1 even mentions the right to an "adequate" supply of food.[54] As a political bill of rights, which is precisely how the Declaration was viewed in 1948,[55] it is "clear that the overriding philosophy . . . is the Western concept of political liberty and democracy, inclusive of property rights in contradistinction to economic rights or egalitarianism."[56]

As the crystallizing document in the recent history of human rights the Universal Declaration does little to ensure that countries like Cuba are protected within their domestic domain so that they in turn can provide the economic wherewithal to their people free of the imposition of Western values that only emphasize political rights. Certainly U.S. interference in the domestic jurisdiction of the affairs of Cuba is self-serving—the United States willingly blinds itself to the actions of other nations with a similar political ideology to that upheld by Cuba because those countries are seen as vital to U.S.

national security. The People's Republic of China and Vietnam are communist states the United States does business with, while even North Korea is provided with foodstuffs to help it overcome the effects of famine. As Ronald Steel, a prominent specialist on international relations has argued, "In truth, no great power is without self-serving ambition. But if American officials seek to wrap themselves in the mantle of morality, proclaiming themselves to be the world's conscience and enforcer, they invite others to hold them to a higher standard than is applied to the normal run of devious statesmen."[57]

Beyond the political failure of the Universal Declaration of Human Rights to even address the issue of hunger and starvation, the fact is that the 1976 United Nations' International Covenant on Economic, Social and Cultural Rights speaks quite dramatically to the point in Article 11 "by recognizing the right of everyone to . . . adequate food . . . recognizing the fundamental right of everyone to be free from hunger. . . . Taking into account the problems of both food-importing and food-exporting countries, to ensure an equitable distribution of world food supplies in relation to need."[58]

For the United States to continue pursuing the embargo in light of its clear violation of international law as seen in the International Covenant and, according to the European Union, as being in violation of the 1994 General Agreement on Tariffs and Trade (GATT),[59] is to discount not only world opinion but universal morality. To support a policy that engenders starvation is to invite comparison to the very oppression the United States claims to find repugnant in other nations. According to Alfredo Duran of the Cuban Committee for Democracy, "the embargo hasn't worked and everyone knows it. The starvation in Cuba is what the embargo has created."[60]

The commanding study on economic sanctions prepared under the auspices of the Institute for International Economics speaks to the astonishing failure of the U.S. embargo on Cuba. As a policy result it has "failed." As a "sanctions contribution" there is none. Its "success score" is close to "outright failure." Its "cost to the sender" virtually a "major loss." And as to the "economic health and political stability of the target scaled from 1 (distressed) to 3 (strong)," the result is estimated as a two.[61] As early as 1977 Secretary of State Cyrus Vance spoke of the failure of economic sanctions as a policy tool against Cuba. Nineteen years later 11 Latin American leaders attending the Rio Group summit in Cochabamba, Bolivia, condemned Helms-Burton and the overall embargo saying the law ignored fundamental principles of respect for sovereignty. Clearly, the policy remains a dismal failure in legal, political, and most especially moral terms, although in economic and foreign policy terms Cuba has been squeezed.

TO STARVE A PEOPLE?

In 1995 Lorenzo F. Delgado, vice chair of the Westchester County Hispanic-American Republican Committee, spoke quite dramatically to the issue of the embargo and starvation. A fierce anti-Castro advocate, Delgado minced no words when speaking about withholding food from Cuba's people. When asked during a televised debate on changing Cuban policy, "Is the human misery involved with the embargo worth it?" Delgado replied,

> Is there a time limit on embargos? Until it works. In South Africa the embargo worked. It should do the same in Cuba. Make sure that embargo is tight. That nothing gets through. I have loved ones in Cuba. I know it hurts. It hurts me very close. I would venture to say a poll of the Cuban people, a true poll of the Cuban people, would say 'strengthen that embargo so we can get rid of Fidel Castro'. We are not talking about the next meal for the Cuban people; we are looking at their future.[62]

As the person he was debating, I sat there aghast. Cubans on the island, whatever their disposition toward Fidel Castro or communism, were frightened to death that the embargo would, as it has, continue to be tightened. Few, if any, favored further tightening of the noose around their necks. Most wanted the embargo to just end so that Cubans could stop being hungry. It was easy enough for Delgado to speak. But the people on the island were the ones without food. Perhaps Cuba's misfortune and the deeper feelings of its people are more accurately reflected in Ousmane Sembene's outstanding novel *God's Bits of Wood,* which depicts a 1947/1948 railroad strike against the French colonial authority in what is today Senegal and Mali, and where famine was used as a tool against the colonized. "Real misfortune," spoke one of the leading voices in the book, "is not just a matter of being hungry and thirsty; it is a matter of knowing that there are people who want you to be hungry and thirsty—and that is the way it is with us."[63]

Ricardo Alarcón's perspective of hunger and human rights reflects the position of the Cuban government and pointedly goes to the political heart of the matter. "We could talk about human rights," he said in 1996, "but it's important to say that although it is a very noble expression, something that no one in the world should belittle, it is also a highly manipulated belief as part of the anti-Cuba strategy, to justify the exulted blockage that pleases certain people so much."[64]

To claim to uphold human rights, as the United States does, while inflicting a policy that imposes starvation on an entire people seems a bit of a contradiction. But it is plainly a circumstance the United States is prepared to accept. As President Clinton indicated in responding to Japan's failing economic policies in 1998, nations should be prepared to dispense with theories that are shown over time to flounder.[65] The president ought to follow his own words of advice to Japan and apply them to Cuba. That he refuses to do so is a chilling reminder of the intensity of the opposition to Fidel Castro among important quarters within the United States.

Given the reality that Cuba poses no threat whatsoever to the United States and is, on the contrary, a Third World nation struggling to survive in the shadow of its mighty neighbor, Washington should allow the country to deal with its own affairs and settle its own disputes. Although the embargo has undermined Cuba's ability to feed itself it has failed to achieve what has always been its real purpose—the removal of Fidel Castro and the "peaceful transition to democracy."[66] Success for its Cuba policy would mean of course that Cuba would once again be incorporated into America's sphere of influence, and the United States and the corporate community would once again direct and monopolize its economy. If the United States has to starve the Cuban people to achieve that end, so be it.

FIVE

THE QUESTION OF RELIGION

WHEN POPE JOHN PAUL II ARRIVED IN HAVANA and disembarked at José Martí International Airport to be warmly greeted by President Fidel Castro, it was an extraordinary event. The two aging but powerful titans of the latter half of the twentieth century, each pursuing their own political and religious goals, had agreed to the visit, after years of negotiations, and this well-traveled and very political pope had finally come to the only Spanish-speaking Latin American country to which he had not yet traveled. For five days—from January 21 to 25, 1998—the world watched with rapt attention, and often with deep emotion, as the head of the Roman Catholic Church and the leader of the Communist Party of Cuba parried with each other to achieve the ends that each was seeking.

Although the agenda and the outcome had largely been predetermined, the spectacle of watching it unfold day by day, as the two political giants jousted, was a lesson in the politics of diplomacy and in the skillful use of political language. Abandoning his usual military fatigues for a specially cut double-breasted blue suit Castro made every effort to accommodate the ailing 77-year-old Vicar of Christ, a powerful political force credited with playing a key role in ending communist rule in Poland. For both the risks of this trip were formidable. The pertinent issues would be human rights, underdevelopment, religious freedom, and the embargo. As reporters invaded Cuba and crowds listened to the many papal Masses delivered in various cities throughout the country (including one in Havana that Castro himself attended) viewers around the globe watched transfixed as the political dance between the Vatican head-of-state and Fidel Castro began. History was also a presence. Although not the first meeting between the two (they had met in the Vatican in 1996), it was almost certainly the only gathering there would ever be in Cuba, and given the age of both men, Castro being 71 at the time, it was quite possibly the last time these two supreme leaders would meet.

Castro and the pope, being political animals with few peers, know their presence in and impact upon history. They are also showmen, in that they understand that symbols and political rhetoric are vital to influencing a constituency. Both have an extraordinary connection with the people—mixing with them, touching and reaching out to them, both use charisma to develop an attachment between themselves and their audiences. Each has many formidable and vocal antagonists but few leaders can match these political artists at work. At their best they can speak for hours on the weightiest political subjects knowing that their audience is not merely those before them, but, particularly in this case, the United States.

Each was trying to gain advantage, to obtain specific political assurances while at the same time understanding that the other also had to attain a measure of success. Both would exit their meetings with something to exult over. Cuba and the Vatican had interests that had to and would be served, and both Castro and the pope understood that the role they were now playing was one that could eventually dramatically affect Cuba's relations with Washington. They also knew that fundamentally this meeting was the last step, not the first one, in a long process, and that it put the pope in the position of affixing his imprimatur to the vast changes in the religious climate of Cuba that had been underway since 1991. The trip thus served many purposes. And the reason it was free of rancor, and why the two appeared so congenial together, is that each knew at the beginning of the journey what he would essentially receive. Each also knew his adversary well.

Castro, born of Catholic parents, baptized in Santiago de Cuba, and, early on, schooled by Jesuits, is no stranger to the rites and politics of the Catholic Church. He knows its virtues, its conservatism, and its power. As early as 1979 he had asked the Vatican to have the pope make a stopover in Cuba on his way back to Rome from a bishop's conference he was attending in Mexico. A papal visit was then denied but in 1985 Castro set forth his views on the pope and why an eventual visit was significant.

> I must acknowledge that this pope is an outstanding politician because of his activities, trips, and contacts with the masses. We revolutionaries meet with the masses . . . but it's a new thing for the head of the Catholic Church to do this. Of course . . . we feel honored by any interest the pope may have in visiting our country—that's beyond question. I would also consider it a courageous action. In fact, visiting Cuba has become an expression of independence. I don't believe it should be just another visit to another country, since Cuba is a state struggling for social justice; a state that's struggling against imperialism; a revolutionary, socialist country. . . . Undoubtedly, we would discuss everything that the pope is interested in regarding the Church in Cuba, the Catholics in Cuba. On our part I'd say that our country's main interest would be related to an analysis of the issues that are of great importance for the underdeveloped nations. . . all the issues that affect our poor world that is exploited and plundered by the industrialized capitalist nations. . . . I think a dialogue with the pope could be very useful. . . . I believe . . . a visit by the pope to our country would have maximum implications and such a visit is something I consider possible.[1]

The 1980s, however, were not appropriate for such a visit. Events in Poland and throughout Eastern Europe absorbed the attention of the Holy See, while the Catholic Church in Cuba was repressed. As Castro indicated in 1985 such a visit would have to be carefully prepared in advance, and, he might have added, a vast improvement in relations between the Cuban government and the Cuban Church would have to occur before the pope would even consider such a trip. It was far too early, but Castro astutely recognized in those early years that a papal visit was of enormous gravity. He also presciently predicted the topics that would be discussed should a meeting ever occur, and undoubtedly he knew the outcome he wanted.

Until the end of the 1980s, however, Cuba was in no hurry to create the conditions for such a visit. The Soviet Union and its East European allies were providing economic subsidies to Cuba, its political influence abroad remained telling, and the population of the country was doing relatively well, even in the face of the embargo. True, Cuba was, to a large degree, a dependency of its patron the Soviet Union; still, because Fidel was who he was, the Soviets were often frustrated by his independence, revolutionary attitude, and activities, which often ran counter to Soviet policies. Moscow tried, for example, to reign in his conduct in support of Grenada's Bishop because Grenada was recognized to be within the U.S. sphere of interest and provoking the United States would not serve the vital national interests of the Soviet Union. Because Castro knew the Soviets needed Cuba politically as much as Cuba needed it economically there was no fear that some Cuban independence in foreign affairs would propel Moscow to substantially curtail economic support. And as long as Cuba was not demonstrably affected by the U.S. embargo, there appeared little need to liberalize the status of the Catholic Church, and therefore there was no interest in the Holy See for a visit to Cuba by the pope.

All that changed irrevocably in 1989, as the Soviet Union entered a period of turmoil with its Eastern European clients, when a Vatican representative to Cuba first raised the issue of a visit by the pope with Fidel, and then again 1991 when the Soviet Union ceased to exist and Cubans were confronted with "an event as inconceivable and shattering as the arrival of the Spaniards on Mexico's shores was for the Aztecs."[2] Cuba's economy went into a tailspin, and the U.S. embargo, in its ruthless progression, began to influence political as well as economic policies. With a restless, shocked, and soon-to-be hungry population Castro quickly moved to create more political space in Cuba so as to mollify his people. As Castro proclaimed, "the revolution was determined to survive in a struggle against a very powerful enemy that wanted to crush it";[3] after 1991 survival would in part be accomplished by moving toward an accommodation with the Catholic Church in Cuba.

THE CATHOLIC CHURCH IN BATISTA'S TIME

Prior to Castro's accession to power, Cubans were a secular people. Although some 85 percent were nominally members of the Roman Catholic Church, "only about 10 percent were active and informed members; at least 25 percent were in practice agnostics."[4] As with most elites of the time the Church leadership was associated with the ruling classes and with the Batista hierarchy, and the Church itself was singularly represented only in the urban areas. It showed little interest and less initiative in expanding into the countryside, "and the formal religious life of peasants was usually limited to the occasional visit of a priest to perform baptisms."[5] As Castro himself scowled, "In our country . . . there weren't any rural churches. . . . There wasn't a single church in the countryside, not a single priest in the countryside! And that was where . . . the people lived."[6]

The 1950s were a time of extreme anticommunist activity throughout the Western world, while nationalist insurgencies were erupting and sometimes succeeding in the Third World. The cold war was heating up in such far-flung places as Laos, Vietnam, and Guatemala. Conservative Catholic prelates, particularly in the United States and Latin America, who feared communist or communist-inspired insurgencies that would threaten the Church's religious dominance in the emerging nations tied themselves ever more closely to governments in power. This was as true of Cardinal Frances Spellman in New York City in his advocacy of America's Catholic client in South Vietnam, President Ngo Dinh Diem, as it was of the Church authorities in Havana in their response to Castro. The ideological struggle was also a class conflict as the Church in Cuba had virtually no connection to the poor in the interior. Each lived in different economic, political, and cultural spheres with the Church taking a patronizing attitude toward its peasant flock. This was not unusual at the time, as there was not even a trace of the liberation theology that would later evolve in Latin America and parts of the Caribbean to draw stronger links between this new and radical church element and the population. In the 1950s the traditional Catholic Church in Cuba ruled supreme, allied and sharing its "aristocratic" values with the government of Batista.

When Castro took power the Church remained quiescent; after all, the revolution's success was now a *fait accompli* and the Catholic Church had to live with the results. Coexistence was the only reasonable attitude, and a "wait and see" approach was taken. Cuba's Cardinal Manuel Arteaga, who was also Archbishop of Havana, and other Church leaders were prepared to accept moderate reforms that would not alter the existing social structure, but as profound and revolutionary changes were implemented that altered the entire basis of society and eliminated the privileges of the upper classes the Church's position shifted to outright opposition. "At the beginning," according to Castro, "the revolution's relations with all the social sectors were very good. The difficulties began with the first revolutionary laws."[7] Castro, who has never opposed religious faith itself, declared in his unique fashion in 1961, "Within the Revolution everything; outside the Revolution, nothing."[8] As long as the Church acquiesced in the policies put forth by the new revolutionary government there would not be conflict; but once it positioned itself to oppose what the revolution was doing and trying to accomplish, it moved "outside the Revolution" and was from then on entitled to "nothing."

THE MESSAGE OF THE REVOLUTION

It became apparent immediately after the success of the revolution that Castro had more in mind than merely reform of the political system. Emboldened by an extraordinary display of public enthusiasm for himself and the 26th of July Movement Fidel moved rapidly to "destroy every vestige of the old social order in Cuba."[9] Revolutionary tribunals were established to try Batistianos, and Castro selected perhaps the most radical and uncompromising of his followers, Che Guevara, "for the indispensable job of purging the old army . . . by exacting revolutionary justice against traitors."[10] The trials, some being televised to publicize the terrors of the *ancien régime*, were a blow to the elites of the country, particularly as by May 1959 some 550 "traitors" had been executed. Government ministries were cleansed of reform elements and replaced by the more radical elements from the 26th of July Movement, or even from the ranks of the communist Popular Socialist Party (PSP). The PSP, perhaps the most organized and certainly the most ideologically acceptable structure to Castro, became a force in society even prior to Fidel's announcement in April 1961, in the midst of the U.S.-sponsored Bay of Pigs invasion, that Cuba had become a socialist state. By December Castro proclaimed a new Marxist-Leninist political party and that "today we shall see to it that to be a Communist is a merit."[11] Already by April 1959, Fidel had associated anticommunism with counterrevolution, although he continuously hedged the issue of Cuba being a communist state until it was clarified once and for all two years later. Marxist-Leninism, though, was clearly on the way as discussions were ongoing with the leadership of the PSP toward that end.[12] By July President Manuel Urrutia was forced out of office and Castro, as prime minister, then announced that since the huge crowds turning out to see and hear him were so laudatory and supportive, and the interrelationship between himself and the people was so unique, that elections, at least for the moment, were unnecessary (and have remained so). The people, he claimed, have spoken through their activity in support of the revolution. Charisma and popular connection *was* the election. Speeches, visits, televised addresses, wading into massive crowds substituted for electioneering. "Revolution First, Elections Afterward" was the rallying cry, and calls for elections were interpreted as indicating counterrevolutionary tendencies. Castro's popularity was prodigious; he seemed to be the living incarnation of the people's hopes and desires. Cubans were thrilled "that they were loved by this colossus" whose refrain was "Man's need is his fundamental right over all others."[13]

A parade of legislation followed that took wealth and power from the few and redistributed it to the many. By 1961 "the government had nationalized the functions of the upper class. . . . Most of the traditional, distinguishing marks of the old upper class were abolished."[14] The new state identified with the lower classes and created INRA in 1959 to absorb 40 percent of the land into cooperatives; restrictions on private ownership of property were severe, and later such ownership was eliminated or "redefined." INRA, which was conceptualized with the aid of Che Guevara, was the heart of the revolution. It seized private lands (although compensation was offered based on valuations of tax assessment, owners rejected it as ludicrous since they claimed it was an undervaluation of the property's real worth), and it helped peasants whose farms had been destroyed during the war. Under INRA's Department of Industrialization, initially headed by Che—a most unlikely bureaucrat, as he came to conclude—major enterprises were seized and then nationalized. Most of the labor force, now working on government or cooperative farms, was under his authority, while his office participated with the Central Planning Council in coordinating the state economy. Essentially INRA was an agency created to operate properties seized for redistribution or for incorporation into cooperatives. There remained little doubt by the end of the first year of the revolution that this was a complete overturning of the old social order. Obviously property owners and conservatives found "all this most distasteful."[15]

In October 1960, under the rubric of the Urban Reform Law, houses and apartments were nationalized, and under the slogan "every tenant an owner" each family could reside in a house, or part of one, or an apartment by paying 50 percent of their former rent to the state through the National Institute of Savings and Loans, and within 20 years, each tenant would receive title to the property. A similar mechanism of attaining "ownership" rights exists to this day; tenants pay rent to the state, and after full payment is made title is turned over to the former renter, and although some housing may often be of poorer quality than others everyone has access and none are homeless. By 1960 Revolutionary Boards were established to purge professional organizations, including medical, legal, business, and university associations, of members whose attitudes or politics were "incorrect."

With the fierce language of the revolution complemented by rapid and striking changes in property rights, the middle class began fleeing Cuba. They had, along with U.S. corporations, more than 2.5 million acres of their land confiscated, and 150,000 Cubans who had worked for U.S. corporations lost their jobs or had their wages drastically lowered when the industries, including United Fruit, Esso, Standard Oil, utility companies, sugar mills, and nickel mines, were nationalized in August 1960. Their professional lives were in disarray.

Then in October 1960 the first of the U.S. embargo laws was generated when President Eisenhower prohibited the export of U.S. products to Cuba. Life was no longer pleasant for the middle and upper classes as they lost power, status, class, and control over their own lives; their life style had been drastically altered. The poorer classes were the primary beneficiaries of the revolution, as was the Black population, which historically had to contend with the yoke of racism. As discussed by political scientist Robert C. Smith, "Fidel did for Blacks in Cuba what LBJ did for Blacks in the United States;"[16] perhaps even more, and a "sense of despair and outrage permeated the *criollo* elite [those born in Cuba but of Spanish ancestry]."[17] The formerly elite whites had seen enough. By December 1959 more than 56,000 Cubans immigrated to the United States; in the spring of 1960 the Soviet Union reestablished diplomatic relations with Cuba (which had been broken off in 1952), which led to a further exodus of Cubans to Miami. By the end of 1960 the total number of Cubans fleeing the country reached 110,000. "Almost all of them were upper- and middle-class Cubans whose livelihoods had been destroyed, or at least severely compromised by the revolution;"[18] their stark bathos is hauntingly depicted in Cuban film director Tomás Gutiérrez Alea's masterpiece, *Memories of Underdevelopment.*

During this time the Catholic Church too lost its exalted rank as it objected to the radicalism evident in the direction of government and the movement toward a Marxist-Leninist order. It would soon be excluded from the new society and its followers banned from participation in the Communist Party, which had the effect of denying them many of the benefits that participation provided.

FIDEL CASTRO AND THE CATHOLIC CHURCH: THE FIRST DECADES

"The problems" with the Church, according to Fidel, "stemmed from the passing of revolutionary laws: the Urban Reform Law and the Agrarian Reform Law. The revolutionary laws produced conflicts without a doubt, because the bourgeois and landed sectors, the rich sectors, changed their attitude toward the revolution and decided to oppose it. That's how the initial conflicts with the Church began, because those sectors wanted to use the Church as a tool against the revolution."[19] In addition, he argued, religion in Cuba "was disseminated, propagated, mainly through private schools—that is, schools run by religious orders . . . which were attended by the wealthiest families in the country, the members of the old aristocracy, or those who considered themselves aristocrats, the children of the upper middle class and part of the middle class in general."[20]

As the Catholic Church "increasingly assumed the task of expressing opposition to the government, . . . denunciations of private schooling—most of which was given by Catholic organizations—were intensified"[21] Thus, the simplest solution but the one most egregious to the Church leadership was taken: in a further effort to destroy the landed and once-powerful classes the private Catholic schools were nationalized in May 1961, although Castro indicated that since churches would remain open, religion but not education could be considered in that environment.

The months surrounding the Bay of Pigs invasion were a difficult time indeed. Many foreign Jesuits, whom Castro referred to as pro-Franco Spaniards holding reactionary, right-wing ideas, were expelled from the country. Castro saw the conflict with the Jesuits as predicated on class, not religion, but the Church leadership was uninterested in such subtleties. The expulsion of prelates—including 131 priests who were labeled "enemies of the revolution"—and the closing of Catholic schools "reduced the clergy from 759 to 200" in 1961.[22] Priests and nuns lost their once-acclaimed status, and, according to Cuban Jesuit Fr. Nelson Santana, who was interviewed in 1997, those adherents "who openly professed their beliefs risked losing privileges such as university enrollment, employment promotions. Catholic children . . . were admonished at school, with authorities insisting their parents were caught in the 'trappings' of capitalism."[23] Those who had to evaluate fellow workers for promotion "or grant them the right to new living quarters . . . would always say no, because they were Catholic."[24] Committees for the Defense of the Revolution (CDRs), established in 1960 to mobilize political participation, also served as instruments of neighborhood social control that to some degree were directed at Catholics. CDRs remain in existence; their signs, usually alongside Cuban flags, hang from apartments and houses for identification purposes. Parishioners had to choose between church and state, between the new ideology and the old. Many Cuban priests and nuns fled to Florida or took refuge in foreign embassies until diplomatic arrangements were made to allow them to leave for Miami or elsewhere.

Catholics, as well as the upper and middle classes, were denied economic rights beyond those entitlements granted to the population as a whole. Practicing believers were even refused many of those prerogatives. With great wealth having been eliminated, "the priority given to economic rights—such as the right to work, the right to leisure, old age benefits, the right to health care and medical services and the right to education—have instilled a sense of dignity, hitherto absent. Particularly in providing for health care, education and housing, Cuba has been remarkably successful."[25] By contrast, the Catholic Church found that its position in Cuban society had been functionally destroyed.

WHITHER HUMAN RIGHTS?

Within the context of the socialist perspective of human rights, the Church had violated a major precept by denying the revolution, thus alienating itself from what was demanded by the community—as articulated by the state, the repository of the people's values. If economic and social rights are primary within the context of what is good for the community as a whole—that is, the group—then individual political and civil rights, which conflict with the paramountcy of the larger group, must be denied. And the 1976 Cuban constitution is very clear on the matter. According to Article 54, "The socialist state . . . recognizes and guarantees freedom of conscience and the right of everyone to profess any religious belief and to practice, within the framework of respect for the law, the belief of his preference." But it goes on to say, "It is illegal and punishable by law to oppose one's faith or religious belief to the Revolution. . . ."[26] According to Fidel Castro, that is precisely what the Catholic Church did. By standing against the revolution, that is, against the people, the Church forfeited its right to participate in the new social order.

> The primacy of the group and the idea of the collective ownership of the means of production represent an alternative to the individualistic, free enterprise system. . . . Under socialism "rights" moved away from the purview of the individual and an "egalitarian" social structure prevailed, at least according to the Cuban constitution.[27]

The problem for the Church as well as for the ruling classes was that the socialist or Third World perspective of human rights violated the natural order of things. According to these classes their wealth, their status, and therefore their power entitled them to certain perquisites, among which control was the most decisive. They accepted as "natural" individual rights for themselves as their value system adhered to that of their patron, the United States. But when Castro and the new socialist world arrived, which accentuated redistribution of rights to the larger group, they rebelled—not in the sense of outright combat, though some did—against the taking of all they had, which bestowed upon them their power and authority. It didn't matter if the larger population would benefit. The other Cuba, the poor and dispossessed, was never of concern to them in the first place, so what Castro was attempting in his revolution was quite irrelevant. Their selfishness or self- interest defined their politics, and their politics demanded they stand against Castro. They could not abide communism, or a different perspective of human rights. So, having lost everything, they fled.

Castro's analysis was more severe. "All of the privileged social classes that had a monopoly on the Church were against the revolution, so when in organizing the party, we excluded those who believed in God, we were excluding them as potential counterrevolutionaries, not Catholics. What we were demanding was complete adherence to Marxism-Leninism."[28] In violating the tenets of the new standard of human rights, the Church and its allies were seen by Castro and the new leadership as opposing the principles of the revolution. That was defined as akin to treason, particularly since counterrevolutionary activity was tied to the United States, which was engaged in a vendetta against Castro in an effort to topple him. The leadership would not divorce dissent from President Kennedy's various attempts through the CIA to assassinate Castro (code-named Operation Mongoose),[29] or his support of the 1961 invasion at the Bay of Pigs. The Church, as a result of its stand against the policies of Castro, was tied to U.S. activity and so its leading role in Cuba was eliminated. Since Cuba was essentially a secular state, the political cost to Castro was minimal. As he said, "If the masses in our country . . . had been active Christians, we couldn't have formed a revolutionary party based on those premises; we couldn't have done it."[30]

To be fair, the Church never had a chance. The Church represented the elites of society; they were its primary constituency. Also, the Catholic Church in the 1950s was far more politically and socially conservative than it is presently, and it could see politics and social change only from its own narrow perspective. Pope John XXIII and his reforms had not yet arrived on the scene, and Catholicism remained confined to the conservatism symbolized by Pope Pius XII, who failed to do very much to deter the mass killing of the Jews of Europe during the Holocaust.[31] This was not a Church that could even comprehend the changes that were taking place in Cuba, much less empathize with the disturbing existence of Cuba's poor. It viewed Fidel Castro, Che Guevara, Camilo Cienfuegos, and all the other guerrillas as ragged roughs intent on destroying the world it knew and benefited from. The Church as it was in that period of history had no choice. It did not even recognize the human rights perspective that Castro was applying; how could it sympathize with it? For 30 years the Church existed on the margins of the new Cuban society, and it is likely that it would have remained in that position for far longer had not Castro been compelled to alter that state of affairs after the Soviet Union collapsed and the people of Cuba saw their world come crashing down.

A NEW BEGINNING

One of the major unintended consequences of the U.S. embargo that correlated with the downfall of the Soviet Union—and that apparently has escaped notice—was the new approach toward religion and religious practices that Fidel Castro and the Cuban Communist Party were compelled to take. From the late 1980s, when Soviet client states in Eastern Europe began to break away from its orbit, through 1991, when the once-superpower itself crumbled, Cuban leaders were confronted with a bleak and desperate circumstance. The subsidies and aid provided by these countries ended, and 90 percent rather than 15 percent of Cuba's international trade outside the parameters of the former socialist market was suddenly affected by the embargo. "The socialist world [had] purchased 63 percent of Cuba's sugar, 73 percent of its nickel, 95 percent of its citrus, and 100 percent of its electronic goods. [They] in turn provided 63 percent of Cuba's food, 80 percent of its nonfuel raw material inputs, 98 percent of its fuel, 80 percent of its machinery, and 74 percent of its manufactured goods."[32] Losing 93 percent of its trade with the former Soviet bloc while being unable to reorient that trade to the West because of the embargo—which also made it close to impossible to obtain loans and credits from the IMF, the World Bank, and other international lending agencies—as well as its lack of hard currency, the desperate straits of its economy, and Europe's refusal to subsidize Cuba, forced the leadership to look into areas that could give some breathing space to the Cuban people.

The opening of the economy to self-employment that had been decided upon, or would soon, could not have the desired effect rapidly enough to satisfy the immediate economic needs of the country. But additional social space could be permitted that might bring once-deviant groups into the fold, while reducing the anger that might arise amongst those who were proud to be Cubans in a socialist state standing up to the United States and who had heretofore supported Castro, or at least remained quiescent. Of concern was not the dissent that could be expected from the usual quarters—the indigenous human rights organizations, those unhappy with a socialist economy or the lack of political rights, and individuals attracted by Western consumerism—but that of the overall population, the people going to work daily whose salary would decline precipitously, who would have little food to eat while watching their children go hungry, who would have no medicine to buy and no gasoline to drive their cars with. With prices certain to increase, and supplies, goods, and services sure to decline markedly, Castro had to be concerned, perhaps alarmed, that this "Special Period in the Time of Peace" might not turn out to be so peaceful. As Castro admitted in his annual July

26 speech in 1995, "Many people . . . believed that the Revolution would collapse in a matter of days or weeks, and here we are not only resisting, but little by little once more beginning to gain ground."[33]

Whether the revolution was ever threatened is doubtful, but the consequences of the U.S. embargo were now of such a scale that to prevent public disenchantment with the economy from turning into wider political dissent—perhaps even public opposition against not only the United States and the embargo, which was not only acceptable but always promoted, but against Castro himself—action would have to be taken and social policy altered. By standing against the embargo as a nationalist as well as a communist so as to draw upon additional support, and by loosening restrictions in the economic and social spheres, Castro, as politically astute as ever, turned the crisis around. In the realm of religion, the embargo impelled Castro to dispense with his hard-line policy and to offer the Catholic Church and its adherents re-entrance into Cuban society.

In 1992, Fidel Castro proclaimed Cuba a "lay" rather than an "atheist" state and lifted restrictions against Catholics joining the Communist Party. The "social pressures against practicing the faith have been reduced. It's like they stopped squeezing our wrists."[34] In turn, 1 year later 11 Cuban bishops published a pastoral letter, later endorsed by the pope, that called for "fraternal dialogue and reconciliation" with the Cuban government. Among the problems cited in the document were "discrimination because of political and philosophical ideas or religious belief."[35] The letter, which also called for an end to the embargo, likewise raised the issue of political prisoners and one-party rule, but Castro chose to ignore the latter two points while he responded to the issue of religious belief. "There have been" he said, "differences and disputes between the Cuban Church and the revolution, but today we must create a climate of confidence and good relations."[36] Havana's Auxiliary Bishop Carlos Baladrón also indicated at the time that the pastoral letter, by modifying the restoration of private Catholic schools to a "second-level demand," a marked change from the past, removed a major obstacle to the rehabilitation of Church/state relations.

By 1996, Church and state had agreed upon a new concord in which the Church was permitted to freely practice its theology as long as it remained out of politics, while an increase in the number of priests and nuns was agreed to. In 1997 Cuba acted to increase the number of priests, which had in any case been growing over the years, by 28 to 268 and the number of nuns by 29 to 429. Cardinal Jaime Ortega, who is also Archbishop of Havana and a consistent and long-time antagonist of the government, was moved to proclaim that "in terms of what faith means, there can be a new understanding of what the church really is" in Cuba.[37] And although the Church has no access to newspapers, radio, or television it is no longer molested. Even U.S. Secretary of State Madeleine Albright was forced to concede in 1998 that the Catholic Church in Cuba now has access to millions of adherents while its priests are free to deliver "uncensored sermons."[38] It is estimated that some 500,000 Catholics now regularly attend weekly religious services.

Castro also wisely attached his new religious policy to the crisis faced by Cubans over the lack of food by permitting Caritas Cubana, the regional branch of the Catholic charity organization, to expand its food distribution centers throughout the country, thereby enlarging its role as the only nongovernmental agency permitted to distribute humanitarian aid in Cuba. Castro believed, probably correctly, that this new policy would bring him support as he would be seen as compromising a religious policy he felt strongly about so as to insure, to the degree he could, the population's nutritional needs. In 1996 the Communist Party newspaper *Granma* went so far as to heap praise on Caritas Cubana for the "noble orientations of this Catholic organization in Cuba."[39]

Clearly, by 1998 a new, and certainly more positive, association had been developed between Castro and the Catholic Church. Negotiations, which were conducted privately but whose results could be publicly appraised, did not go unnoticed in Vatican City. Indeed, it can be assumed by the support given the 1993 pastoral letter by Pope John Paul II that he was aware of the nuances within the agreements the conferees reached. And he gave his assent to them. In October 1996, in a 35-minute meeting with Castro held at the Vatican, which itself indicated a policy change, the pope accepted Castro's invitation to visit Cuba. Around this time the Vatican also publicly condemned the Helms-Burton Act for the first time. The papal visit Castro had sought in 1979 and spoken of in 1985 would soon occur. And Cuba's reorientation of its relationship with the Cuban Church was fully responsible. The Cuban president and the very political Holy Father would now spend a year preparing for the pope's trip to Havana, so that both could achieve the results they needed and desired.

In its own way, though probably quite inadvertently, the United States, through the use of the embargo, had forced Castro's hand. Capitulation to Catholicism might never have occurred at all had Castro not been pushed into taking a new approach because of the economic chaos that shook the island after the disappearance of the Soviet Union. Liberalization may still have come eventually, no one can really know, but its timing in relation to events in the Soviet Union make it highly likely that there was a very strong interconnection between the embargo, the death of the Soviet Union, and the new opening to the Catholic Church.

CATEDRAL DE LA HABANA

In my own travels in Cuba, stopping off at Havana's main cathedral to stare at its beauty and observe the crowds, indication as to the renewed presence of religion was striking. Built by Jesuits between 1748 and 1777 the massive stone church has been beautifully restored as a symbol of Cuban history. "Architectural restoration has become a national obsession, the most visible, talked about and hotly debated activity in urban Cuba. Those preservation efforts have multiplied dramatically since 1990, when the Soviet Union began to crumble . . . [i]n an effort to supplant Soviet subsidies with tourist dollars."[40] Financed in part by Cuba, foreign investment companies, and UNESCO (which has designated Old Havana a World Heritage Site), the edifice is of spectacular baroque style of exuberant shapes; it stands at the end of the reconstructed cobbled square the Plaza de la Catedral.

While in 1995 Sunday Mass was sparsely attended, by 1998 the church was packed. Now a center of religious activity, it is visited not only by the elderly, as Cuban officials like to declaim, but by scores of young parents with children, young couples, and smatterings of tourists. The plaza itself is now alive as a crafts center where artists, in a private market opened in 1994, sell their crafts and paintings. Cubans and tourists crowd both the church and the plaza as Catholics, reveling in their new-found freedom, take advantage of the more open climate. Although religion may not be "free" in terms of how freedom is defined in the West, it is certainly far more open than it has ever been since 1959. And while some observers may decry the cathedral's refurbishment "as so pretty it sets the teeth slightly on edge,"[41] others "are constantly amazed at the juxtaposition of the beautiful with the improbable."[42] Undoubtedly, the Cubans who fill the pews on Sundays appreciate the restored quality of their surroundings as they contemplate their renewed ability to practice their faith openly.

THE JEWISH COMMUNITY

Prior to 1959, the Jewish community numbered more than 15,000, some of whose ancestors immigrated from Turkey after World War I, while others are of Eastern European origin whose forebears settled on the island in the 1920s and 1930s. A prosperous, relatively middle-class community, most Cuban Jews joined the exodus to the United States after Batista's fall, not because of anti-Semitism, but because their lifestyle had collapsed. Presently some 1,200 Jews remain, with more than two-thirds living in Havana while more than 300 sephardim dwell in the eastern cities of Santiago de Cuba and Guantánamo, and some 50 in the central city of Cienfuegos. Although many are still well off relative to Cuban society at large, predominantly those in Havana, the Jewish community is a mere shadow of what it once was. After 1992 "Jewish life began to revive in Cuba . . . when the government permitted members of the Communist Party to be religious observers."[43]

Although there are two small Orthodox synagogues in Old Havana, Shevet Achim and Temple Adath Israel, the primary center of Jewish life is the Conservative Patronato Synagogue in Vedado, the stylish, middle-class section of town. A modern, well-appointed building with "Gran Sinagoga De La Comunidad Hebrea" written over the glass entranceway, an arch, looking very much like half the icon of McDonalds, stretches high above the temple. The synagogue houses a community room in which programs are conducted for children and young people and a sizable library that is clearly lovingly tended. Perhaps a few thousand books spanning the centuries of Jewish culture in and out of Cuba are squeezed into the library's scores of stacks. And though one would expect the edifice to be run down—given the effects of the embargo, much of Havana is architecturally dilapidated—it is not. Rather than being neglected, it appears very well cared for.

Located only a few blocks from the U.S. Interests Section, which overlooks the Caribbean Sea, the synagogue stands around the corner from the Jewish Community Center (Comunidad Hebrea), the Jewish community's largest building in Havana. When I visited the center for the first time in 1995 there was a large poster advertising the presentation of a play by Bertolt Brecht.

Attending Friday evening services in 1995 (and then again more than two years later), I was impressed by the religious openness that exists in Cuba and the composition of the synagogue's congregation. Of the some 70 people, many were young, in their teens and 20s, informally but well dressed and looking much like young people anywhere in the world. Others, in their 40s and 50s, were very well attired. Few elderly Cubans were in attendance.

The sanctuary itself has the dimensions of only an overly large living room, and the *bimah,* with the ark and enclosed Torah, was no wider than about 15 feet. We were all tightly squeezed into the pews, with some dozen people having to stand in the back. Since the synagogue is without a rabbi—"Cuba has no rabbi—only one who visits four times a year from Mexico"[44]—the services were conducted by a young woman and man in their twenties. Very informally attired, they took turns leading the congregation in song and prayer, sometimes in Hebrew, sometimes in Spanish. Virtually the entire service was sung and, except for the use of Spanish, almost replicated Friday evening *Shabbat* services on the Upper West Side of New York City.

Speaking with some of the people after the service it was clear to me that "the maintenance of Jewish life in a communist state has real resonance."[45] No one I spoke with complained about the difficulty of being Jewish in Cuba. Indeed, another observer found that "Jewish life seems to be thriving in Communist Cuba. Virtually none of the Jews I spoke with professed any desire to leave."[46] A 27-member mission from the United Jewish Appeal-Federation of New York that traveled to Cuba in 1997 "saw no evidence of anti-Semitism; in fact, every Jew they met wore a Star of David necklace."[47] Jews are quite free to practice their religion with few constraints. No person I spoke with, in visits from 1995 to1997, indicated otherwise.

Judaism is not merely a lip-service religion in Cuba and "There's a definite sense that vibrant Jewish life has returned."[48] The religion is taken seriously and respondents felt strongly about the continuity of their religion and their practices. Although the embargo affects Jews along with other Cubans in a physical sense, in that goods are either not available or rationed, many Jewish organizations outside of Cuba contribute medicine, food, clothing, and books to Cuba's Jews. In fact, the Patronato Synagogue runs a pharmacy from which contributed medicine is distributed to the community. Most communities have a Jewish cemetery.

The kosher butcher shop in Old Havana is one of the few places in the city that has a regular supply of meat, a product few in Cuba enjoy on a regular basis. In Havana, for example, the yearly ration per person is half a pound of beef (18 pounds for a pregnant woman) and 7½ pounds of soy-enriched ground beef. Fidel Castro committed himself after the revolution to have the government supply meat to the kosher butcher shop, with the cost to be paid by the Jewish community. More than 150 families purchase meat there.

The Cuban Jewish community never had the venomous relations with the Castro government that were experienced by the Catholic Church. A society that had always encouraged social democratic values, its leadership did not publicly condemn the revolution, and whatever views it had of events at the time it kept to itself. Although the state has granted Jews the freedom to practice their religion, their strength lies within their own community. This is reaffirmed by the large number of conversions to Judaism of non-Jewish spouses as a result of the extensive rate of intermarriage, a common event also reflected in the tiny Jewish community of Sosua in the Dominican Republic. The Jews of Havana, more so than others in outlying regions who feel quite secluded, are comfortable with who they are and remain quite relaxed about being Jewish in Cuba. Though under siege, as all Cubans are, as a result of the U.S. embargo and Cuba's state-controlled economic policies, and though isolated from the Jewish community in the United States, there is a revitalized spiritual and cultural existence among Cuban Jews even in the face of economic adversity.

SANTERÍA

Santería is a belief that first arrived in Cuba in the sixteenth century via African Yoruban people (largely from what is today Nigeria) who were taken to Cuba by the Spanish during the African slave trade. For the following 300 years the Spanish "would consider its victims, not as servants or domestic slaves who deserved respect in spite of their servile condition, but as chattel slaves, commodities that could and should be sold at whim or will."[49] The Catholic Church in Cuba "had no objection to masters trading in slaves [and] remained steadfast in upholding the slavery institution."[50] "King Tobacco" in the eighteenth century and "King Sugar" in the nineteenth provided the impetus for an explosion in the number of imported slaves, and in 1880 when slavery finally ended in Cuba there were approximately 250,000 slaves on the island, primarily along the Havana-Matanzas corridor.

In remarking on this extraordinarily destructive era Castro commented, "When Columbus arrived here with his Church—the Catholic Church—he came bearing the sword and the cross. With the sword he sanctified the right to conquer; with the cross he blessed that right. . . . We had an African legacy, a legacy of animist religions which later mixed with the Catholic and other religions."[51]

Santería comprises a number of groups that vary according to the heritage of the slaves' origins in West Africa. Decentralized and with a history of secrecy, Santeros, who are predominantly black and who probably comprise anywhere from 5 percent to 15 percent of the population, believe in a supreme being and a pantheon of *orishas,* sprits of kings and founders of tribes who are prayed to for aid in dealing with life's struggles. The world is seen as a place for the evolution of the soul and to achieve completion using magic, music, dancing, and spiritual possession. Because of the terror and brutality directed toward slaves by their Spanish conquerors, the Africans cloaked their religion in the paleography of Catholicism so as to protect themselves from abuse. Thus, as the religion has evolved through the centuries it has taken on a Catholic/animist form that reflects Roman Catholic imagery. Santería has "incorporated items of Catholic ritual and mythology. Their devotees regard themselves as Catholics and believe that the names of the Catholic saints are translations into Spanish of the Nigerian names of African gods. Catholicism is viewed as the Spanish tribal version of Santería."[52]

Prior to 1992, Santeros were repressed in much the same manner as were Catholics, in large part because of their spiritual interconnection with Catholicism. But because so much of the ritual is individually-based and takes place inside the homes of Cubans the state was not as successful in eradicating the institutions and fetishes of the religion. When the era of religious liberation was set in motion there began to be seen "an invasion of medallions and crucifixes, of the beads of *santería*."[53] Once again practices could be openly engaged in.

PROTESTANTISM

With the loosening of restrictions an explosive enthusiasm for Protestant churches, most notably evangelical churches, erupted. Seen by government authorities after 1959 as a small group, marginal and sympathetic to the aims of Castro, much like the Jewish community, Protestants were pretty much left unhindered as long as the practice of their religion remained out of sight. Since 1992, however, Protestant congregations jumped from 900 to 1,700, which excludes the numerous evangelical house churches—which require government permits—while some 400,000 adherents attend weekly services. Castro has usually been quite supportive of Protestantism, seeing it as a more liberal challenge to Catholicism: "The Protestant Churches took a different attitude. . . . As a rule, [they] spread more among the poor sectors of the population."[54] Indeed, the "spread of Protestant churches has also been aided by support of the Castro regime, which has openly favored them over the Catholic Church for their focus on faith instead of politics."[55] Perhaps the fastest growing religion in Cuba, Protestantism is now free to proselytize and advance its beliefs.

THE POPE IN CUBA

When the pope stepped off the plane onto a red carpet provided by a member of the U.S.-Cuba Trade and Economic Council, a private and corporate-funded U.S. organization that provides economic and commercial information for the U.S. business community, he was greeted by a Christian hierarchy from South and North America. In fact, the U.S.-Cuba Trade and Economic Council had provided $100,000 in funding, products, and services in support of the pope's visit, including two aircraft to transport U.S. Catholic Cardinals, Archbishops, and Bishops within the Republic of Cuba.[56] The U.S. business community, which had been pressing the United States to end the embargo since at least 1995, was doing its part to influence the debate over the embargo.

The sparring between Pope John Paul II and President Castro began at the welcoming ceremony at the airport and was seen on television by millions of people around the world. The embargo, underdevelopment, religious freedom, human rights, and political prisoners were the issues both men had planned to discuss, and they got right down to it. In his greeting, Castro led off the discussion by raising the matter of exceptional concern to him—the embargo:

> Holy Father, genocide is attempted again when by hunger, illness and total economic suffocation some try to subdue this people that refuses to accept the dictates and the rule of the mightiest economic, political and military power in history; much more powerful than the old Rome. . . . Like those Christians horribly slandered to justify the crime, we who are as slandered as they were, we choose a thousand times death rather than abdicate our convictions.[57]

As to the issue of repression of Catholics, Castro maintained, "if there have ever been difficulties the revolution is not to blame."

For his part, the pope began his comments during the flight from Rome to Havana. Regarding the embargo, when asked what effect his visit would have on U.S. policy he responded by saying, "To change, to change. It seems to me that for the United States, the papal visit to Cuba is very interesting. Perhaps both Cuba and the United States are looking for a better future."[58] As to the issue of human rights, the pope was just as forceful in condemning Cuba as he was honest in criticizing the embargo: "Human rights are fundamental rights, the foundation of all civilization. . . . I brought this conviction, the engagement for human rights with me from Poland, in the confrontation with the Soviet system, the Communist totalitarian system."[59] Regarding the Catholic Church and its historical role in Cuba, the pope spoke directly to the Cuban people at the opening ceremony:

> I come to share your profound religious spirit . . . in order to make it more deeply present in the life and history of this noble people who thirst for God and for the spiritual values which in these 500 years of her presence on this island the Church has not ceased to dispense. Therefore, from my very first moment of my presence among you, I wish to say with the same force as at the beginning of my pontificate: Do not be afraid to open your hearts to Christ.[60]

In conclusion, the pope critiqued both Cuba and the United States. "May Cuba," he spoke, "with all its magnificent potential open itself up to the world, and may the world open itself up to Cuba."[61]

Both leaders were fully aware of the momentous religious changes that had been occurring in Cuba since the early 1990s; had such changes not taken place this meeting may well not have transpired. Castro was grateful, he said, to this Bishop of Rome because he spent his life reaching out to the people of underdeveloped nations and had the courage to stand against Washington by coming to Cuba despite the embargo. As Fidel declared, "we feel the same way you do about many important issues of today's world and we are pleased it is so."[62] The criticism of Cuba's stand on religion was no longer pertinent to Castro so he let that issue wash right over him. In fact, in anticipation of the visit and at the pope's behest, in 1997 he permitted Christmas to be celebrated in Cuba for the first time in three decades. As far as human rights were concerned, Castro, a firm believer in the socialist / Third World perspective, knew that his arguments on the matter would fall on deaf ears, so that irritant was left hanging.

After four days of delivering open-air Masses in different cities throughout Cuba, the pope once more spoke to the pestiferous issues. With the metal sculpture of Che Guevara as the "heroic guerrilla" staring down at him from the Ministry of the Interior, and the image of Jesus, drawn for the occasion, flanking it, the pope spoke at a televised two-and-a-half-hour open-air Mass before hundreds of thousands of people at Havana's Plaza of the Revolution, the site of numerous political speeches given by Castro in the past. The imagery, quite frankly, was incomprehensible and spoke to the surreal quality of the entire visit. With warmth amidst criticism; Castro introducing the pope to his siblings, including his politically hard-line brother Raúl Castro; the visages of Che (who would surely be aghast) and Jesus abutting one-another; open-air Masses in the heart of this Marxist/Leninist nation; with cries of "freedom" ringing the air as the pope spoke and Castro, attending the Mass and apparently enjoying it thoroughly, applauding; the atmosphere was one of contradiction and improbability.

"True liberation," the Pope maintained as he raised the issue of political prisoners, "cannot be reduced to its social and political aspects" but must also include "the exercise of freedom of conscience—the basis and foundation of all other human rights."[63] In an appeal on behalf of the estimated 500 political prisoners the pope said:

> There is also suffering of the soul such as we see in those who are isolated, persecuted, imprisoned for various offenses or for reasons of conscience, for ideas which though dissident are nonetheless peaceful. These prisoners of conscience suffer an isolation and a penalty for something for which their own conscience does not condemn them. What they want is to participate in life with the opportunity to speak their mind with respect and tolerance. I encourage efforts to reinsert prisoners into society.[64]

In framing his demand, the pope left no doubt that he wanted release to mean reentry into Cuban society and not exile to the United States or elsewhere. Before leaving Cuba the Vatican secretary of state,

Cardinal Angelo Sodano, handed Castro's representatives a list of 300 political prisoners that the pope wanted freed.

Finally, upon his departure on the evening of January 25 the tired septuagenarian spoke sternly and emphatically about the embargo in a way that was meant to capture the attention of Washington. He claimed that "Cuba's material and moral poverty" arose not merely because of "limitations to fundamental freedoms . . . but also from restrictive economic measures—unjust and ethically unacceptable—imposed from outside the country."[65] Castro could not have been more delighted; those were the very words he wanted spoken and in the very fashion that he wanted them heard. It was perhaps the main reason he wanted the pope to come to Cuba in the first place.

PURPOSES, GOALS, AND RESULTS

According to the Vatican, the pope's primary aim in visiting Cuba was "to give the Cuban people a new perspective on life—on what the pope calls the human reality."[66] Lorenzo Albacete, author of "The Poet and the Revolutionary," maintains that Fidel Castro wanted above all to publicly tie the pope to his vision that they are "the only world leaders willing to condemn the triumphalist neoliberal capitalism that both believe is widening the gap between rich and poor."[67] "Both men, after all, are visionaries, and both, as a matter of philosophical belief, reject the free market's implicit view of mankind as the sum of its material wants."[68] Whether Cubans gained a "new perspective" is at least arguable and will be determined by history. But certainly both leaders condemned, as both men had previously, the huge gulf that now exists between North and South. That critique was certainly not novel but by giving it in tandem with the pope Castro may have achieved a moral victory of sorts.

But the decisive results came both prior to the visit and immediately afterward. In terms of religion, and specifically Catholicism, the pope had achieved most of his goals before his arrival in Havana. By his very presence he sanctioned the openness and liberalization that had been ongoing since 1992. But he expected more and he got it. Just prior to the pope's arrival Cuba announced that an additional 28 priests and 29 nuns would be permitted entrance from Colombia, Haiti, and Spain, bringing the total number of clergy to 754. And given the pope's presence and pronouncements regarding religious liberty, as well as the fact that Cuba is a relatively secular state in which Fidel believes ethical values are being lost, it is highly unlikely that there will ever be a return to the religiously repressive period that existed prior to 1991. In that regard, the pope's desire to give Cubans a new perspective may have matched Castro's own aspirations. Regardless, the changes that have occurred, for all religions, would be hard to retract, and it is doubtful that they will be.

In the domain of human rights, that is, political and civil rights as opposed to Castro's perspective of economic and social rights, very little is likely to change, at least in the near term. It is improbable, as long as Castro remains active, that there will be an enlargement of the political space to the degree that the United States has demanded.

As an adjunct to the matter of human rights, however, Castro promptly responded to the pope's appeal for the release of political "prisoners of conscience." On February 12, just a month after the pope left Cuba, the government announced that it would free 299 inmates, including 70 political prisoners, in response to the pope's appeal for clemency, the most sweeping release that the Cuban government had granted in years. Several dozen of the prisoners were on the list given Cuba by the Vatican. Although the United States, through its State Department spokesman, praised Castro's decision only faintly, claiming that most prominent political dissidents remained incarcerated and that many of those released were being "forced" into exile, the Vatican announced that it was "delighted with this notable step, which represents a concrete prospect of hope for the future of this noble nation. There is no precedent for this in 40 years. It was a gesture to the Holy Father, but the eloquence of this gesture goes further, to a wider audience. We see it as a strong and eloquent statement to those who want to see a better future in their relationship with Cuba."[69] Shortly thereafter Canada announced that it would accept 17 of those freed prisoners who were released on condition that they leave Cuba. Canada's prime minister Jean Chrétien, who later in the year paid a state visit to Havana, in a sideways swat at the embargo said of the release that it showed the value of "constructive engagement" with Cuba. By mid-summer Canada announced a five-fold increase in its economic investments in Cuba.

Of the freed prisoners 280 were permitted to remain in Cuba. Many had been serving 5-year sentences for spreading "enemy propaganda," while Omar del Pozo Marrero, a well-known political dissident, had been serving a 15-year term for "revealing state security secrets." He was among those who went into exile in Canada.

Castro got almost everything he expected regarding the U.S. embargo. The pope had denounced it in many venues, and the trip itself sent the strong message that the pope would not be held back by America's insistence that foreign leaders not travel to Cuba—which bestowed upon Fidel a great breadth of legitimacy, added to his allure, and strengthened his international standing vis-à-vis his critique of the embargo.

Perhaps the most stunning result of the journey came from Washington. During the first week of March, Madeleine Albright met in the Vatican with the pope to discuss Cuba. Upon returning to the United States she drafted a memo to President Clinton that said that since the Cuban Catholic Church has achieved access to the people and could deliver uncensored sermons, and at the urging of Pope John Paul II, the U.S. should respond to the Pope's trip.[70] He must certainly have exerted some pressure on the secretary of state, a fierce exponent of the embargo, since her view of Fidel Castro is that of a totalitarian presence in a newly "democratic" Latin America. President Clinton then announced on March 20 that in response to the pope's encouragement the United States would (1) restore the daily U.S. charter flight from Miami to Havana; (2) permit Catholic relief organizations, such as Caritas, to charter flights directly from the United States to carry goods for relief purposes and passengers in emergencies (which, in any case, they had been doing from third countries); and (3) streamline the licensing procedure for nonprofit organizations to sell pharmaceuticals to Cuba, although they still could not do so unless they could verify that the goods were used for the intended purposes (which meant that medical supplies would still be virtually impossible to distribute, thus indicating very little change in this part of the policy). Although the embargo and the Helms-Burton Act remained unaffected, this Executive Order, limited as it was, clearly reflected an unmuffled response to the pope's attack on the embargo and his plea to open up to Cuba. For the pope and parenthetically for Fidel Castro this was quite an accomplishment. Later in the year and without publicity, the United States was reported to have approved Cuba's long-standing request that its commercial airliners be permitted to fly over U.S. territory on their way to and from Canada.

The two had gotten much of what they had wanted. Castro acquired a formidable ally in his cause against the embargo. The pope sanctified, as it were, the religious reforms implemented throughout the decade, which were expanded even further as Cardinal Jaime Ortega celebrated Easter Sunday 1998 with an unprecedented outdoor Midnight Mass in the Plaza de la Catedral. And both stood together condemning the harshness of the intensified nature of capitalism and its corrosive materialism, exemplified particularly by the IMF's structural adjustment program, which ravages workers and peasants in emerging nations. The pope's solicitation for the release of political prisoners was partially met, while the Catholic Church's liberalized position in Cuba was secured and its growth was seen to by Castro's permitting more priests and nuns to come to Cuba. Each did not get everything, but they came out of their discussions with more than they probably expected. For both, the trip was a success, while the long-term ramifications are still to be calculated.

Perhaps the real impact of the meeting between Pope John Paul II and President Castro is that it took place at all. The images of these two twentieth-century colossi politically working each other—Castro patting the pope on the back and being solicitous of his infirmities, the pope caressing his audience at the various Masses by telling them he liked to be interrupted by their music and cheering so he could catch his breath, as well as graciously meeting with Fidel's hard-core communist cohorts—are the memories that will last beyond the political results that were achieved. The man in the blue suit, one of the last surviving communist leaders, and certainly the longest in power, dueling with the pope in his white cassock, and both in the very twilight of their lives, is what in time will be most remembered.

SIX

POLITICAL DISSENT

TOWARD THE END OF 1997, the United States Coast Guard intercepted a cabin cruiser near the coast of Puerto Rico that was manned by four Cuban exiles, three of whom resided in the United States. Its navigational coordinates were set for Margarita Island, Venezuela, where Fidel Castro was to attend a summit meeting in November, and the Coast Guard, its suspicions aroused, searched the vessel and found an arsenal of weapons that it suspected were to be used in an assassination attempt against Castro. Most of the crew, self-declared Castro antagonists, along with the registered owner of some of the weapons and the director of the corporation that held title to the vessel, were either connected to the anti-Castro Miami-based Cuban American National Foundation or had taken part in the 1961 CIA-sponsored Bay of Pigs invasion. By 1998 the U.S. Customs Agency; the Bureau of Alcohol, Tobacco, and Firearms; the CIA; the FBI; the Maritime Enforcement Agency; the State Department; and the Justice Department were well into an investigation of the circumstances with an eye toward eventual prosecution.[1]

Earlier, in the summer of 1997, a former Salvadoran army paratrooper and sharpshooter who had, according to Cuban officials, attended U.S. army training courses in Georgia set off a series of explosions in Havana's Hotel Nacional, Hotel Capri, the Copacabana Hotel, and the La Bodeguita del Medio, one of Ernest Hemingway's old haunts and perhaps Cuba's most famous bar and restaurant. Alpha 66, a militant anti-Castro organization headquartered in Miami, claimed "that it was in contact with clandestine cells inside Cuba that were responsible" for organizing the explosions which killed one Italian tourist and caused extensive physical damage.[2] According to the Cuban government the perpetrator was part of a "network of mercenaries operating out of El Salvador, dedicated to terrorism and international drug trafficking, closely linked to counterrevolutionaries in Miami."[3]

Ever since the first embargo act was implemented in 1960 Fidel Castro has claimed, quite correctly, that the United States was intent on subverting his government so as to remove him from power, which would permit Washington to restore its tight control over Cuba's economic and political affairs. Indeed, Castro was off by only one year as already in 1959 the United States had, according to Assistant Secretary of State Roy R. Rubottom Jr., initiated an effort to overthrow Castro and have him replaced by a government friendly to the United States by "covertly supporting the build-up of anti-Castro elements. Leading Cuban dissidents are now organizing outside of Cuba as well, and we [the State Department and the CIA] have reason to hope that their strength will reach such proportions as to bring about his downfall. Perhaps within a period of months. This would be the *most desirable* end to the Castro menace, assuming that he is replaced by elements friendly to the U.S."[4]

Certainly the Bay of Pigs invasion, and in its wake, the establishment of paramilitary exile groups such as Alpha 66, the Second Naval Guerrilla Group, and later the Union of Former Political Prisoners, all headquartered in Miami, gave credence to Castro's speculation that the United States would be satisfied with nothing less than his overthrow. President Kennedy's campaign to have Castro assassinated via Operation Mongoose and the fact that by "the early 1960s an astonishing 12,000 Cuban emigres were on the CIA payroll"[5] only added legitimacy to Castro's acute mistrust of the United States.

America's war against Fidel Castro, which nine presidents have pursued, has presented Castro with the opportunity to still the voices of virtually all political dissidents in Cuba. The fact that the United States has repeatedly violated international law, and even its own domestic laws, in its effort to evict Castro from power has only weakened its arguments that Cuba unjustifiably disallows political dissent. Even Human Rights Watch, the nongovernmental organization established in 1978 "to monitor and promote the observance of internationally recognized human rights . . . ,"[6] has indicated that "The Cuban government's justification for repression can be largely encapsulated in three words: the United States."[7]

Castro's paranoia is well founded and is supported by history. Presidents from Eisenhower to Clinton have unrelentingly intruded in Cuba's internal affairs and have done what they could to destabilize Cuba and to see to it that the basis of Castro's legitimacy is eroded. Clinton's Department of Justice, for instance, refused to halt the flights of Brothers to the Rescue that had been buzzing Havana for two years prior to February 1996, when two of its civilian aircraft were shot down. Cuba's Foreign Minister Roberto Robaina argued,

> We actually begged the United States Government to do all in its power to prevent those flights, which violated not only our own laws but also the laws of the United States. It was not us who could prevent those violations from happening. Only the United States had the power to do so.[8]

But the United States remained unwilling to stop the unscrupulous activities of Brothers to the Rescue, thrusting full blame on Cuba for *its* illegal actions in having military aircraft shoot down "civilian" planes. Although hardly innocent civilian aircraft—Ricardo Alarcón called them "paramilitary aircraft, devoted to subversion, sabotage"[9]—the United States had allowed previous Brothers to the Rescue overflights, hoping they would help its destabilization policy succeed.

Cuba cannot be blamed for still seeing the United States as a promoter of terrorism on the island: as late as 1997 terrorist activity against Cuba inside the country and on the high seas was linked to Miami-based exile groups and remnant participants in the Bay of Pigs invasion; the United States was viewed as doing nothing to prevent such activities even when fully cognizant of them, the Venezuela indictments notwithstanding. By actively promoting and sponsoring actions to get rid of Castro and by pursing a policy of benign neglect toward expatriate anti-Castro groups, Washington has granted Cuba a logical rationale by which to discredit and prohibit Cuban political dissidents from engaging in any display of opposition to Castro's policies

As stated in the Cuban constitution citizens have freedom of speech as long as it adheres to the objectives of socialist society.[10] But when virtually all public criticism is tied to "imperialist intervention"[11] of the kind exhibited by the United States for 40 years that is meant to obstruct the objectives of Cuban socialism it is clear why Cuba pitilessly restricts such behavior. All dissident groups and individuals within Cuba are categorized as being nourished by or serving the interests of Washington and Miami, and so long as the United States and the Miami-based conservative Cuban political establishment continue to push for Castro's removal little movement toward liberalization ought to be expected; indigenous organizations will continue to be harassed and individual actors will often be jailed. The Cuban Democracy Act and the Helms-Burton Act, buttressed by appeals from the Vatican, may have led to the early release of some political prisoners, but they can do little to fundamentally alter the generic policy that closely monitors all dissident activity and comes down hard on those seen as violating the objectives of socialist society as articulated by the Communist Party and the Cuban constitution.

Dissidents are denied the political right to oppose the values and norms of Cuban socialism because the overriding value system is directed toward collective economic and social rights. If they seek to pursue their individual "rights" they are defined as stalking horses for the United States, even if their motives are otherwise. Cuba's penal code allows charges to be brought against anyone who "incites against social order, international solidarity or the socialist State" and also defines as crimes "illicit association" and creating "public disorder."[12] Those found in violation of these edicts of the penal code can be imprisoned for up to 8 years, while those who through the use of the media spread "false news or malicious predictions that tend to cause alarm or discontent or public disorder" may be jailed for 15 years. At the present time, Cuba has about 350 political detainees, some of whom are serving up to 20-year sentences. In all cases Cuba has defined them as representing imperialist interests, that is, acting to further the purposes of the United States. And although that is certainly not always true, Castro's government finds itself unable or unwilling to separate acceptable behavior regarding political rights from past historical actions of the United States in which it has violently tried to overthrow and even kill Fidel Castro.

The political and oft times militaristic activities of the Miami-based exile organizations only serve to harden Cuba's attitude, leaving little space for those Cubans who oppose Castro's policies or for those wishing to provide a nongovernmental and alternative approach to political, social, and economic issues of the day. Internal dissidents and Miami are seen as two halves of a whole, which eliminates any singular role Cuban oppositionists may wish to play. They are not seen as actors whose primary interest is Cuba but as parties speaking for exile interests who themselves are seen as only furthering the goals of the United States.

THE CUBAN-AMERICAN NATIONAL FOUNDATION

The most right-wing, powerful, and politically effective lobby group representing the voice of Cuban-Americans is the Cuban American National Foundation (CANF). Set up in 1981 at the suggestion of President Ronald Reagan it claims to have been founded "for the purpose of gathering and disseminating data concerning the economic, political and social welfare of the Cuban people, both on the island and in exile [and] to promote respect for human freedom, democratic values and the pursuit of prosperity with dignity and justice for all."[13] To that end its goal is "to maintain a relentless call for political, economic, and moral pressure on Castro's regime until his unconditional withdrawal from power, so that the Cuban people may exercise their right to self-determination. Cuba will be free. Whether it is tomorrow, next month, or next year, we will not stray from our course. Freedom and respect for human dignity will revisit us once Castro is gone. . . ."[14]

Until his death in November 1997 CANF was led by Jorge Mas Canosa, who in 1961 had been part of the exile network that participated in the Bay of Pigs invasion. He was a furious and unrelenting antagonist of Fidel Castro (mentioned by the self-proclaimed Cuban exile terrorist Luis Posada Carriles as financing assassination attempts directed against Castro), and the organization he led "built a power base that resembles a government in exile, to the point of bestowing medals on visiting heads of state, warning foreign governments that they will be punished if they trade with Cuba and writing a new Cuban constitution."[15] Through a political action committee CANF has donated millions to congressional and presidential candidates of both the Democratic and Republican parties, and with a membership base of more than 50,000, while also claiming to represent the more than 1.3 million Cuban-Americans predominately in Florida (65percent) and New Jersey (20percent), CANF wields extraordinary power. In fact, because Florida is always a key state in the presidential election candidates of both parties have vied for Mas Canosa's approval, seeing him as vital and influential to winning the state.

In 1985, CANF was given responsibility to operate Radio Martí and in 1990 Television Martí as propaganda outlets broadcasting reactionary anti-Castro venom from the United States to Cuba. Although supposedly under the authority of the Voice of America, both Radio and Television Martí have been essentially unregulated and autonomously run by an advisory board supervised by Mas Canosa and subsidized by the United States to the tune of more than $286 million since 1985. According to a 1992 General Accounting Office study, "TV Martí lacked balance and did not meet established Voice of America standards."[16] When the Soviet bloc began to disintegrate CANF's intent, according to a former director of Radio Martí, "was no longer limited to the liberation of Cuba. Instead the Foundation became a political organization whose goal was to take power after Fidel Castro"[17] and to regain control of all properties nationalized after the revolution.

Since CANF was also given funding by the U.S. government to resettle Cuban refugees who found their way to Florida, the foundation not only had a huge supply of available capital provided by Washington, but its direct access to the refugees allowed it to be a sort of Tammany Hall, providing help in locating housing and a job, and in integrating into the larger Miami-Cuban community. In return, as the exiles became citizens, they were expected to vote as CANF demanded. As more refugees arrived, more money flowed from Washington, additional votes were garnered, and the leverage of CANF kept increasing. Under the Cuban Exodus Relief Fund CANF also received $588 in Federal support for each Cuban refugee it brought in from a third country. As families were united under this program CANF gained many more supporters, and according to Wayne S. Smith, "I don't know of any other political organization that has ever received this kind of privilege. It is one they have clearly used to their advantage, saying to people, 'We can get your uncle in Madrid to the U.S. and oh, by the way, you do support the Foundation, don't you?'"[18] In 1993, after complaints by other Miami-based organizations, the third-country resettlement subsidy was ended.

Mas Canosa's power was prodigious and he used it unsparingly. He was seen as someone whose support for or rejection of a candidate could swing elections. And it often could. During the various election seasons Reagan, Bush, Clinton, Vice President Albert Gore Jr., Dole or whomever was running for office would fly to Miami to have very public meals with Mas Canosa and his entourage in Little Havana, after which a virulent anti-Castro speech would usually be given by the candidate, sometimes even in the massive Orange Bowl. Congressional candidates in Florida normally fell all over themselves to cater to Mas Canosa's whims, while leading anti-Castro politicians such as Jesse Helms, Robert Torricelli, and Jeb Bush bestowed plaudits and power upon him. His support was considered to be worth at least one million votes, particularly as the Cuban-American community in Miami comprises more than one-third of the population of that city, an immense voting bloc in Florida, which has a population of 14 million people. Securing the state in November via its Cuban-American community is every politician's desire.

Since the early 1980s, the Cuban American National Foundation has more or less been able to frame the foreign policy debate over Cuba. It led the call for the creation of the Cuban Democracy Act and it lobbied hard for the Helms-Burton bill, which was eventually signed by President Clinton on the heels of the shooting down of the Brothers to the Rescue. It has concentrated the minds of politicians to such a degree, and it is so well endowed and well organized, that it has been able to establish the parameters of foreign policy toward Cuba for each president since 1981. Its resources have been made available to those seen as supportive, and with chapters in Los Angeles, New York, New Jersey, Texas, and in assorted foreign lands CANF is able to call on an array of supporters who clearly have had the ability to influence any politician vis-à-vis Cuba. All presidents have heaped praise upon or saluted CANF and Mas Canosa, no matter their real political desires, and once in the grip of the foundation politicians have found themselves unable to extricate themselves politically. Even foreign dignitaries such as Russia's Boris Yeltsin and President Václav Havel of the Czech Republic have passed through Miami and paid their respects to Mas Canosa.

There is little doubt that Mas Canosa saw himself succeeding Castro as President of Cuba. To that end, in 1991 he established a Blue Ribbon Commission on the Economic Reconstruction of Cuba to develop a blueprint for a post-Castro Cuban economy. It was made clear to all foreign leaders and businesses that investment in Castro's Cuba meant exclusion in a Mas Canosa regime. Corporations joining the commission would, for a $25,000 fee, be entitled to participate in establishing new economic guidelines, but in fact, according to one U.S. business executive, the "fee" was little more than an entitlement offering access to "these guys [who] were going to be the leaders of Cuba when Castro goes down and that we would be in their good graces by being part of this committee. That was the pitch."[19] Or as CANF put it, in no uncertain terms,

> Investments made in Cuba under the present circumstances should not benefit from any laws passed by a future Cuban government for the protection of private property. We feel that these investments should be considered as state property and disposed of accordingly. We will do our utmost to insure that no foreign investment made in Castro's Cuba will enjoy the protection of the law, and that the validity of every agreement be questioned.[20]

Clearly, Mas Canosa saw himself as the person who would eventually invoke this new economic standard in Cuba. Even in Miami he played the role of a president who was merely temporarily in exile. Residing in a mansion surrounded by high walls, he had a chauffeur-driven Mercedes and was always surrounded by bodyguards and sycophants. It was extremely difficult to even gain entrance to see lower-level bureaucrats in his offices without a prior appointment. And he made it clear to both domestic and foreign leaders that called upon him and that often depended upon his largess that he was the political leader to be reckoned with. George Bush declared in 1992, while signing the CDA, "I salute Jorge Mas"; that statement could as easily have been made, and often was, by every politician who came to Miami to obsequiously bend before Mas Canosa. His formidable position only lent authority to his own vision of replacing Fidel Castro.

Since Mas Canosa was *the* primary force behind CANF his death at the youthful age of 58 will certainly have the effect of weakening the leverage once wielded by the organization. No replacement, including his successor Alberto Hernández, can hope to attain the immense dominance of Mas Canosa or display the singular energy he provided that made the Cuban American National Foundation so feared in Washington. It is also unlikely that any future U.S. president will again bestow such prestige on Mas Canosa's successor and remain imprisoned within the confines of CANF's policies. Mas Canosa's demise provides liberals in Washington the opportunity to reach out to the more moderate Miami-based organizations so as to eventually develop a more reasonable policy toward Cuba. And that is vital if other voices are to be heard.

MIAMI'S OTHER EXILE COMMUNITY

Most Miami-based political organizations and their membership reflect the conservatism of CANF. Usually based in the ethnic enclave of Little Havana, economically successful to an extraordinary degree, and "in terms of racial composition, overwhelmingly white,"[21] most consider the removal of Castro and the destruction of communism "to be the central missions in their existence."[22]

Brothers to the Rescue, led by its president, José Basulto, was initially organized to rescue Cuban boat people who were fleeing the island. Spotter planes were used to direct assorted yachts and cruisers to the refugees so that they could be picked up and brought to Florida. This noble response to a refugee crisis, however, was complemented by something dramatically different and quite ugly as the spotter planes alternated between rescue and provocation, often illegally flying through Cuban airspace and even at times, as some have reported, dropping political leaflets and spreading propaganda.[23] The U.S. Justice Department and the Federal Aviation Administration (FAA) did nothing to inhibit these activities until the passage of Helms-Burton, which itself was a result of the provocative and truly alarming actions of Brothers to the Rescue. Indeed, Basulto was the pilot of the only surviving plane and according to Ricardo Alarcón the United States never "took any steps in relation to the violators of Cuba's air space."[24] Though he was not prosecuted Basulto's pilot's license was suspended in May 1996 and the FAA now keeps very close tabs on the air and sea activities of Brothers to the Rescue.

Among other anti-Castro associations in Miami are more than 120 *municipios en el exilio* that function under the umbrella organization Municipios De Cuba En El Exilio. While organizing individuals via the townships they fled and offering various social services they also coordinate voter registration drives, enlist their members to support this or that candidate, and dogmatically socialize their constituents into maintaining a fierce anti-Castro position.

Cuba Independiente Y Democratica; Agenda: Cuba, whose motto is "No Castro, No Problem"; the Organization of Cuban Educators in Exile; and Corriente Agramontista, a lawyers group with representation in Cuba (but which has not been granted legal recognition) that provides support to Cuban lawyers defending political cases—all are notable for their antagonism toward the current government. Anti-communism and anti-Castro attitudes are hallmarks of these organizations, which largely disallow moderate political views from being represented within their constituency.

The Cuban Committee for Democracy and Concilio Cubano are two significant moderate organizations—along with close to a score of others—whose emphasis is on dialogue with Castro's government so as to develop a strategy acceptable to all parties that can lead to policy to be implemented presently or in a post-Castro Cuba. According to Alfredo Duran of the Cuban Committee for Democracy, who is highly critical of the obstinacy and dogmatism articulated by the conservatives in Miami, "the only way to achieve dialogue is through engagement" with Castro.[25]

His position is echoed by Concilio Cubano, whose official statement issued by its representative in Havana in 1995 argued that there "is a compelling need to find a consensus by all democratic forces, inside and outside the island . . . to create an appropriate framework for debating and designing common strategies." To that end, it agreed "to work for a totally peaceful transfer toward a democratic society under the rule of law, devoid of any vindictiveness, and equally comprising all citizens; equal participation by all Cubans . . . that will lead to economic independence [and to] guarantee participation for all Cubans, with no exclusions whatsoever."[26]

Until after the death of Mas Canosa, those individuals and organizations displaying a more tolerant view of Cuban/American relations were physically roughed up and politically and economically repressed. The conservatives participating in the overall anti-Castro movement were as dictatorial and oppressive to their opponents as they maintained Castro was to his; the irony of Miami is that the thuggery directed against representatives of moderation gives little credence to the conservatives' claim that political democracy would be restored should they ever find themselves in charge of decision-making in Cuba. Should the violence be resurrected it would only serve to buttress Castro's unwavering position that internal dissidents are not independent actors but are only influenced by those right-wing elements in Miami who refuse to entertain any reasonable dialogue. Anyone who strolls through the streets of Little Havana and whose views of Castro differ markedly from the prevailing conservative sentiment has to be very wary about airing those views. Differing opinions are still not welcome and one has the distinct sense that it would be rather unwise, perhaps even unsafe, to do anything but keep quiet. In 1998 the recently stifled violence still seemed at the edge of incipiency.

INTIMIDATING THE LIBERAL MIAMI-BASED CUBAN COMMUNITY

During the Fall of 1994, a series of bombings occurred in Miami that were coordinated with attacks on individuals whose political stance mostly reflected the exact opposite perspective of Alpha 66, CANF and Brothers to the Rescue. The harassment against those seeking dialogue with Castro's government was a direct result of a meeting held in Havana the previous April that was sponsored by the Cuban government, as well as a subsequent video, furtively shown some months later, of a reception in which participants were shown kissing and greeting Fidel Castro—some were even heard thanking him for what he had done for Cuba. "The Nation and Immigration" conference was called to initiate a discussion on exile/Cuban relations, and some 200 exiles, many from the Miami area, even some who opposed Castro and had been imprisoned by him, were invited and attended the conference. From that point on their lives changed dramatically; they came under attack by right-wing, anti-Castro thugs, while the FBI and local authorities did very little to investigate the crimes.

Alpha 66 had issued a warning, a death threat to be precise, to those who planned on traveling to Havana for the conference by indicating that they would be considered "a military target and will suffer the consequences inside or outside of Cuba."[27] It was no idle threat. On September 6 the Miami office of *Réplica* magazine was bombed after its publisher, who supported dialogue with Castro, attended the meetings. A businessman belonging to a professional association that advocated an end to the U.S. embargo—Profesionales y Empresarios Cubano-Americanos—and a Jewish couple who had earlier founded Jewish Solidarity, which delivers food and medicine to Cuban Jews, had their lives threatened, while bomb threats were phoned into their respective offices. Acts of Repudiation occurred—a form of punishment that ironically also takes place in Cuba using different slogans—in which the identified person is surrounded by a mob, trapped, and then overwhelmed with insults such as "Communist traitor, get out of Miami," "If you like Fidel so much, go live in Cuba," "Only vermin like Fidel will kiss Fidel."[28] After being verbally assaulted the individuals were often beaten.

Local Spanish radio stations identified the participants to the conference, referring to them as jackals, communists, or agents of Fidel, and as a result some people were fired from their jobs and blacklisted from economic access as, according to some, "government positions and contracts at all levels, but especially at the state, county, and local level, are awarded and denied on the basis of political viewpoint and activity."[29] That is, whether or not one stands against Castro. According to Human Rights Watch these radio stations contribute mightily toward the repressive climate that clearly tends to restrict freedom of opinion and expression. The repression was compounded by the fact that local officials often encouraged the attackers with their disparaging comments about the conferees, including Republican Congressman Lincoln Diáz-Balart—the nephew of Fidel's ex-wife—who "asserted that conference participants should be registered as foreign agents."[30]

These violent attacks were neither the first nor the last to occur against those favoring a more measured response to Castro's Cuba. Some years earlier Marazul Tours, the sole U.S.-based travel agency licensed by the United States Treasury Department to arrange legal travel to Cuba for citizens or residents of the United States, had its offices bombed and destroyed. Through 1997 Cuban entertainers visiting the United States and booked to perform in Miami would often find the theater closed down due to pressure by local officials, or by bomb threats, or by such huge numbers of demonstrators violently railing against the presence of Cuban artists—who had the audacity to actually live and work in Cuba!—that the performance would have to be canceled. Even the office of the French Counsel, which organized a Latin film festival in Miami in 1996 and 1997, was careful about including Cuban films in its repertoire, fearing a backlash by the community.[31]

Mas Canosa, when asked by a journalist, "the fact is there were Molotov cocktails tossed [in 1996]; are they, is there intolerance or not in Miami?" responded, "Absolutely there is tolerance in Miami. When a Molotov cocktail is tossed, the perpetrator must be an inciter or maybe a Castro agent, because he sends these people to Miami to provoke the victims of his system into that type of protest." Regarding attacks against visiting artists Mas Canosa replied in all seriousness that "they are victims who come here to provoke the Cuban exile community."[32]

It was only in 1998 that a change in the prevailing climate of Miami took place, although how deep-seated and long-lasting remains in question. According to Manning Salazar, a young Cuban-American music promoter based in Miami and intent on spreading Cuban culture in the United States, "A lot of things, big and small have happened over the last year or so. Jorge Mas Canosa, the leader of the right-wing Cubans died."[33] For the first time in decades Cuban artists came to Miami and to New York without the normally attendant death and bomb threats. Alicia Alonso's world-renowned National Ballet of Cuba performed for one week at New York's City Center without incident,[34] while musical ensembles such as the all-female quartet Gema 4, Havana's popular band La Charanga Habanera, and the Cuban singer Isaac Delgado performed in Miami Beach without violence and to great acclaim; Los Muñequitos de Matanzas, a percussion vocal and dance group, played to standing room only crowds at New York City's Hostos Community College, the dance band Los Van Van performed at the JVC Jazz Festival in New York City, and the percussionist Pancho Quinto was featured at Manhattan's Symphony Space Theater. The Center for Cuban Studies, an organization established in 1972 by Sandra Levinson, its Executive Director, which publishes the bi-monthly *Cuba Update* and is "dedicated to providing information and activities relating to contemporary Cuba and contributing to a normalization of relations between Cuba and the U.S.,"[35] sponsored a series of artistic exhibits. José Fuster, a ceramicist and painter, appeared together with his work at New York's Metropolitan Arts Center, which is linked to the Center for Cuban Studies, while in late 1997 the Center for Cuban Studies Art Space put on a display of 15 Cuban artists on the subject "Naive Art From Cuba." In all these cases the events took place without any outside fuss. The once large but now very small groups of anti-Castro protesters who gather each Thursday in front of the New York City offices of the Permanent Mission of Cuba to the United Nations on Lexington Avenue and 38th street (although the police force them to stand across the avenue on 39th) shouting "No Castro, No Problem" and holding aloft anti-Castro banners and posters appear to have had the wind knocked out of them by Mas Canosa's death. The

New York presentations, as well as those in Miami, came off without disturbance.

Despite the only very recent decline in violence directed at Cubans or Cuban-American supporters of negotiation with Castro, the uncompromising madness of those U.S.-based partisans whose ideological stance is supported by those Washington politicians intent on seeing Castro dethroned certainly validates, although it does not excuse, Fidel's stance on internal political dissent. The connections, or claimed links, between the reactionaries in Miami and some opposition groups in Cuba only serves to harden Castro's stance—on July 26, 1998, Castro labeled CANF a CIA-supported "terrorist mafia." These are definitely not individuals or organizations that anyone can work or negotiate with, and any reasonable person can only view their actions with the greatest alarm. That wariness clearly spills over into Cuba and determines the treatment of political dissidents, even those with the purest motives. If the Miami organizations, who still today despite the decline in violence view even the Visual and Performing Arts as a threat to their control and domination of the Cuban diaspora, can not accept peaceful co-mingling in Miami with Cuban artists, musicians, and painters then Castro must approach the issue of political dissent with a particularly wary eye, repugnant as that may seem to Americans.

THE STIFLING OF POLITICAL DISSENT IN CUBA

In 1996, Ricardo Alarcón said of Elizardo Sánchez Santa Cruz, Secretary General of the Cuban Commission for Human Rights and National Conciliation, who was alleged to have provided information to Miami's Radio Martí and Television Martí during the time of the Brothers to the Rescue event: "Don't make a mistake. We know how to deal with these people."[36] And unfortunately, Cuba does. Since the monitoring of human rights by indigenous groups on the island is illegal and Cuba disallows legal status to opposition or pro-democracy organizations, political dissidents in Cuba are treated harshly and given very little political space to register their views. Associations that demand the implementation of human rights based largely on the Universal Declaration of Human Rights are either brusquely shut down or repressed by the Cuban security services. Their leadership is often jailed with or without trial (although not usually immediately) since judicial independence is constrained by the constitution of Cuba.[37] Preventive detention for as long as four years is often imposed for "anti-social" acts while stiff prison sentences are handed down for those who produce "propaganda" and try to distribute it publicly. Since requests for legal status for political and human rights organizations are always rejected virtually all those who press for change or apply to register their associations with the state are immediately marked and monitored. CDRs, the Federation of Cuban Women, the security network, and neighborhood Acts of Repudiation are then utilized to isolate and identify individuals, which earmarks them to the larger community as political pariahs.

If arrest is not in the cards surveillance, wire taps, loss of employment, refusal of social services, the denial of travel visas, and overall ostracization are instruments used to harass and intimidate individuals. Sánchez Santa Cruz, for example, who spent more than two years in prison, is disallowed from traveling outside Cuba. Prison conditions, according to Human Rights Watch, violate the UN's Standard Minimum Rules for the Treatment of Prisoners. Beatings, harsh confinement in isolation cells, denial of medical attention, and incarceration far from places of residence are the norm.[38]

Marta Beatriz Roque, a former professor of mathematics and statistics at the University of Havana, who in 1994 co-founded the National Association of Independent Economists of Cuba and in 1996 the Internal Dissidence Working Group, was arrested and imprisoned without trial in July 1997. In a letter smuggled from prison in 1998 she "spoke of cruel prison conditions, political indoctrination and inadequate medical care."[39] Arrested along with her were Vladimiro Roca, who is the son of Cuba's prerevolutionary communist leader and Castro-supporter Blás Roca, and who in 1991 founded the illegal Social Democratic Party; René Gómez Manzano, co-founder in 1990 of the independent lawyers' group Corriente Agramontista; and Félix Bonné Carcasses, who in 1992 founded Cuban Civic Current, a professional think tank for academics. All were arrested for distributing a document in June 1997 entitled "The Homeland Belongs to All of Us" that called for an expansion of human rights, democratic elections, and an even greater opening up of the economy. It is more than likely that the prison conditions the three must contend with parallel those of Marta Beatriz Roque.

For the most prominent jailed dissidents forced exile, usually to Spain or the United States, is a tool used by the state to get rid of its antagonists. But this mechanism, which blatantly violates the Universal Declaration of Human Rights,[40] is conditioned on acceptance by the prisoner and most have been unwilling to voluntarily abandon their country of birth. Sebastián Arcos Bergnes, who was arrested in 1981 for helping to organize the Cuban Committee for Human Rights in Cuba, released in 1988, and rearrested in 1992 for disseminating "enemy propaganda," spent a total of ten years in prison. He rejected an offer of early release if he would leave Cuba, "insisting that he preferred to remain and resist."[41] He was eventually freed in 1995 for health reasons and reluctantly moved to Miami after a Cuban doctor who had treated him upon his release was dismissed for "ideological incompatibility with the national health system."[42] He died of cancer in Miami in 1997. Yndamiro Restano Díaz was sentenced to ten years in prison in 1992 for "rebellion" for trying to create a democratic socialist movement to bring about governmental change. A noteworthy political prisoner "adopted" by Western human rights agencies he refused banishment but was unconditionally released in 1995. More than a dozen of the political prisoners set free after the Pope's visit in 1998 loathingly accepted exile in Canada. One, Edelberto del Toro Argota, who had been serving a four-year sentence for "enemy propaganda" and was freed only on condition he leave the country, said, "I am leaving because I cannot live in peace. I am going so I can work and support my family."[43]

The leaders of organizations such as the José Martí National Commission of Human Rights, the Máximo Gómez Human Rights Front, the Cuban Human Rights Party, the Harmony Movement, Alternative Criteria, the National Civic Union, the National Council for Civil Rights in Cuba, the National Commission of Independent Unions, the Democratic Civic Party, and the Association of Independent Journalists—all of which endure outlaw status—remain either politically terrorized or jailed for their activities. Francisco Chaviano

González, president of the of the National Council for Civil Rights in Cuba, for example, was imprisoned for 15 years in 1995 on charges of revealing state secrets and falsifying documents for Cubans seeking U.S. visas. According to Human Rights Watch prior to his arrest in 1994 "he had been the target of constant government harassment, including frequent surveillance and acts of vandalism to his home."[44] Usually, Human Rights Watch explained, these

> human rights workers are imprisoned on vague and malleable political charges that violate basic political and civil rights. Typical charges include "illicit association," "clandestine printing," and "disrespect to the head of state." After completing their sentences, dissidents may be kept in prison under the commonly used provision of "high dangerousness," which can add as much as four years to the original period of incarceration. "Spreading enemy propaganda," one of the most common political charges, carries prison sentences that frequently reach ten years; more when combined with other crimes.[45]

The response of Cuban authorities reflects not only their rejection of the political/civil rights perspective as articulated in the Universal Declaration of Human Rights, but their analysis that the United States and the exile community in Miami is closely connected to human rights activities on the island, linking indigenous human rights advocates with America's 40-year long war against the government of Fidel Castro. Therefore the Cuban government maintains that

> any objective analysis of human rights in Cuba and, in particular, of persons sentenced and held in the island's penitentiaries, must take at its point of departure a full understanding of the political situation in which the Cuban Revolution has developed since its accession to power in 1959. The situation is characterized by an uninterrupted series of aggressions of all types from the United States, whose resources do not need to be emphasized. [The activists'] purported status as defenders of human rights is no more than an unusual facade for hiding the work that they do in close coordination, and under the direction of foreign enemies of Cuba, with the goal of

> establishing internal conditions to facilitate the United States' well-known plans to destroy the Cuban Revolution.[46]

The argument, although an accurate reflection of historical circumstance, does not fly. Clearly not all activists can be painted with the same brush of sedition and not all of them are connected to the United States. It is highly likely that many of those attempting to achieve alternate political or economic goals are acting in the interests of Cuba and its people. Indeed, many even reject the capitalist framework. It is doubtful that *every* human rights devotee under surveillance or house arrest, under detention, or in prison is acting to further the interests of the United States, or that their activities would even indirectly bolster U.S. policy toward the island. Although Cuba's leadership has every reason to be paranoid about the United States and the Miami exile community, they have been in power now for 40 years and surely ought to have developed a more precise, reasonable, and insinuated response to those political advocates who want some change but do not wish to see Cuba's independence and sovereignty impugned. An experienced leadership that has singularly sought to create new economic and social opportunities for Cubans outside the purview of America's historical repression ought to be able to do no less.

Conditions of imprisonment for political actors can not be rationalized. Whether they are truly guilty of political crimes against the state or not, there is no reason to subject them to the harsh circumstances verified by outside observers. The United States, it is true, displays incredible hypocrisy when it comes to political acts, political prisoners, or political killings. It says little about Kurdish insurgents liquidated by Turkey in Iraq or journalists jailed in Peru, deported by Panama, or murdered in Mexico and Turkey; it supports loans to Indonesia, whose human rights abuses are legion; and it has a broad array of relations with China, which in 1998 forced Wang Dan, its most noted of many dissidents in prison, into exile in the United States. Many of its allies hold political prisoners, while in the Democratic Republic of the Congo and Rwanda it supports governments that have murdered and supported the killing of tens of thousands of Hutus.

Still, that neither rationalizes nor excuses the treatment of political prisoners in Cuba. If Cuba does not want to be put into the same category as some of those regimes—and there is little reason it should given the number of political prisoners it holds (although 350 is a lot in absolute terms it hardly compares with the many thousands once held and often horribly tortured in Nigeria or Indonesia) and the complete absence of the torturous and deadly methods applied by some of America's friends (Liberia, Israel in the West Bank and Gaza Strip)—it ought to move rapidly to improve the conditions of incarceration for political inmates. Not doing so only serves to validate Washington's criticism, hysterical and sanctimonious as it may be.

The fortieth anniversary of the revolution serves as a propitious moment for revising the laws dealing with proponents of human rights. Distinctions regarding the activities of different organizations and individuals ought to be advanced. Without subverting the emphasis on economic and social rights Cuba can easily liberalize its grim point of view of political and civil rights and create a frame more in harmony with its overall approach of trying to radically redistribute goods and services to the entire people. Political rights, at least to a degree, can also be safely redistributed. Those who can be proven to have links with the United States and who unmistakably act to further the vengeance of Washington should be treated differently than those whose interests are far more benign.

THE VISUAL AND PERFORMING ARTS

Almost all citizens are affected by the restrictions on speech, opinion, association, and the press. Since they are aware of the limits on dissent they normally only discuss real politics within the sanctity of their homes or with close friends. Criticism of some policies is acceptable, but notably it most often occurs within the confines of party or state organs, in which the discussion can become quite heated. As the Cuban constitution indicates, "The social and mass organizations have all the facilities they need to carry out those activities in which the members have full freedom of speech and opinion based on the unlimited right of initiative and criticism."[47]

Public figures, however, cannot escape scrutiny. That is particularly true of cultural figures and educators. Since there is in reality "little freedom of expression and no freedom of the press at all,"[48] one would assume that all cultural icons and educators would be severely restricted within the context of their professions. Yet that is not the case. Cuba retains a contradictory position regarding its "stars" whereby some are discredited if they stray too far from revolutionary dogma while others are given a wide berth for displaying their talents.

Despite the fact that Cuba's detractors insist that art in Cuba is not free, that in fact is hardly the case. The Cuban constitution, certainly in this matter, quite accurately portrays reality when it says "artistic creativity is free as long as its content is not contrary to the Revolution. Forms of expression of art are free."[49] According to Luis Camnitzer, author of *New Art of Cuba,*

> Fidel Castro's famous statement in 1961, 'Within the Revolution everything; outside the Revolution nothing' can be seen as more ambiguous and less ominous than it has generally been portrayed outside of Cuba by those unsympathetic to the revolutionary process. The context of the quote was one to ensure respect toward those artists who were not militant revolutionaries, explaining that nonrevolutionaries were not counterrevolutionaries. . . . As Castro himself underlined once more 'Nobody should fear that the Revolution or socialism may asphyxiate artistic freedom.'[50]

Other than the first years of the1970s and for a time during the convulsions in Eastern Europe and the Soviet Union in the late 1980s and early 1990s, Cuban artists have been free to produce their art pretty much as they see fit, even if until 1994 they were unable to sell it on the open market. Representational, modern, primitive, and Afro-Cuban art, as well as abstract expressionism, exists alongside the more contemporary poster, performance, kitsch, and installation art. Tame topics are encountered side-by-side with political ones that are often highly critical of the government or leadership. According to Havana art critic Gerardo Mosquera, "The 'art of the Revolution'—like the Revolution—turns out to be something very different from what the leftists dreamed or what the rightists railed against." Cuban youth, he continues, are "allergic to rhetoric" and in their art they "delight in dismantling ideological constructions and mechanisms of manipulation."[51] In 1989, for instance, a painting by Eduardo Ponjuán and René Francisco Rodríguez was exhibited at the Castillo de la Real Fuerza showing Fidel in drag with oversized breasts and leading a rally of followers.[52] Although censorship was demanded by some, ultimately nothing came of it.

In 1976, Castro organized a Graduate Institute of Art, which offers 12 years of free education to those with the talent to gain entrance and which "helped create a sophisticated and competent generation of Cuban artists who were in touch with their own popular culture."[53] The Casa de las Américas, which was established in 1959 as an institution devoted to Latin American culture, complements the Institute by giving artists the opportunity to exhibit their work and to present lectures about it.

The state-owned Cuban gallery network is quite extensive and is where artists apply to have their work presented in a traditional and legitimizing forum. Major galleries "aspire to museum-quality exhibitions,"[54] which effectively constrains politics from playing an oversized role in the selection of pieces. Poster art, photography, and paintings are exhibited in the multiple galleries that are spread throughout Vedado and Old Havana, as well as the few in Trinidad and Santiago de Cuba. The more traditional and historical art can be seen in Havana's stiflingly hot National Museum of Fine Arts, although post-revolutionary art of a far superior quality is found in the art galleries. The sequence of photographs taken by Roberto Salas in 1997, in which nude male and female bodies are enveloped by the sensual transparency of membranous cigar leaf and swirls of tobacco smoke, would be far more likely to be exhibited in a gallery; so too the colorful and dramatic Picasso-like *Fumadora* series of oils painted by Leonel Lopez-Nussa in 1996. Many artists also use their own homes or studios as galleries in which profits produced by sale, normally to foreign buyers, remain untaxed and need not be shared with the state. Some, such as Juan Manuel Hernández, who creates papier-mâché folk art, display and sell their work at Havana's Plaza de la Catedral.

Street art on city walls or billboards has an earthier quality to it, reflecting a kind of graffiti/poster art. Its colorful spreads are often directed against the United States or its embargo and are usually splashed with a sizable dollop of humor. Pop art, often produced by graphic artists, is usually also public art as it can be found in the lobbies of apartment houses or government offices. José Martí and Che Guevara seem to be the two most popular subjects, usually in the form of a montage of facial reflections combined into a single composition. Oddly enough images of Fidel are rare as he frowns on and has belittled the establishment of a cult of personality.

Art, therefore, seems to have escaped the suffocating atmosphere that otherwise envelops social existence. Social and political criticism does exist as many painters, including Kadir Lopez ("Kdir") in his 1997 watercolor *Casi Todo* ("Almost Everything"), depict birds and people caught in mazes that they are unable to escape from, while others use their art as a symbol of rebellion. European and American influences are profound, while a distinctly Cuban art, based on its culture and heritage, is just as vital. There is no single ideological style or technique in which art is presented, and certainly the Latin impact on what has often been in other societies the sterility of communism has a lot to do with the freedom and ongoing renaissance that is Cuban art.

Music and dance reflect the same tendencies. Cuba's National Art Schools of Cubanacán, opened in 1965, provides music and dance as well as art facilities and is architecturally designed to "create a mood conducive to both, meditation and creation."[55] The National Ballet of Cuba has its classrooms, workshops, and theaters at the school, while its public performances are presented at Havana's neo-baroque-styled Gran Teatro, which contains several performance auditoria. Acclaimed throughout the world, Alicia Alonso's ballet troupe is free to develop and present whatever she sees fit, although she usually produces classical ballets such as *Carmen, Giselle,* or *Cinderella.*

A wide variety of musical groups performing everything from pop to salsa, opera to rap, religious to street music—and many of which, like the National Ballet, tour throughout the world—attests to the unconventional nature and openness that has allowed an explosion of alternate styles and techniques. In Cuba music is everywhere: on the radio, in streets, in theaters and clubs, and it has both a public and private face. Street groups who perform in public parks are available to all, while a more select audience—one that has the financial wherewithal—goes to the Gran Teatro for classical opera or to the nightclubs for more contemporary music. Musical limitations in terms of ideological conformity do not exist.

The motion pictures of Tomás Gutiérrez Alea, particularly *Strawberry and Chocolate,* which extends the revolution to incorporate gays, and *Guantanamera,* push and reflect the expansiveness of cultural freedom of expression in Cuba. Incorporating a sense of historic obligation to support the revolution and widen its parameters, he was rooted in Cuba's national culture and saw himself as a revolutionary artist. His death in 1996 was felt in Cuba and abroad, where many of his films were received with passion and praise. Fernando Pérez's film *Madagascar,* which was shown at the Film Society of Lincoln Center in New York City in 1996, depicts the harshness of life in revolutionary Cuba. It was met with approval by critics who saw it as an eloquent metaphor for the loss of revolutionary hope.

The major constraint that all in the performing and visual arts face is the same confronted by all Cubans. The drastic economic situation brought on by the embargo limits the ability to acquire supplies and equipment. Alonso's troupe, whether in Havana or New York, appears shabby, while the ballet company is limited in the productions it can stage because of its inability to create proper scenery or lighting or even to provide appropriate costumes. Artists are always short of watercolors, oils, acrylics, or even bathroom tile for those ceramicists working with that medium. Paint brushes are not available and when they are, which is rare, remain far too expensive and thus old ones must be kept until they are useless. Film, flashbulbs, and dark-room equipment for artistic photographers are either nonexistent or too costly for the artists to create their work easily or even appropriately. Cinematography is a hugely expensive enterprise even in countries in which everything is available, which is far from the case in Cuba. Some artists who perform or exhibit and sell abroad are able to keep some of their earnings in foreign countries and have an easier time of it, but in most cases all artists suffer economically. The embargo has an enormous impact on the arts, far more than outsiders are conscious of, even though art itself remains relatively free of government censorship.

BASEBALL

Baseball originally arrived in Cuba in the late nineteenth century via U.S. soldiers and businessmen. The first stadium was constructed in Matanzas in 1874, and in the 1940s and 1950s major league teams from the United States periodically held spring training on the island. From the beginning baseball "had gripped Cuba from sophisticated Havana to the most humble provincial settlement."[56] A baseball-crazed nation, in part because the sport linked Cuba closely to the United States, its ballplayers are arguably the most loved or hated (depending on the score or the standings) cultural icons on the island, and to attend a game is truly a thrilling experience.[57] Even Fidel Castro, who now and then frequents games, was said to have been offered a minor league contract sometime around 1950 to pitch in the United States. Although players, umpires, coaches, and managers receive very little money (as do virtually all workers in Cuba) their love of the game as well as the status they receive from rapturous fans partly compensates for their economic deprivation. Indeed, the fantastic salaries received by players in the United States only seems to add to the respect garnered by all those involved in baseball. For some however, status, respect, and pride in country is not quite enough. The multi-million-dollar contracts available in the United States to the most skilled and talented athletes have created tensions between Cuban baseball figures and the government of Fidel Castro.

Two highly skilled and popular ballplayers in particular have raised the ire of Cuban officials, which has led to a tightening of restrictions on those who participate in the game. In 1996 Orlando Hernández, whose brother Livan had defected to the United States in 1995 while the Cuban national team was playing in Mexico, was accused by the government of providing aid and advice to other players intent on defecting. Orlando was suspended from baseball and went to work as an orderly in a mental hospital for some $14 a month, while his brother Livan had signed on as a pitcher with the Florida Marlins for a salary in the range of $6 million. In 1997 Livan led his team to victory in the World Series and was its most valuable player.

In December 1997 Orlando was one of a group of eight people who fled Cuba on a small rickety boat, eventually washing up ashore in Anguilla Cay, the Bahamas. Joe Cubas, a baseball agent on friendly terms with the Cuban American National Foundation, brought Orlando to the attention of the New York Yankees and obtained a pitching contract for him worth $6.6 million. Although the United States was obligated by terms of its 1994 agreement with Cuba to repatriate all illegal entrants or, if a well-founded fear of persecution was found to exist, to settle them in a third country it made an exception in this case.[58]

The Hernández brothers' defection, rightly or wrongly, even perhaps understandably given the millions of dollars at stake, was seen by Castro as having been engineered by CANF because the first phone call made by Orlando in the Bahamas was to the foundation, which in addition to putting him in touch with his family in Cuba and the United States apparently directed his attention to Joe Cubas, who was also Livan's original agent. Castro clearly views Cubas, CANF, and Washington as in cahoots to bring about further defections to add to the luster of CANF and create embarrassment for Cuba.

The issue for Castro is politics rather than sports. For Cuba, which expends state monies toward the training and development of its sports figures, defection by such professionals purely for outlandish salaries is defined as an act of perfidy that gives aid and comfort to the enemy. If Cuba's teachers and doctors, who have offered their skills in the scores of thousands over the years to well over 40 Third World countries pass up more than ample opportunities to defect, then as Castro most likely sees it, the Miami organizations must be held largely responsible for the actions of the baseball players. Once again the rich North Americans used their clout and their wealth to outmaneuver Cuba. The result of it all is that the freedom of Cuban sports figures is now far more restricted.

EDUCATION

According to Article 38 of the Cuban constitution, education is a function of the state, is provided free of charge, and is accessible to males and females equally.[59] At the age of 45 days infants are enrolled in preschool nurseries, and at age 4 they are transferred to one of more than 1,000 preschool centers organized by the Federation of

Cuban Women. Six years of primary school, 3 of high school, and 3 more at the intermediate school level follow. Continuing Education courses for working people are also conducted throughout the nation. The extraordinary emphasis on education has given Cuba a literacy rate above 96 percent, by far the highest in Latin America.

By the time students begin attending college they will have also received hundreds of hours of instruction on Marxism-Leninism in their schools as well as through the Union of Pioneers of Cuba, the mass organization of young people whose foremost role is to integrate them into becoming productive members of socialist society. In addition, the Young Communist League, the "organization of the vanguard youth, under the direction of the Party, works to prepare its members as future members of the Party and contributes to the education of the new generations along the ideals of communism. . . . "[60] Once enrolled in college or at a university the mass student organization Federation of University Students seeks to "improve their political and ideological education [by] the creation of a 'new man' willing to support and fulfill the needs of the Revolution, to live the principles of proletarian internationalism, and to defend the country."[61]

Although scores of newspapers, magazines, and journals are published in Cuba that often provide "levels of agreement [that] do not appear to be consistently greater than for similar . . . non-Communist media systems,"[62] virtually no divergence from the accepted ideology exists. Cubans can often catch local radio broadcasts from Miami, watch snippets of CNN from a hotel room or lobby, and can even purchase the *New York Times* and the *Wall Street Journal* twice a week in the major Havana hotels (at three dollars a copy) or the weekly edition of *Newsweek*, but it is the Cuban mass media that provide the "essential channel for mass mobilization and control."[63] The Communist Party daily newspaper *Granma* and the multiple radio and television stations provide the ideological message that complements all the doctrinal lessons learned in school and via the mass organizations. There is little real deviation from normative values by the media.

Teachers and professors as a group probably accept the premises of Cuban socialism and nationalism. But even if they don't they have very little option but to follow a curriculum that toes the ideological line. Being in the limelight with an audience made up of many students in different classes teachers can never be sure that what they say will not come back to haunt them. They must, if they are critical in their analysis, be vigilant and careful. Since most teachers in rural areas also reside in their villages, conformity with prevailing values is a given. Even at the University of Havana courses dealing with history, politics, and economics study the world from the ideological spectrum of post-1959 Cuba. As Article 38a of the Cuban constitution maintains, "the state bases its educational and cultural policy on the scientific world view established and developed by Marxism-Leninism."

Since education is viewed as among the key agents of socialization, as decisive as the media or parental guidance, the professorate is taken seriously. Liberals or reformists in the educational structure would certainly be seen, in Raúl Castro's phrasing, as "fifth columnists" intent on subverting the revolution. Raúl in particular appears to mistrust intellectuals and he and the circle around him are suspicious of those they term reformers.[64] Teachers at all levels of education are professionally and ideologically trained to be concerned both with order and revolution; in Cuba the creed of revolutionary order leaves no room for a revolution within the revolution. In a society little differentiated by income but largely stratified by profession teachers are rewarded with relatively high status. To maintain it, particularly if they hold opinions that contradict prevailing attitudes, requires self-censorship. In Cuba, education is politics and one's politics defines one's stance within the revolution. As Fidel Castro proclaimed, to be inside it is "everything," to be outside, "nothing."

CONCLUSION

As early as 1979, at a time when the embargo's effects were still quite minimal, Wayne S. Smith, then America's leading diplomat in Havana, reflected on life in Cuba.

> One saw no beggars in the Havana of 1979, nor any of the poverty and misery which abound in so many other Latin American cities. In

> Cuba the basic needs have been provided to all. Everyone is guaranteed enough to eat, adequate clothing, access to education, medical care, and a place to live. The diet is monotonous, and one may have to stand in line to buy food; some of the housing remains substandard. Still, that no one goes hungry or homeless is no small achievement.
>
> The Cuban people of course paid a high price in political and civil liberties. There is little freedom of expression and no freedom of the press at all. It is a command society, which still holds political prisoners, some of them under deplorable conditions.[65]

The trade-off between economic/social rights and political/civil rights could be presented neither more starkly nor more accurately. Revolutionary Cuba made its choice regarding the two alternative models of human rights, no matter how reductive the options appeared to be. It made it in 1959, it maintained it in 1979, and it adheres to it still in 1998. And despite what Cuba's detractors may say, it was a choice that was received with approval by Cuba's people. Smith said in 1979 that in his judgment there was little doubt "that Castro could easily win a fair and honest election. The majority is still with him. The U.S. government deludes itself in choosing to believe otherwise."[66]

Although it might be reckless to speculate, I would say that Castro could still win that election, although the vote count might be narrower than it would have been in 1979. Surely it would be a landslide if the other contender was a Miami representative, something few Cubans would welcome and most fear. But it would certainly be a sizable victory if Fidel Castro moved to refine his interpretation of human rights and granted more political space to critics of the government who remain inside the revolution. Every critique is not concocted in Washington, and not every human rights advocate is on Washington's or Miami's payroll. If political rights, including press freedoms, were broadened to correspond to the creative rights enjoyed by some of Cuba's artists Castro's popularity would surely increase dramatically, while Cuba's national security could still be guaranteed.

Castro has achieved more than anyone would have believed in 1959. He has freed Cuba from America's economic domination and political repression, and he has seen to it that goods and services are shared more or less equally among Cuba's people. He has destroyed the structure of the Cuban elite that before the revolution so oppressed and terrorized the population. In international affairs Cuba has a standing and reputation far beyond what a nation its size should expect—and that remains the case despite Cuba's relative isolation from the world community due to America's embargo policy. For the Third World Cuba has not only provided a model for the delivery of health care but has shown emerging countries how to stand up to the United States. And of course Fidel is perhaps the charismatic leader of our time. Havana is not only a capital city, but also a romantic symbol of independence and fortitude. It is Fidel's city and it represents his values. If those values were shifted somewhat to include greater political freedom, to enlarge the arena of human rights, it is more than likely that Castro's popularity inside Cuba would skyrocket.

In such a scenario, although the United States might still hold on to the embargo it would find that its reputation would be even more stigmatized vis-à-vis Cuba than it is already. Expanding political liberties would, I believe, augment Castro's legitimacy and increase the likelihood of ensuring the stability of the political and economic institutions he has created. It would at the same time pull the rug out from under the exile establishment in Miami and weaken its relations with Washington. It would also be the morally right thing to do.

All that being said, it remains doubtful that any fundamental change regarding human rights will occur so long as Washington and Miami insist that Castro must go and that communism be eviscerated on the island of Cuba. Unless that happens the framework of political rights is not likely to change in any radical or fundamental way.

SEVEN

CONCLUSION: CUBA'S FUTURE AND THE EMBARGO

ALMOST FROM THE ONSET OF THE 1959 CUBAN REVOLUTION, the United States has been in the throes of a national paranoia, what Richard Hofstadter referred to in 1965 as the paranoid style of American politics.[1] In his classic work on the subject of right-wing political paranoia, Hofstadter speaks to the hostile and conspiratorial world seen to be directed specifically against the United States, which is "aroused by a confrontation of opposed interests which are (or are felt to be) totally irreconcilable, and thus by nature not susceptible to the normal political processes of bargain and compromise."[2]

Virtually from the moment Vice President Richard Nixon first met Fidel Castro U.S. policy toward Cuba began to be framed in the language of mistrust and fear for America's vital interests. On April 23, 1959, merely four days after Nixon's discussions with Castro in the Capitol, a memorandum prepared in the Department of State indicated,

> despite Castro's apparent simplicity, sincerity and eagerness to reassure the United States public, there is little probability that Castro has altered the essentially radical course of his revolution. It

> would be a serious mistake to underestimate this man. While we certainly know him better than before, Castro remains an enigma and we should await his decisions on specific matters before assuming a more optimistic view than heretofore about the possibility of developing a constructive relationship with him and his government.[3]

One day later, Assistant Secretary of State for Inter-American Affairs John C. Hill Jr. sent a memorandum to Assistant Secretary of State Roy R. Rubottom Jr. suggesting, "we should examine how we might, as the situation matures, identify and develop an alternative acceptable to us."[4]

Although Hofstadter's analysis related specifically to extremes of conservatism the attitude evident in U.S. policy toward Cuba had all the hallmarks of a national rather than a specifically partisan paranoia. Castro uncontrolled was equivalent to losing Cuba and its sources of wealth. The vision so clearly articulated by John Adams in 1783 of Cuba as America's "natural extension" would be obscured if Cuba exited the sphere of interest of the United States. The initial antagonism, therefore, had little if anything to do with anti-communism and everything to do with the potential of Castro being totally independent and thus an unpredictable and uncontrollable presence. As Carlos Lage indicated to the United Nations, "The policy of blockade and aggressions pursued against the Revolution right from its inception was established before its socialist orientation had been declared."[5] Two years before to be precise, merely a few months after Castro took power.

The radicalization of Cuban politics as it evolved from May 17, 1959, with the creation of INRA, but long prior to the signing of the trade agreement with the Soviet Union in February 1960, led the U.S. State Department in the summer of 1959, as Rubottom indicated to Secretary of State Christian Herter, to decide "along with CIA, that it would be impossible to carry on friendly relations with the Castro Government in Cuba and that, as a consequence, we should devise means to help bring about his overthrow and replacement by a government friendly to the United States. This decision has been implemented. . . ."[6] The memo went on duplicitously to state that security and secrecy in the execution of the various programs relating to the overthrow of Castro should be stressed "if we are not to lose incalculably through destruction of the U.S. image as a defender of the principle of non-intervention."[7] In order to prevent Cuba from falling away from U.S. control, irrespective of the potential of having a communist state influenced by the Soviet Union, the United States moved finally to break diplomatic relations with Cuba on January 3, 1961, in an effort, according to the U.S. Embassy in Havana, "to further the U.S. objective of securing a change in the Cuban Government in that it would signal to the Cuban people and the world our conclusion that the Castro regime is not a representative Cuban Government. . . ."[8]

The primary goal of U. S. sanctions against Cuba was always and from the earliest the removal of Fidel Castro, a leader Washington was unable to "orient in the right direction." Nixon's injunction injudiciously spelled out quite clearly that it was control of the man and the country he led, rather than the inherent fear of communism, that fundamentally led the United States to take the fateful first steps in its anti-Castro crusade.

Once Castro moved toward the Soviet Union in 1960—accepting $100 million in credits and establishing diplomatic relations—the United States found a more valid rationale to justify its activities against Cuba. With the Soviets poised at the doorstep of the United States and with Cuba seen as their puppet, the jingoistic attacks against Castro found support among the general U.S. population. The embarrassing 1961 Bay of Pigs invasion and the hugely popular outcome of the 1962 Cuban Missile Crisis only increased the pace of America's war against Castro. As elections and "democracy" seemed to recede further into the future the rallying cry became the restoration of political liberties.

By the 1970s and into the 1980s, Castro developed a policy of trying to export his revolution, giving support to radical, leftist, or even communist governments and movements in such far flung places as Angola, Ethiopia, Jamaica, Grenada, the Bahamas, [9] Nicaragua, Chile, El Salvador, and Panama. As President Kennedy said at his news conference of February 8, 1961, as Cuban advocacy for revolutionary activity was advanced in Venezuela, the Dominican Republic, and Bolivia,[10] but years before Cuban foreign intervention and/or support became a coordinated policy, "We are giving the matter of Cuba and its export of its revolution throughout Latin America a matter of high priority."[11]

By 1962 the United States had slapped a total embargo on trade with Cuba in order to "deprive the Government of Cuba of the dollar exchange it has been deriving from sales of its products in the United States."[12] Yet when the Soviet Union and its Eastern-bloc allies collapsed from 1989 to1991 and the Soviet-puppet theory disappeared along with Castro's support of foreign revolutionary movements the United States did not relent. Indeed, the Cuban Democracy Act and the Helms-Burton Act only imposed harsher limitations on Cuba. Not even the increased liberties offered the Cuban people in terms of social issues such as religion or economic programs relating to the development of aspects of capitalism could modify America's paranoid fixation with Fidel Castro.

At the end of the 1990s the Soviet Union was gone, many political prisoners had been released, Cuba had receded into developing a Cuba-first-and-only policy, its economy was in shambles, its health care system was paralyzed, its population was ever on the brink of starvation, and "Cuban diplomacy in the English Caribbean [and elsewhere], like its relations with Latin America was in shambles."[13] A desperately poor Third World nation, Cuba could no longer conceivably be considered a threat to the United States—and yet Washington continued to characterize Castro in terms so absolutist that little if any room was left for negotiation.

True enough, there is little in Cuba of what Westerners refer to as political democracy, but neither is there such democracy in Indonesia, where President Suharto had ruled from 1966 to 1998 without a democratic election but with the support of the United States. In 1998, along with the IMF and the World Bank the United States even provided long-term debt relief for Indonesia's wrecked economy. It is also true that Fidel is an outspoken advocate of communism, but as Sam Farber commented, "not many people can take seriously the [U.S.] Administration's breastbeating over the absence of freedom and democracy in Cuba when it is at the same time wheeling and dealing with Vietnam, Indonesia, and China as well as with brutal repressive regimes in Turkey and the Middle East."[14]

Obviously, the variables that set Cuba apart from the rest are Cuba's small size and population—limiting, in relative terms, its prospects for trade—its location within what has historically been considered America's backyard, the right-wing and once-powerful but now less so "domestic political lobby of the Cuban reactionaries,"[15] and of course the most important issue of them all, Fidel Castro.

As many of the policies of Castro that were used as arguments to eliminate the man disappeared the United States reverted to its original doctrine that it could neither abide nor ever accept the existence of Fidel Castro in power. Fundamentally, "adios, Fidel," the auspicious announcement of Jesse Helms at the time of the passage of Helms-Burton, has since 1959 been the paramount and arguably most honest goal of American foreign policy as regards Cuba. That has always been the expectation of Washington's decisionmakers, and as each additional embargo act was generated Castro's imminent fall was expected. For 40 years the United States has been unable to escape from its obsession with Castro's survival, a compulsion eclipsed only by its own frustrating failure through legal, illegal, and dubious actions to even come close to achieving success.

Still, if the U.S. embargo on Cuba ultimately failed in its primary intent it has vastly succeeded in its vigorous attempt to cripple the country. Fidel Castro rules over a Cuba that is only a mere shadow of its vast potential. In 1998 survival, rather than revolutionary expansion, is the order of the day. With food, clothing, shelter, and health care in short supply the nation hobbles along in the expectation, or rather hope, that expanded worldwide trade or a lessening of the most virulent aspects of the embargo will lead to a better life. Indeed, discussions in the United States Congress supported by Jesse Helms to weaken Castro by channeling $100 million in food and medical assistance to Cuba through the Catholic Church or other relief organizations, or as others would have it to even remove food and medicine from the strictures of the embargo, have been ongoing since 1998, and Cubans pay close attention to that debate. But whatever hope Castro had in 1959 to bring to Cuba an existence free from U.S. power has faltered as each new aspect of the embargo has only irritated island life ever more. True, the United States no longer owns and controls the means of production or the economic and political institutions of Cuba, but through the embargo it still exerts extraordinary influence. It has been able to keep Cuba in a state of economic contraction and depression since at least 1991. Cuba remains unable to fully control its present or its future and has failed to break the chains of oppression so tightly held by the United States. Even political decisions are sometimes swayed by the embargo's effects.

The radical perspective of social existence has also, probably quite inadvertently, been reined in by the impact of the embargo. Despite Castro's disapproval he has been forced to implement policies augmenting the economic sphere to incorporate private enterprise, and he has labored hard, one suspects somewhat unwillingly, to expand the frontiers of religion in an effort to reintegrate Cuba into the good graces of international public opinion. Freedom for artists and writers is also affected by the ebb and flow of the U.S. antagonism as internal criticism as well as dissidents and human rights activists are tied to the United States and the Cuban-American community's activities against Cuba.

Toward the same end, although political prisoners remain they are fewer in number than the 20,000 that were imprisoned in the 1960s. In fact references by the United States to the 350 or so inmates still held are a major point of annoyance for Cuba's leadership. As Ricardo Alarcón angrily expressed to Walter Russell Mead in a profile in *The New Yorker,* "You just have to ask a simple question: Is it really your business? The U.S. never cared about elections in Zaire or Morocco or Saudi Arabia. You never interviewed dissidents in Zaire—because they were buried underground. You were the main supporter of Mobutu for years and years."[16] Nevertheless release of prisoners has been generated by the embargo as

> to facilitate its full integration into the world community—and thus the world economy—the Cuban government is trying to improve its human rights image. To a limited extent, the government's concern with image has given rise to some concrete improvements. These include, most notably, the release of some political prisoners prior to the expiration of their sentences, a decline in the number of political prosecutions and "acts of repudiation," a commitment not to prosecute for "illegal exit" persons who have been repatriated to

> Cuba by the United States. . . . These positive developments, which show the impact of international pressure, are welcome.[17]

American decisionmakers from Eisenhower to Clinton may very well have been disappointed in that Castro has been able to elude Washington's ultimate prescription, but nevertheless the United States has certainly insured through its embargo that Cuba remains a negligible actor on the international scene and that its internal policies have been stymied. Yet Castro has disallowed Washington success in reincorporating Cuba into its pre-1959 framework, and his very survival in the face of America's paranoia and destructive policies has given him a cachet throughout the Third World that is presently unrivaled. He is a singular leader and a political role model that the United States has been unable to fathom. To the United States he is an enigma, but to the underdeveloped countries and peoples of the world who resent America's post–cold war imperial and intrusive policies he stands alone as a beacon, though in many ways a tenebrous one.

CASTRO, THE UNITED STATES, AND HISTORY

Fidel Castro's place in history is secured by the stand he has taken against the U.S. policy of Manifest Destiny in Cuba. No leader in the Western Hemisphere has so successfully stood against the United States for so long. But his achievement is not simply in defying Washington but in articulating the views of all Third World peoples who have historically felt oppressed and overburdened by the expansive and often unruly actions of the United States. "Cuban Communism has based itself primarily on nationalism directed against the historic oppressor—the United States. Thus, the embargo is the primary reason for the significant . . . support for Castro inside Cuba today."[18]

When Castro stepped out of the mountains and into the glare of history on January 1, 1959, he not only altered Cuban history dramatically but by first defeating an American-client government and then moving on to combat somewhat successfully the superpower itself he alerted the Third World that the United States, even in its own hemisphere, could be constrained. In that context he stands alongside the Vietnamese nationalists who defeated American aggression in Southeast Asia in 1975. Arguably, Castro's success is almost as powerful and important an event, as it resonates less than 100 miles from America's shores and has been ongoing for 40 years.

Most leaders of emerging countries who kowtow to the United States and fall all over themselves to satisfy Washington's most inconsequential whims appear as political pygmies when contrasted to Fidel Castro. As Tad Szulc, author of the significant study *Fidel: A Critical Portrait,* indicated when speaking of Castro's initial trip to the United States in 1959: "Most new Latin American leaders made a pilgrimage to Washington as soon as possible to curry official favor and seek emergency economic aid. However, Fidel Castro was an exception in his refusal to ask for money, or even talk about it. That threw American officialdom off balance."[19] From the earliest Castro kept the United States off balance and he has never relented. Even those leaders firmly in the grasp of the United States have had to admire his pluck and his determination and have felt proud that a spokesman existed that was able to embarrass the United States by articulating the needs of the peoples of the Third World evermore being trampled on by the United States. Some in the Eastern Caribbean have at times even admitted to their mortification in having been forced to mortgage their countries to the United States. As a victorious revolutionary, a political radical who for four decades has stood against the United States, and as an exemplar of Third World values Fidel Castro is, as Szulc stated in 1986, one "of the greatest political actors of our time."[20] Albert Fried, author and editor of *Socialist Thought,* has labeled Castro "one of the greatest statesmen of the 20th Century."[21]

Certainly, not all agree. Andres Oppenheimer, in his book *Castro's Final Hour* (1993), whose book title infers Castro's imminent demise,[22] speaks of the purging of a nation and the selling out of the Cuban revolution in his extremely critical discourse on Castro; Alexander Haig, secretary of state under Ronald Reagan, spoke of "putting fear into the hearts of Cubans and getting results" since Castro and Cuba could "never stand up to the 'geostrategic assets' of the United States."[23] Jorge Mas Canosa cremated Castro historically in 1996 when he declared, "I believe that the people of Cuba cannot continue to be the victims of a system that remains stagnant in history, that has failed because of its political and economic contradictions."[24] Clearly, all opposed to Castro expected him to fall when confronted with the overwhelming military and economic might of the United States. How wrong they all were.

A leader so controversial, adamant, and pugnacious cannot accurately be categorized by history during his time. But Fidel's long rule and legendary political performance will have a lasting impact in Cuba and in a future Cuban-American dialogue. His stinging attacks on the behavior of the United States in Cuba and in the Third World have had impact because they have so often found their mark. A radical and a communist to be sure, which has often found him opponents who might otherwise be sympathetic, Castro, unlike most Third World leaders, is a lightening rod because so often his political attacks are methodical and reasonable.

This is a leader who will not be judged solely on his domestic policies, but whose place in history will also be determined by larger, more universal concerns. In the mono-polar world of the twenty-first century, where the United States rules relatively supreme, at least for now, Castro's position vis-à-vis the United States does call into question the real as opposed to publicly stated purposes of U.S. foreign policy, particularly as it relates to the most substantial part of the earth, the political entities that comprise the Third World. If there is no Fidel Castro to stand against the United States and articulate the vision of the poorest peoples on this earth, who will? That voice will, I believe, vindicate him historically and in the final analysis absolve him.

His stand, as it applies to a different perspective of human rights, one based primarily on economic need, should also be viewed more fully by history than it is at present. Although economic and social dislocations insofar as they do exist in Cuba can be judged, as they are by some, as failures of a domestic government and political party, over time it will have to be accepted that the rotten state of Cuba's economy is predominately a result of the frightening, mean-spirited, and 40-year- long war against Cuba conducted through the U.S. embargo. The United States has tried often, and in violation of international and domestic law, to kill Castro; it has supported and organized an invasion of the country; it has stood silent while Cuban-American organizations in Miami have tried to organize violent antigovernment activity in Havana and hysterical attacks against Cuban-Americans in Florida more sympathetic to Castro[25]; and it has conducted a major four-decades-long offensive against Castro and Cuban society via the embargo. Few countries, if any, could long stand against that kind of behavior and have their indigenous structures emerge intact. To blame Castro for Cuba's economic demise, without fully taking into account U.S. activity, is disingenuous and a travesty of analytic judgment.

It is in Cuba and its subsequent relationship with the United States that Fidel Castro's historical influence will be felt most. Whoever succeeds him will never be able to avoid his shadow. Even as relations with the United States improve, as they must eventually, a new leadership will not be in a position to ignore Castro's redefinition of the Cuban-American association. So too the United States will surely not again, at least in the foreseeable future and hopefully longer, be able to walk all over Cuba, as it did from 1898 to1959, oblivious to the needs and lives of the Cuban people. By his very existence and his forthright stand against U.S. imperialism, Castro has distanced Cuba from such an ignominious future. Cubans would oppose it and Americans, with Castro's colossal image always reflecting on America's ignoble purposes, would be discomforted by it. A mended relationship should not and will not mean Cuba's engulfment by the United States. "The ultimate goal," as Ricardo Alarcón has indicated, "is a rapprochement that would lead to the repeal of the Helms-Burton bill and the normalization of relations."[26] But normalization means just that, not a plutocratic dependence in which power and authority are exercised in Washington rather than in Havana. Pre-1959 Cuba will never again be seen, and Fidel Castro, along with the heritage he will leave behind, will be responsible for that fortuitous new standard.

THE OLD GUARD OR THE COSMOPOLITANS?

One Fall evening in 1996, a harried Ricardo Alarcón, at a reception sponsored by the Permanent Mission of Cuba to the United Nations at its offices on Lexington Avenue in New York City, was busy stuffing the proffered business cards of American investors and businessmen into his shirt pocket. Surrounded at all times by crowds of entrepreneurs, some of whom had often appeared in the pages of the premier financial news weekly *Barron's*, Alarcón was given no respite by the hordes of potential investors swarming all around. Clearly, whenever the United States was ready to lift the embargo these piranhas, mostly oblivious to Alarcón's amusement, wanted in.

As a member of the Politburo of Cuba's Communist Party since 1992—its most powerful deliberative body—and the elected president of the country's National Assembly of People's Power, "the supreme organ of state power and . . . the only organ of the Republic invested with constituent and legislative authority,"[27] this former foreign minister and ambassador to the United Nations was certainly the person to see. Gracious with his time and always generous with his smile while posing for snapshots with these supplicants, many of whom he clearly didn't even know, Alarcón, the 61-year-old diplomat and reform-minded politician, has been rumored to be in line to succeed Castro whenever he retires or passes from the scene, and of that these people surely were aware.

As cosmopolitan as any of Cuba's leading political figures, Alarcón has been the person, second only to Fidel, who has publicly and articulately railed against the embargo while annually guiding the United Nations General Assembly to vote for resolutions demanding that Washington end its economic embargo against Cuba. In November 1997 the General Assembly voted 143 in favor of such a resolution, with 3 against (the U.S., Israel, and Uzbekistan) and 17 abstaining. The entire membership of the European Union along with Japan voted for the resolution. In 1998 the vote to end the embargo was 157 for and 2 opposed, with 12 abstentions.

Alarcón has been the most persistent Cuban personage on the international scene when it comes to revealing the layers of hypocrisy that surround the rhetoric of the embargo. A man who has asserted "The Cuban Revolution means everything to me,"[28] Alarcón can easily lay claim to the support of the younger pro-reform bureaucrats throughout Cuba who run most of its social and economic institutions and who are themselves proud of how the Cuban revolution has stood up to the United States. These youthful urban and rural professional stalwarts, who range in age from twenties to forties, speak proudly of Alarcón's representation of Cuba to the world community. A true dynamo he has both a domestic and an international constituency while he is also part of Castro's most inner circle of advisors. Due in large part to his influence, the Ministry of External Relations (MINREX), under the authority of the stylish, engaging, and flamboyant 41-year-old Foreign Minister Roberto Robaina and dominated by "thirty-something" bureaucrats, has made great efforts to network with American universities so as to publicize Cuba's reformist direction among U.S. intellectuals. Shaped and organized by Havana-based Raúl Rodríguez Averoff, MINREX's outreach aspirations are strongly supported by its youthful diplomats based at Cuba's UN Mission in New York City who are overseen by Ambassador Bruno Rodríguez Parrilla. Similar efforts are directed at America's national news media.

Since 1993, Carlos Lage, vice president of the Council of State, an elected body chosen by the National Assembly of People's Power from among its deputies, and "for national and international purposes . . . the highest representative of the Cuban state,"[29] and who also serves as secretary of the Executive Committee of the Council of Ministers as well as being a Politburo member has been catapulted into the public eye by having been selected to oversee Cuba's newly reformed economic paradigm. Forty-seven years old, this former doctor who also makes intermittent appearances at international gatherings speaks of the embargo's effects to the world at large, directing his comments most often to the issues of health care and hunger. As he proclaimed before the United Nations in 1996:

> Accusing Cuba of human rights violations is an unprecedented affront that we denounce here with our heads held high. The total Cuban population has access to free health care services. Our infant mortality rate is eight per one thousand live births. If Latin America registered Cuba's current infant mortality rate, five hundred thousand children who might have otherwise enjoyed human rights but are dying a few months after birth would be saved each year. And Cuba is not rich; it is a poor country under blockade.
>
> Today, two hundred million children of the world sleep in the streets. None of them is Cuban.

> One hundred million children below the age of thirteen are forced to work to survive. None of them is Cuban.
>
> Twenty-five thousand children in the world die every day from measles, malaria, diphtheria, pneumonia and malnutrition. None of them is Cuban.
>
> The world is very complex and difficult. It is absurd and inconvenient to have a single model imposed like a straitjacket on all nations, under any circumstances, and in disregard for their economic and social development, history, and culture.[30]

A youthful technocrat, Lage has also been given the authority to oversee the administration of government, and as such he too now functions in both the domestic and international arena and in a sense parallels and complements the role represented by Alarcón. Seen as a strong proponent of the economic reforms advocated earnestly by Alarcón he is however neither as widely known nor nearly as highly regarded and has therefore received far less attention from Western reporters and commentators. The author of a slim pamphlet on Cuba's recent economic strategy [31] he is not seen as being a prominent politico who could advance to the highest political sphere in a post-Castro era unless he was part of a group organized to function collectively during a transitory period. That most certainly could change, but at the moment Lage is an important government technocrat and political figure who has the potential for a future leadership role.

To a large degree Lage's political future will certainly be determined by the success or failure of the economic reforms he is charged with overseeing. Yet success may also eventually doom his prospects as numerous party hard-liners are opposed to the reforms that have been developed since 1993 and may neither look fondly upon nor approve further extensions of capitalism in this socialist state. In fact at the 1997 Cuban Communist Party Congress, which had last gathered in 1991, the party "balked at taking further steps that might open up the economy or reduce government control."[32] The privatization of state enterprises, which had been discussed during the Party Congress, was also repudiated. As long as Castro is on the scene to lend his support to economic reform Lage's future seems secure, but thereafter his position and future role will obviously depend on the whims of any new leadership's perspective regarding economic reform. As point man of the economic changes Lage might ultimately be caught between a rock and a hard place since attacks on the reformist principles will certainly be directed at him if the hard-line Marxists come to dominate a Cuba without Fidel Castro.

By 1997 additional technocrats and some reformists were promoted to positions of authority, indicating that a core group of more liberal-minded ideologues are in place to influence Cuba's future. General Ulises Rosales del Toro, the military chief of staff and member of the Politburo, was moved from the Council of State and made minister of sugar replacing Nelson Torres, who was blamed for the poor 1997 sugar harvest that helped reduce Cuba's GNP growth rate to 2.5 percent (the reduction was due in part to adverse weather conditions, but Torres nevertheless was blamed for the shortfall). Jorge Luis Sierra, a provincial party secretary, who is in his forties, was advanced to the Politburo while Pedro Saenz Montero, Havana's provincial Communist Party secretary; Abel Prieto, the minister of culture and president of the National Union of Writers and Artists; and Marcos Portal León, minister of basic industry and a major actor in the economic reform movement, reaffirmed the move to a generation of leaders whose philosophy is far less hard-line than those "históricos" who fought with or supported Fidel and are now often being shunted aside. Caridad del Rosario Diego Bello of the Communist Party's Central Committee, María Caridad Abreus, and Regla Martínez, all of whom were elected to the Council of State in 1998, are three professional women who complement the technocratic skills of this group; while Carlos Manuel Valenciaga Díaz, president of the University Students Federation, and Otto Riverio Torres, First Secretary of the Union of Young Communists, who were also elected to the Council of State in 1998, represent a young leadership who have been praised by Fidel.

To a large degree, however, these younger and more reform-oriented party loyalists must take into account the political clout of those hesitant to move too rapidly away from the dogmatism of communist ideology. Economic reform and an easing of relations with the United States are not the sole or loftiest goals of the hard-core activists. Purity of ideology and the maintenance of power are ends that may not, after all, be compromised, but as Alarcón has stressed a way to accommodate the hard-liners will be sought "because we will have to find a way."[33]

Keeping the revolution "immune from ideological viruses" was the 1997 catchphrase of Raúl Castro, the most senior Communist Party official after Fidel. Although a proponent of the 1993 economic reforms he has been ever vigilant against outbreaks of "Glasnost"—the policy of political liberalization propelled by President Mikhail Gorbachev in the former Soviet Union that was seen in Cuba as leading to the downfall of communism in the nation. Both Fidel and Raúl viewed the changes in the Soviet Union as a heresy to Marxism, and by mid-July 1989 a purge of many of Cuba's military and political leaders ensued—accusations of drug smuggling and abuse of authority were leveled, but many of the "conspirators," including General Arnaldo Ochoa Sanchez, the commander of Cuba's troops in Angola who also led military missions to Ethiopia and Nicaragua, were supportive of Gorbachev's reforms and had prodded Castro to follow his example. General Ochoa was tried and executed by firing squad July 13, 1989.[34] The others were either executed or received lengthy jail terms, while Raúl Castro remained singularly unsympathetic, believing they had committed treason against the state and against his brother.

At the 1997 Communist Party Congress Fidel reaffirmed that Raúl, defense minister and deputy general secretary of the Communist Party, was his designated successor, his "relief pitcher"—which "gives us great tranquility and continuity."[35] Yet already by 1960 Fidel had chosen Raúl as his heir, proclaiming "if he died, Raúl would take his place."[36]

As Fidel's 68-year old younger brother, and a man seen as more ideologically dogmatic than Fidel, Raúl wields enormous clout. Often in the past he has chastised liberal forces in the arts and in Cuba's research institutes as being "fifth columnists" who if given free reign would impugn the Cuban revolution. A man who has traveled abroad only very infrequently, and primarily to the former Soviet-bloc countries and China, he has little of the cosmopolitan aura evidenced by the younger reformers. He is a leader whose interests are largely ideological and military and his concentration is on domestic security and maintaining the sanctity and purity of the revolution. A person of great Marxist fervor, he has been called "a colossus in the defense of revolutionary principles. Raúl is Fidel multiplied by two in energy, in inflexibility. . . . Raúl is tempered steel."[37]

The essence of his power resides within the armed forces, and General Ulises Rosales del Toro's promotion to sugar czar in 1997 was seen as an effort to increase Raúl's influence within and outside the military, perhaps even eventually among the reformers, and to develop further the prestige of the armed forces, which after pulling out of Angola and Ethiopia early in the decade have had little to do internationally. Any increase in the power and influence of the military would redound to Raúl's advantage.

Raúl Valdés Vivó, a proponent of Raúl Castro's hard-line stance, is also a force to contend with. A member of the Central Committee of the Communist Party, former ambassador to the Democratic Republic of Vietnam, and prior to that ambassador to the National Liberation Front (in its jungle redoubt), he presently oversees the Communist Party school for the Young Communist League. His doctrinaire fervor can be illustrated by the concluding paragraph of the book he authored on Ethiopia's Marxist revolution of 1974: "It is fitting here to recall the beautiful, passionate words of Karl Marx. . . . He said, 'Citizens, let us think of the fundamental principle of the International, solidarity! It is by establishing this vivifying principle on a strong basis among all the working people of all countries, that we shall achieve the great goal we have set ourselves.'"[38] Valdés Vivó has harshly attacked the economic reform movement, often in language reminiscent of the bleakest years of the cold war. He is no friend of the reformers and has recently insisted that the private economy "would introduce a social force that sooner or later would serve the counterrevolution."[39] Whatever his influence upon Raúl Castro it is likely far from negligible and certainly of a severely conservative coloration.

The most prominent woman in revolutionary Cuba is Vilma Espín, the 69-year-old president of the Federation of Cuban Women who has led the organization since its founding in 1960. A former July 26th Movement activist she joined the rebel army in 1958, serving in Raúl Castro's "Second Front" in the Sierra Maestra and then marrying him in 1959. She is a member of the Central Committee of the

Communist Party, serves on its Politburo, and has been a member of the Council of State since 1976. One of the more important symbols of revolutionary women in Cuba, she continues to be a major influence on both Fidel and Raúl as regards the role and position of women. As she has argued:

> For the essential goals that socialism seeks, the social equality of women, our full participation in economic, political, cultural and social life and the full exercising of our rights are fundamental and are principles laid down in the policy of our party and state, which each of our institutions and the society as a whole has the task of concretizing, and which, of course, is the whole reason for the existence of our organization, the Federation of Cuban Women.[40]

Her influence in a post-Fidel Cuba will probably be quite enormous due not only to the fact that she is Raúl's wife but because she is a political force of her own and is singularly the most important factor regarding women and politics in Cuba. Espín's comments can often be pretty hard-line, as when she wrote in 1991 that it "is our ideology that makes [women] invincible, together with the precise and powerful proof that socialism is a superior system in every field. Paraphrasing Lenin we could ask ourselves: 'What is to be done?'"[41] No doubt her own views on what needs to be done, not only for the rights of women but insofar as the future of Cuba is concerned, are exacting.

According to the Cuban constitution upon the death of the president the first vice president of the Council of State would assume presidential duties.[42] But since the constitution also proclaims that "The Communist Party of Cuba, the organized Marxist-Leninist vanguard of the working class, is the highest leading force of the society and of the state, which organizes and guides the common effort toward the goals of the construction of socialism and the progress towards a communist *society*,"[43] it is from the party that a new post-Fidel leadership will be selected. Although the Council of State may be the "highest representative of the Cuban state" it is the Communist Party that is the "highest, leading force of the state"; therefore the first vice president who might move into the presidency would be inferior to the head of the party, which would be Raúl

Castro, presently the number two man after Fidel. Since Raúl is momentarily also first vice president no conflict exists.

It is therefore highly likely that in the near term Cuba without Fidel would find itself being led by Raúl Castro. However, that certainly does not by itself indicate that the reformers would have no place in society. On the contrary, with the military in hand Raúl would most likely have to reach out to the economic reformers as they presently have a substantial constituency that is likely to only grow in size. He will need their support, and they will need his patronage and leverage if they are to continue to develop their policies. But the reformers will most probably have to move more slowly than they would choose to because the circle that surrounds Raúl is apparently more conservative than that presently encircling Fidel. Although many commentators in the West have already adopted the scenario of a collective government that will rule during a "transition" period, which seems less than likely, though certainly it remains a possibility. But "collective" meaning rule by consensus without a quintessential leader is doubtful as long as Raúl Castro remains within the power structure.

The Alarcóns of Cuba would most likely want to move further along the road of economic reform and would like to conclude the hostile relationship between the United States and Cuba. Given that prospect the position of dissident groups in Cuba could be transformed, since any improvement in the Cuban/American relationship would surely reduce the impact of the Cuban-American community in Miami. But neither Raúl Castro nor Ricardo Alarcón have thus far indicated any desire to loosen the strictures surrounding political rights, that Western perspective of rights that includes elections, speech, association, and so forth. All decisionmakers in Cuba have witnessed what happened in the Soviet Union, and if any foreign model is appealing it is more than likely the Chinese experience of expanding economic responsibilities but continuing the sharp curtailment of political rights. But the Chinese model, which in any case has already been to some degree accepted, would continue to be only partially adopted. Cuba, with only 11 million people, would be swamped and overwhelmed by American private enterprise and thus any opening to the United States would place sharp limits on its economic possibilities. Privatization of state enterprises is conceivable but expansion of political rights, if it occurs at all, will be held closely in check.

To that end the hard-liners and the reformers may not be so very far apart in political philosophy. Economic reform is acceptable as long as the socialist character of the state is maintained. Political reform along the lines demanded by the United States will most likely continue to be rejected, with the emphasis being on first meeting the economic and social needs of the Cuban people. As Alarcón angrily commented in 1997 in memorializing the thirtieth anniversary of the death of Che Guevara, for the United States "to come to tell Cubans that the Cuba of 1958 was prosperity and democracy is really an insult and an affront that this people cannot allow. The Cuba of 1958, the 'prosperous democratic' Cuba, was furthermore, the Cuba of latifundia, of evictions, of murders, tortures, repression, robbery, of all those things they wish to reinstate here. And in addition, they expect the Cuban people—as if they were a group of idiots—to finance the reinstatement of those things here. And later they would applaud it, I guess. It was the Cuba of corruption, of embezzlement, and of submission to Washington."[44]

Whether Alarcón's influence in a government led by Raúl Castro would be stronger or weaker, or even if there would be a consortium of leaders, a sort of political directorate, the likelihood of vast economic or political changes taking place in Cuba on the heels of Castro's replacement is more a hope of outsiders than a reasonable prediction of what is likely to occur. All will be careful to prevent what in their minds would be a return to pre-1959. And although Western analysts may view that as an irrational perspective, as Alarcón indicated in his 1997 speech, these revolutionaries who supported and participated in the struggle for independence find 1959 and Fidel Castro to be the touchstone of their politics.

Raúl Castro as general secretary of the Communist Party and Ricardo Alarcón, or any other reformer for that matter, as president of Cuba is not an unlikely outcome. But expectations that the nation will undergo radical change should be held in check as both will be very careful to ensure that the socialist direction of Cuba continues, while whatever relationship exists with the United States will be determined by the Cuban leadership and not dictated by Washington. Alarcón and the other reformers are in many ways as hard-line as is Raúl. They may be softer when it comes to limited and controlled economic change, but they remain resolute that Cuba retain its socialist framework and that distribution of wealth, goods, and services remain the hallmark of the state. Political liberation as seen by Washington is viewed as folly in Havana; any new leadership is highly likely to remain adamantine in maintaining its own interpretation of political rights and human rights, even if it does not include Raúl, should he pass from the scene before Fidel.

These men have been shaped by Fidel Castro and his heritage, an influence that will remain seductive, and it is unreasonable to expect that they can, or even wish to, avoid his adumbrative counsel. Cuban sovereignty as it exists today is purely a result of Fidel Castro, and no future leader who has gone through the headiness of the 40-year-old revolution or is a product of its success is likely to sell that legacy to Washington—negotiate certainly, but sell, hardly.

THE FUTURE OF THE EMBARGO

Richard Nixon, who during his presidency had asked Secretary of State Henry Kissinger, "what can CIA do to support *any* kind of action which will irritate Castro,"[45] had by 1990, while he was deep into the process of trying to resurrect his image as statesman, changed his mind and declared in reference to Cuba that "sanctions will almost never succeed in altering the *domestic* policies of a hostile Communist state."[46] Long before 1999, the fortieth anniversary of the Cuban revolution, Cuba's involvement on the international stage had been crushed, many of its domestic policies, if not altered, had been modified, and the 37-year-old embargo had clearly taken its toll on Cuba and its population. The question, then, is Why continue the embargo? If Nixon was finally correct that sanctions will not force a political opening in the domestic political policies of Cuba, as is apparent from the embargo's failure in that regard, the maintenance of the embargo can be considered purely a maleficent policy targeted solely at the Castro brothers' retention of power.

Although the primary object of the embargo has not been achieved, its secondary successes have been so effective that Fidel Castro's ability to threaten the national security of the United States is extinct. No rational excuse remains for continuing the embargo. Soviet missiles and troops are no longer in Cuba while the Soviet Union lies in the dustbin of history, Castro has been and will remain unable to directly influence radical movements elsewhere in the world, communism itself, in the new financial/capitalistic world of the late twentieth century is, at least for the time being, a casualty of history, and Cuba is an impoverished nation. Even the once noteworthy leverage of the Cuban American National Foundation has been sharply reduced, as its previously feared and influential leader, Jorge Mas Canosa, is dead. Not only are most underpinnings of the U.S. embargo no longer relevant but its very existence, with no compelling raison d'être, has only buttressed Fidel's popularity in Cuba and elsewhere, which eviscerates the very purposes the embargo was set up for. If the national security of the United States is the primary concern of America's leadership then any rational policy ought to lead to the elimination of the U.S. embargo against Cuba, or at the very least to the beginning of a process whereby its various acts will be gradually lifted.

However, rational behavior leading to intended consequences has not always been the hallmark of the embargo laws. Based in large part on the animus directed against Fidel Castro's survival, as long as he remains on the scene it is unlikely that the embargo will be lifted in one fell swoop. But since there is presently enormous pressure being placed on the United States by the membership of the European Union and by many influential Latin American countries to dilute the extraterritorial elements of the Cuban Democracy Act and Helms-Burton it is not unlikely that even during Fidel's lifetime that particularly peculiar aspect of the embargo, which clearly violates international law,[47] may be adjusted or perhaps even lifted. President Clinton has repeatedly, although only temporarily, waived Title III of the Helms-Burton Act, which allows civil suits against persons or corporations "trafficking" in nationalized properties to which the U.S. or its citizens hold a claim,[48] but the strained relations between the United States, Europe, and Canada are such that either he or the next president may very well be pressured to go to Congress to seek permanent curtailment of the strictures of third country application. In fact, in May 1998 Clinton asked a reluctant Congress to pass legislation required to support an agreement he made with the European Union to amend and waive indefinitely Title IV of Helms-Burton, which requires the U.S. to deny visas to executives in foreign countries that profit from nationalized property. In return, the European Union's members would "discipline" foreign investment in expropriated property by limiting somewhat government support for such activity and would agree not to take the United States before the WTO for violating international law. Pressure from the same sources and the United Nations General Assembly has emphasized hunger and the reduced medical care available to the Cuban people, and it is probable therefore that *if* there is modification of the embargo it will initially be moderated to allow third countries to provide aid in and sales of food and medicine. Beyond that, it is unlikely that so long as Fidel Castro survives any other substantial measures to reduce the impact of the embargo will be taken.

It is just as unreasonable to assume that if Raúl Castro takes the helm in a Cuba without Fidel that the embargo's impulses would be mitigated beyond the scope of third country application. Prior to Helms-Burton the Cuban embargo had to be renewed annually and its authority rested within the Executive Office, but under Helms-Burton the control over sanctions was transferred to Congress, investing only the legislature with the power to permanently reduce the embargo's effects or eliminate it altogether. Additionally Helms-Burton stated rather emphatically that the embargo will remain in place until a democratically elected government, excluding Fidel or Raúl Castro, is in power in Cuba. Since after the fall of the Soviet Union Congress has invoked a pretty conservative ideological approach to most foreign policy issues the likelihood of any diminution in the embargo should Raúl be selected as the paramount political force in Cuba is slim, particularly since he is viewed in Washington as merely the alter ego of his brother. Should, however, the complexion of Congress change, a review of the policy that provoked the embargo in the first place might conceivably be conducted that could lead to an alternative approach toward Cuba.

In another scenario, a political reordering that has Ricardo Alarcón or any representative of the reform movement taking power would lead to a speedy resolution advancing the embargo's demise. Without either Fidel or Raúl mucking up the picture all evidence points to the prospect that the embargo would be terminated, either gradually or, perhaps, immediately. Even though limitations on the political rights of Cubans would likely be retained, reformers would be willing to negotiate the entrance of U.S. business interests into the economic fabric of Cuba, which private investors in the United States have been seriously lobbying for since 1995 when they complained that "all deals down there are being cut by foreign competitors."[49] And since the United States has proper diplomatic relations with numerous countries whose governments, in its view, violate the political rights of their own citizens that would no longer by itself be cause for continuing the disruption of ties between Cuba and the United States. The Castros would be gone, erasing the primary impediment to restoring diplomatic relations. Resolution of the compensation issue within the context of an overall diplomatic settlement could also be expected.

Raúl Castro's participation in any future government will be the key to what occurs. Even if he is merely a participant in a "transitory" political structure the United States would tend to look quizzically at any negotiations or even restoration of relations with the new government, and the embargo would most likely endure as a mechanism to pressure the political forces in Havana to remove him from the political scene. Should Raúl remain a fixture then clearly the embargo would be maintained to one degree or another.

A patterned decline or even the rapid elimination of the embargo, negotiated with Cuba, will lead to the swift normalization of relations between the two countries. But that will not mean the United States will get what it wants in terms of political rights. It will probably have to compromise that plank of its policy and be satisfied with the removal of Fidel and Raúl Castro from the stage of Cuban politics; while it could always maintain that it is negotiating that specific issue and expects that changes will occur in the future. The U.S. public's concentration on that issue would no doubt dissipate over a decent interval of time. The Cuban government, whatever its ideological composition, will keep strict controls over political participation and will disallow the United States influence in that realm of politics. Even so, a restored connection to Washington "could lead to a total transformation in the legal and political situation of dissidents on the island"[50] as their perceived linkage to the reactionary elements of the Miami Cubans would be broken, and since the more liberal dissident groups in Florida would gain far more leverage the dissidents in Cuba would not be seen as so threatening by Havana.

With the end of U.S./Cuban animosity and hostility, U.S. tourists will flock to the island, a situation that will also encourage Cuba to use more subtle tactics in restricting its human rights advocates. Even if political liberalization is not in the cards, a lesser degree of constraint might be expected, even as relatively tight controls are maintained. That alone would go far in satisfying the United States, even if in absolute terms its political desires remained unmet.

Cuba, however, will not turn the country over to America's investment community, particularly "as when the American embargo goes [Cuba] will become one big magnet for American tourists and American cash."[51] Fearing being overwhelmed by the U.S. corporate community Cuba's leaders will insist on controlled and conditional U.S. participation in the Cuban economy. Pre-1959 is the penumbra of Cuban politics, indeed the very basis of the revolution, and no Cuban leadership will ever again sell the country to the United States. Fidel Castro's political visage will always be retained and will morally disallow the United States from attaining the dominant and oppressive position it held in the societally crushing years prior to the revolution.

U.S. investments and tourist expenditures will surely help the economically ravaged island recover from its damaged state, which by itself will still those dissidents whose primary concern is the state of the economy. After all, whether Fidel Castro would win a presidential election or not he is still extremely popular on the island and is alone seen as responsible for shaking off America's tyrannical exploitation of Cuba. An economically revitalized country would restore much of the glitter to the image of Fidel that has been tarnished as a result of Cuba's recent economic collapse, and the dissident movement would probably be greatly reduced. Economic development, however, will not necessarily lead to the establishment of political rights despite what Western analysts argue. On the contrary, it may provoke the Cuban government to be ever more vigilant when the United States again becomes a presence on the island.

Cuba and the United States will in the not-too-distant future see their historical connection revitalized. But the relationship will be on a sounder, more equitable footing, as Cuba will certainly retain the essence of what Fidel has bequeathed. It will be a truly sovereign state that will insist on retaining its human rights perspective of economic and social rights taking precedence over political rights. Socialism will remain the overriding framework as the nation will continue to maintain its emphasis on seeing to it that all, rather than a few, benefit from whatever the system can generate economically. That in turn means that collective needs as opposed to individual rights will remain sacrosanct. On social issues the same parameter will apply.

The United States will have a new and different role to play, one that will allow its citizens to invest in and travel to Cuba, but on a basis negotiated by both countries that will recognize Cuba's sovereign rights and respect whatever limitations it chooses to place on the relationship. Additionally, Cuba will be reincorporated into the international community and will once again participate in the regional organizations of Latin America and the Caribbean, becoming gradually integrated into the African, Caribbean, and Pacific group of 71 countries who are signatory members of the post-Lomé trade and cooperation accord. And it will in the future be permitted to join the other 34 countries meeting at a Summit of the Americas in order to establish a free-trade area from the Yukon to Tierra del Fuego by the year 2005. The reestablishment of diplomatic relations with the United States will also permit Cuba the opportunity to apply for loans from the World Bank and the IMF, thereby also opening up other avenues for foreign loans and economic aid.

However the country evolves it will be a Cuba that has been created by Fidel Castro through the aegis of the revolution. No official in the United States, or any leader in Cuba for that matter, will ever be able to ignore or avoid the historical and political importance of Fidel. As Jean-Paul Sartre said as early as 1961, "We have seen how a lucid practice has changed in Cuba even the very notion of man";[52]

that proud personification of the Cuban revolution will ever haunt a Cuban or American leadership that contemplates overturning the essential parameters of what Fidel Castro has delivered to Cuba. Fidel Castro and Cuba will always be inseparable as far as history is concerned, and that linkage will continue to set the standard for what can and can not be done in and to Cuba.

NOTES

PREFACE

1. *CIA Targets Fidel,* 1996.
2. Beschloss, 1997: 87.
3. Schlesinger Jr., 1965: 220.

ONE

1. *Universal Declaration of Human Rights,* December 10, 1948.
2. Halberstam, 1973: 135.
3. Kennedy, 1961: 63.
4. Taft, 1989: 269. For the consummate account of the Roosevelt/Batista connection see Gellman, 1973.
5. Pollis and Schwab, 1979: 1.
6. Ibid.: 2.
7. Wright, 1979: 20, 21.
8. Pollis and Schwab, 1979: 9.
9. Pollis, 1996: 319.
10. Pollis, 1982: 10, 18.
11. Scali, 1976: 567-568, 570. Excerpts from address at the Shoreham-Americana Hotel, Washington, D.C., March 6, 1975.
12. Lazreg, 1979: 37. The *Universal Declaration of Human Rights* was adopted by the General Assembly of the United Nations on December 10, 1948, by a vote of 48 for, none against, and 8 abstentions. It had been recommended to the body by the United Nations Commission of Human Rights, chaired by Eleanor Roosevelt.
13. Charter of the United Nations, 1945: Chapter IV.
14. Goodrich, 1964: 249.
15. Pollis and Schwab, 1979: 6.
16. Pollis, 1981: 1014.
17. "The Federalist No. 10," 1961. *The Federalist Papers* were originally published in 1787 and 1788.
18. *New York Times,* April 30, 1998: A16.

19. Szulc, 1986: 547.
20. Smith, 1987: 280.
21. Cited in Franqui, 1980: 326.
22. *Constitution of the Republic of Cuba,* 1976: Articles 8 and 12.
23. Ibid.: Article 61.
24. Ibid.: Article 12.
25. Ibid.: Article 38.
26. "A Survey of Cuba," 1996: 4.
27. Camnitzer, 1994: 129.
28. Remirez de Estenoz, 1998.
29. *Constitution of the Republic of Cuba,* 1976: Article 1; Article 16.
30. Ibid.: Article 15.
31. Ibid.: Preamble.
32. Pollis, 1982: 18, 16.
33. See *Constitution of the Republic of Cuba,* 1976: Articles 7 and 43; *Mapping Progress—Cuba,* March 1998: 61; *United Nations World Statistics Pocketbook,* 1997: 47; Espín, 1991: 21, 57; Rudolph, 1987: 74, 121.
34. *Constitution of the Republic of Cuba,* 1976: Article 8.
35. Domínguez, 1979: 62-63.
36. "Fidel Castro Gives Dynamite Six-Minute Speech in Turkey." *Cuba Update,* September 1996: 17.
37. Robaina, March 20, 1998: 10.
38. Ibid.
39. *New York Times,* April 22, 1998: A5.
40. *New York Times,* April 27, 1998: A9.
41. Charter of the United Nations, 1945: Preamble.
42. Charter of the United Nations, 1945: Chapter I, Article I.
43. See Kissinger, 1979: 632-652.
44. Rudolph, 1987: 221.
45. Smith, 1987: 108.
46. Ibid.: 110.
47. Vance, 1983: 131.
48. Smith, 1987: 117-118.
49. For analyses of the Angola and Ethiopia issues, see Falk, 1986, and Domínguez, 1989. Smith, 1987 reflects on how the relationship among Cuba, Angola, and Ethiopia influenced the dialogue between Cuba and the United States. Korn, 1986, looks at Cuba's role in Ethiopia.
50. Rudolph, 1987: 221.
51. *New York Times,* April 28, 1998: A6.
52. Taft, 1989: 269.

TWO

1. The Eastern Caribbean includes the semi-circle arc of eight states and ten

colonial territories identified also as the Lesser Antilles, made up of the Leeward and Windward Islands. It is bordered by Venezuela in the south and Puerto Rico and the Virgin Islands in the north, and to the east it faces the coast of West Africa. Popularly known as the West Indies, it has been largely ignored by scholars, who tend to study and write about the islands in the northern Caribbean—Cuba, Jamaica, the Dominican Republic, and Puerto Rico—that are part of the chain of islands in the Greater Antilles. The western and southern Caribbean, or the Caribbean Basin, is made up of those states on the mainland of South America, Central America, and Mexico. On any regulation map the countries of the Eastern Caribbean appear merely as dots separating the Atlantic Ocean from the Caribbean Sea. Among the regional organizations to which the Eastern Caribbean nations belong are the Caribbean Community (Caricom), made up of 13 countries of the former British empire plus Haiti and Suriname, grouped together for the purpose of economic cooperation; the Association of Caribbean States (ACS), which includes all the countries of the Caribbean and Central America, along with Mexico, Colombia, Venezuela, the Dominican Republic, and Cuba; and the Organization of Eastern Caribbean States (OES), made up of Trinidad and Tobago plus the nations of the Eastern Caribbean Regional Security System (RSS), a U.S.-supported and -sponsored military security pact whose members are Barbados, Antigua and Barbuda, Dominica, St. Lucia, St. Vincent and the Grenadines, St. Kitts-Nevis, and Grenada.

2. Watson, 1986: 34.
3. Halliday, 1983: 5.
4. DeMar, 1995: 52.
5. *New York Times*, October 24, 1996: A13.
6. Prior to the Cuban revolution the United States intervened militarily in the Caribbean and Central America almost 50 times.
7. Feinberg, 1981: 1124. See also *New York Times*, March 24, 1983: 15.
8. As cited in Krinsky and Golove, 1993: 159.
9. *Hearings Before a Subcommittee of the Committee on Appropriations*, 1985: 281. See Gonzalez, 1982: 194-197.
10. Ibid., 1985: 260.
11. Watson, 1986: 25.
12. Barbados' action is pretty well known. The French operation was discussed by Dominica's Minister of Health Ronan David during an interview with the author in Dominica's capital, Roseau, in March 1987. David, who at the time was acting prime minister, maintained that French troops were requested because of their proximity to Dominica. He claimed that "if we had asked the British [the former colonial power] we would still be waiting."
13. *New York Times*, March 24, 1983: 15.
14. Cracknell, 1973: 12.

15. The operation was discussed in Dominica's weekly newspaper the *New Chronicle*, March 20, 1987: 1. On June 18, 1988 the *Democrat for St. Kitts* exposed information about Eastern Caribbean war games conducted in Puerto Rico. For additional information on Exotic Palm see Boodhoo, 1986: 88.
16. Phillips, 1986: 61.
17. Pattullo, 1996: 136.
18. See Pattullo, 1996, and Kincaid, 1988.
19. *Hearings*, March 28, 1985: 306.
20. Ibid.: 307.
21. Greene, 1985: 45. Although Jamaica is not in the Eastern Caribbean it is a major actor in its military and political affairs. Also see LeoGrande, 1982: 181.
22. *NACLA, Report on the Americas*, 1985: 33.
23. *New York Times*, October 24, 1996: A13.
24. *New York Times*, October 14, 1996: A4.
25. Interview conducted by the author in Roseau, March 1987. See "Dominica: Seeking Prosperity Through Self-Reliance," 1986, the interview with Prime Minister Charles.
26. Pattullo, 1996: 182, 202.
27. *Caribbean Contact*, March 1987: 3.
28. St. Lucia also participated in the 1983 invasion of Grenada.
29. Ambrose, 1971: 148.
30. Trefousse, 1966: 101 (the Truman Doctrine speech in its entirety: 97-102). Although the Truman Doctrine dealt specifically with aid to Greece and Turkey its implications were universal.
31. The English-speaking states of the Caribbean, formerly under the colonial administration of Great Britain, are now mostly independent but are still as a group known as the Commonwealth Caribbean and retain membership in the British Commonwealth.
32. *Economic Survey of Latin America and the Caribbean, 1983*, 1985: Volume II.
33. *United Nations Statistical Yearbook 1993*, 1995: 746-750. In 1995 Dominica had a *total* balance of payments deficit of $195 million; its imported goods were valued at $317 million while its exports totaled $122 million. *United Nations Monthly Bulletin of Statistics*, October, 1997: 134.
34. Pattullo, 1996: 39, 156-175.
35. *United Nations Statistical Yearbook 1993*, 1995: 237.
36. Richardson, 1983: 47. See too Domínguez and Domínguez, 1981: 53-63.
37. Boodhoo, 1986: 83.
38. Interview conducted by the author in Roseau, March 1987. In 1985 merely 1.6 percent of Dominica's exports went to the United States, while 26.6 percent of its imports came from there. In 1991, 31 percent of imports came from the United States. In terms of imports the United States remains its largest supplier, while the percentage of its exports

makes the United States virtually its most inconsequential trading partner. *The World Bank,* 1985: 59. See also *World Bank,* "Dominica Economic Memorandum," 1983, and *United Nations World Statistics Pocketbook,* 1997: 52.

39. See *Statistical Yearbook for Latin America and the Caribbean 1996,* February 1997.
40. *Hearings and Markup,* March 1 and 16, April 12 and 13, 1983: 23.
41. Ibid.
42. *NACLA,* 1985: 30. The competitiveness of CBI is seen from the full listing of states and territories eligible to receive funds. They include Antigua and Barbuda, Barbados, Belize, the British Virgin Islands of Tortola and Virgin Gorda, Costa Rica, Dominica, the Dominican Republic, El Salvador, Grenada, Guatemala, Haiti, Honduras, Jamaica, the British Crown Colony of Montserrat, the Dutch islands—Aruba, Bonaire, Curacao, St. Maarten (which shares its island with the French territory of St. Martin)—Panama, St. Kitts-Nevis, St. Lucia, St. Vincent and the Grenadines, Trinidad and Tobago, and the Bahamas (which was designated in 1985).
43. For an excellent analysis of the impact of the United States on the political systems of the Eastern Caribbean in pressuring them to become even more conservative then they already were, see the *Bulletin of Eastern Caribbean Affairs—Special Issue,* January/February 1986. The issue also discusses the amount and direction of U.S. military aid.
44. *Economic Survey of Latin America and the Caribbean 1983,* 1985: 3.
45. Pattullo, 1996: 80-101. Kincaid, 1988, begins her book, which relates to Antigua, with reflections of the overpowering impact of the British and Americans.
46. Pattullo, 1996: 121.
47. Chomsky and Prieto, 1995: 28.
48. Gunn, 1993: 28.
49. Ibid.: 32.
50. Schwab, 1995a: 17A, and 1995b for descriptions of what life was like in Cuba during that time. See also Anderson, 1998: 62-68.
51. Murray, 1993:16-18; Gunn, 1993:20-21. For the full text of the CDA see Krinsky and Golove, 1993:147-155.
52. *New York Times,* October 24, 1996: A13.
53. Comment made by Jamaican prime minister P. J. Patterson at the summit meeting of Caribbean Community leaders and President Clinton held in Bridgetown, Barbados, May 10, 1997. *New York Times,* May 11, 1997: 6.
54. *New York Times,* October 24, 1996: A13.
55. *New York Times,* May 11, 1997: 6. In 1998, Patterson was less diplomatic. In welcoming Castro to Jamaica, he maintained, "We are implacably opposed to the economic blockade of Cuba, which is morally wrong. The blockade constitutes a threat to the sovereignty of other states." *New York Times,* August 2, 1998: 3.

56. Ibid., 1997.
57. Ibid.
58. *New York Times,* December 21, 1997: 8.
59. Ibid.: Statement by Prime Minister P. J. Patterson. The *Grenadian Voice,* June 27, 1998: 3. According to *Grenada Today,* June 26, 1998: 2, Mitchell invited Castro because, as the prime minister said, "We have been helped tremendously [by Cuba]. That international airport has been one of the shining economic activities for this country's development and Cuba has played a major role and it doesn't matter what your views are, the facts are the facts." In contrast, however, postcards are still sold in Grenada that thank the "U.S.A. for liberating us" in 1983 and "thank God for U.S. and Caribbean heroes of freedom." Castro arrived in Grenada August 2 for a goodwill visit that lasted two days.
60. In a communication to the World Trade Organization, Cuba denounced the proposed legislation as "a demonstration of the arrogant and hegemonic character inherent in U.S. foreign policy." *World Trade Organization,* June 18, 1997: 3.
61. Gunn, 1993: 33.
62. Smith, September 1996:14. By 1998, according to Cuba's Washington-based chief of Interests Section, Cuba had substantially diversified its foreign trade; 40 percent of its export and import markets were with Canada, Latin America, and the Caribbean, and 33 percent were with the European Community: Remirez de Estenoz, 1998.
63. Schwab, 1997a: 21A. *Caribbean Compass,* June 1998: 1, 3.
64. "Fidel Castro Gives Dynamite Six-Minute Speech in Turkey." *Cuba Update,* September 1996: 17. The same message was articulated in the summer of 1998 when Castro visited Barbados, Grenada, Jamaica, and the Dominican Republic.
65. *World Trade Organization,* October 8, 1996: 1. *New York Times,* April 6, 1996: 3.
66. Cohn and Berlin, 1997: S2.
67. Krinsky and Golove, 1993: xvii.
68. For a description of life during this period see Schwab, 1997a: 21A.
69. Schlesinger Jr., 1974: 178.
70. Hufbauer, Schott and Elliott, 1990a: 71.
71. Lieuwin, 1961: viii.
72. Ibid.: 223.
73. *New York Times,* February 29, 1996: A6.
74. Erisman, 1998: 91.

THREE

1. Szulc, 1986: 463.
2. Ibid.: 480.

3. *Foreign Relations of the United States 1958-1960: Cuba,* 1991: 476.
4. Eisenhower, 1965: 525.
5. *Foreign Relations of the United States 1958-1960: Cuba,* 1991: 1090.
6. Murray, 1993: 17.
7. Eisenberg, 1997: 1250. See also Schwab, 1997b.
8. Sweig and Bird (editors), 1997: 16.
9. Eisenberg, 1997: 1249.
10. Schwab, 1997b: 23-25.
11. *New York Times,* March 8, 1998: Section 4, 1.
12. Peréz-Stable, 1993: 29.
13. Ibid.: 31.
14. Sartre, 1961: 41. For an exceptional pictorial essay on Cuban life prior to 1959, see *Walker Evans: Havana 1933,* 1989.
15. Huberman and Sweezy, 1960: 4-5.
16. Mills, 1960: 58.
17. Paterson, 1994: 36, 40.
18. Matthews, 1970: 49. See Smith, 1962.
19. Szulc, 1986: 537.
20. Castro, 1972: 183-184. July 26, 1953, is the official beginning of the revolution. Although sentenced to 15 years for organizing and leading the attack Castro was released from the Isle of Pines prison on May 15, 1955, after receiving amnesty from Batista.
21. Pollis and Schwab, 1979: 8.
22. Ibid.
23. Ibid.: 10.
24. Pollis, 1981: 1011.
25. Pollis, 1982: 5.
26. Arat, 1991: 4.
27. Pollis, 1982: 16.
28. Sweig and Bird (editors), March 1997: 11. See *Avances Medicos De Cuba,* 1997.
29. *Constitution of the Republic of Cuba,* 1976: Article 49.
30. "One Thing Cuba Does Right." *Economist,* September 7, 1996: 42.
31. Dale, 1997: 22. The United States has approximately one physician for every 350 people.
32. Frank and Reed, 1997: 34.
33. Cuban National Budget, 1996. According to Remirez de Estenoz, 1998, 32 percent of the 1997 budget was allocated to health care, social security, and education while only 5 percent was assigned to military expenditures.
34. *United Nations Statistical Yearbook 1994,* 1996: 84.
35. Sweig and Bird (editors), March 1997: 12.
36. Frank and Reed, 1997: 140.
37. *Cuba Update,* Winter 1997: 21.
38. Frank and Reed, 1997: 140.

39. *The World's Women 1995: Trends and Statistics*, 1996: 71.
40. *United Nations Statistical Yearbook 1994*, 1996: 75.
41. Guillermoprieto, 1998a: 22.
42. Frank and Reed, 1997: 34.
43. Ibid.: 182.
44. Cuban Ministry of Public Health, 1996.
45. Ibid.
46. Frank and Reed, 1997: 233.
47. *Economist*, September 7, 1996: 42.
48. Frank and Reed, 1997: 261.
49. Schwab, 1997b: 17.
50. Smaldone, 1996: 28.
51. Frank and Reed, 1997: 103.
52. Nash, 1996: 20. See Frank and Reed for the full 301-page report of the American Association of World Health, 1997, and Feinsilver, 1995.
53. Murray, 1993: 25.
54. Garfield and Santana, 1997: 6.
55. Frank and Reed, 1997: 35.
56. Ibid.: 65.
57. Ibid.: 235.
58. Murray, 1993: 26.
59. *Disarm Education Fund Cuban Medical Project*, 1997.
60. Sweig and Bird (editors), 1997: 31.
61. Eisenberg, 1997: 1249.
62. Wallop, 1997: editorial page. For a detailed listing of embargoed medicine and technology see Permanent Mission of Cuba to the United Nations, 1997: *The U.S. Embargo is a Deliberate Crime Against the Cuban People's Health.*
63. *What You Need to Know About the U.S. Embargo: An Overview of the Cuban Assets Control Regulations*, 1996: 1.
64. For a discussion of illegal travel to Cuba, see Parsa, 1997: 36-43.
65. Garfield and Santana, 1997: 6.
66. *Universal Declaration of Human Rights*, 1948: Article 25.
67. *International Covenant on Economic, Social and Cultural Rights*, 1976: Articles 10, 12.
68. Lazreg, 1979: 40.
69. Ruffin, 1982: 115.
70. Pollis, 1998: 9.
71. Pollis, 1996: 319.
72. Anderson, 1997: 457.

FOUR

1. *Cuba News*, March 1998: 10-11; Rosset and Benjamin, 1994: 13, 21;

Gunn, 1993: 27-28.

2. Hufbauer, Schott, and Eliott, 1990b: 200. Rudolph, 1987: 207.
3. Rosset and Benjamin, 1994: 13.
4. Haufbauer, Schott, and Elliott, 1990a: 71, 41.
5. Krinsky and Golove, 1993: 149. For the full Act see 147-155.
6. Ibid: 148.
7. Frank and Reed, 1997: 121-122.
8. Murray, 1993: 17.
9. Traub, 1998: 80.
10. Ibid.
11. Quirk, 1993: 327.
12. LeoGrande, 1981: 252.
13. Koont, 1994: 2. Also see Falk, 1995: A11, and Scrinis, 1995: 1-46.
14. LeoGrande, 1981: 252.
15. Rosset and Benjamin, 1994: 11.
16. *United Nations World Statistics Pocketbook,* 1997: 47.
17. *Financial Times,* March 1990: 6.
18. Frank and Reed, 1997: 133.
19. Ibid.: 129.
20. *United Nations World Statistics Pocketbook,* 1997: 47.
21. Frank and Reed, 1997: 123.
22. Rosset and Benjamin, 1994: 11; Frank and Reed, 1997: 133-134.
23. Schwab, 1995b.
24. Frank and Reed, 1997: 133-134.
25. Miller, 1996: 321, 26.
26. Koont, 1994: 6.
27. Anderson, 1998: 62. For a harsh view of prostitution in Cuba, see Guillermoprieto, 1998b.
28. "A Country Frozen in Time," 1995: 3B.
29. "Fidel Castro Attacks 'Track Two' Policy on July 26." *Cuba Update,* October 1995: 8.
30. Iyer, 1996: 59.
31. Prada, 1995: 23.
32. Prada, 1995: 40. See also León Cotayo, 1991.
33. Pattullo, 1996: 38.
34. Ibid.: 83.
35. Aron, 1974: 329.
36. *New York Times,* August 15, 1995: A6.
37. Ibid. For Mariel, see Smith, 1987: 197-237.
38. *Cuba Update,* October 1995: 8.
39. Falk, 1995: A11.
40. *New York Times,* October 12, 1997: 5.
41. *Correo de Cuba,* n.d.: 32. *Cuba News,* March 1998: 7.
42. *New York Times,* October 12, 1997: 5.
43. Lage, 1993.

44. *New York Times,* February 1, 1998: 3. See also Valdés Vivó, 1978.
45. *New York Times,* February 29, 1996: A6.
46. *CIA World Fact Book,* 1996: n.p.
47. *Cuba Economic Report, Summary,* 1996: 1, 5. During this period greater emphasis was also placed on organic/traditional forms of agriculture; see Scrinis, 1995, and Rosset and Benjamin, 1994. See also *Cuba Update,* winter 1997: 33-38.
48. *Economic Survey of Latin America and the Caribbean 1996-1997,* 1997: 198. See also *United Nations Statistical Yearbook for Latin America and the Caribbean 1996,* 1997.
49. "A Country Frozen in Time," 1995: 3B.
50. Mead, 1996: 10. See also LeoGrande, 1998, and Alarcón, 1996.
51. *Reaffirmation of Cuban Dignity and Sovereignty Act,* December 24, 1996.
52. Alarcón, 1997b: n.p.
53. McNamara, 1995.
54. *Universal Declaration of Human Rights,* 1948: Articles 17, 23, 24, 25.
55. Schwelb, 1964: 32.
56. Pollis and Schwab, 1979: 5.
57. Steel, 1998: (4) 15.
58. *International Covenant on Economic, Social and Cultural Rights,* 1976: Article 11.
59. *World Trade Organization,* May 13, 1996: 1.
60. "The Cuban Embargo." *The News Hour with Jim Lehrer* (television program): March 20, 1998.
61. Hufbauer, Schott, and Eliott, 1990b: 202-203.
62. "Should We Change Our Policy Toward Cuba?" *Critical Issues* (television program): November 1, 1995.
63. Sembene, 1970: 101. Miller, 1998, speaks of the enduring lack of food and medicine in Matanzas.
64. Cuban American National Foundation, 1996: 6.
65. *New York Times,* April 4, 1998: 1.
66. Krinsky and Golove, 1993: 148; see 148-149 for Section 1703 of the CDA.

FIVE

1. Frei Betto, 1990: 222, 224, 225, 226. Fidel's conversations with this sympathetic Brazilian Dominican friar regarding religion and the Catholic Church are fascinating.
2. Guillermoprieto, 1998a: 22.
3. Frei Betto, 1990: 198.
4. MacGaffey and Barnett, 1965: 236.
5. Ibid.: 243. For a discussion of the traditional Catholic Church in Latin America during the period, see Vallier, 1967: 203, who maintains,

"traditional Catholic elites in Latin America are oriented to the power structure of secular society . . . [and] the reference group of the traditional elite is the upper class, from which many of them come."

6. Frei Betto, 1990: 147.
7. Ibid.: 137, 138.
8. Camnitzer, 1994: 129.
9. Szulc, 1986: 463.
10. Anderson, 1997: 376.
11. Szulc, 1986: 568.
12. Ibid.: see pages 471-478.
13. Sartre, 1961: 125, 134.
14. MacGaffey and Barnett, 1965: 325.
15. Huberman and Sweezy, 1960: 118.
16. Smith, 1996: 8.
17. Olson and Olson, 1995: 53. See also, Gimbel, 1998: 51–80.
18. Ibid., 1995: 55.
19. Frei Betto, 1990: 146-147.
20. Ibid.: 147.
21. MacGaffey and Barnett, 1965: 346.
22. *National Catholic Reporter,* July 4, 1997.
23. Ibid.
24. Guillermoprieto, 1998a: 24.
25. Pollis, 1981: 1014.
26. *Constitution of the Republic of Cuba,* 1976: Article 54.
27. Ruffin, 1982: 124.
28. Frei Betto, 1990: 173.
29. *CIA Targets Fidel,* 1996; Ratner and Smith, 1997. See, too, *Possible Actions to Provoke, Harass or Disrupt Cuba,* 1997.
30. Frei Betto, 1990: 173.
31. See the Vatican's apology, its "act of repentance," for its behavior during the period in *We Remember: A Reflection on the Shoah,* March 16, 1998.
32. Gunn, 1993: 28.
33. *Cuba Update,* October 1995: 8.
34. *National Catholic Reporter,* July 4, 1997.
35. See the *National Catholic Reporter,* March 7, 1997: 10.
36. Ibid.
37. Ibid.
38. *New York Times,* March 20, 1998: A8.
39. *Granma,* November 13, 1996: 3.
40. Lowinger, 1997: 42, 47.
41. Guillermoprieto, 1998a: 20.
42. Lowinger, 1997: 42.
43. Margolis, 1996: 1.
44. "This Year in Havana," 1997: 12.
45. Schwab, 1997c.

46. Margolis, 1994: 3.
47. "This Year in Havana," 1997: 12.
48. Margolis, 1994: 3.
49. Davidson, 1961: 46.
50. Simons, 1996: 101. Also see Klein, 1986: 100-102.
51. Frei Betto, 1990: 149.
52. MacGaffey and Barnett, 1965: 246.
53. *National Catholic Reporter,* July 4, 1997.
54. Frei Betto, 1990: 151.
55. *New York Times,* January 29, 1998: A8.
56. U.S.–Cuba Trade and Economic Council, 1998.
57. Castro, 1998.
58. *New York Times,* January 22, 1998: A14.
59. Ibid.
60. John Paul II, 1998.
61. Ibid.
62. *New York Times,* January 22, 1998: A14.
63. *New York Times,* January 26, 1998: A1.
64. *New York Times,* January 25, 1998: A1.
65. *New York Times,* January 26, 1998: A1.
66. Albacete, 1998: 41.
67. Ibid.: 37.
68. Ibid.
69. *New York Times,* February 13, 1998: A9.
70. *New York Times,* March 20, 1998: A1, A8.

SIX

1. *New York Times,* May 5, 1998: A1, A10.
2. *New York Times,* September 5, 1997: A14.
3. *New York Times,* September 12, 1997: A6. Apparently Castro was correct. The Cuban exile, and self-proclaimed terrorist, Luis Posada Carriles, told The *New York Times,* July 12, 1998: 1, 10, 11, that he organized the wave of bombings with money partially supplied by Jorge Mas Canosa, then the head of CANF. He and CANF later denied the accuracy of the report.
4. See Assistant Secretary of State Roy R. Rubottom Jr.'s note of June 27, 1960, in *Foreign Relations of the United States 1958-1960: Cuba,* 1991: 955-956.
5. Olson and Olson, 1995: 57.
6. Human Rights Watch, 1994b: 9.
7. Human Rights Watch, 1995: 10.
8. *New York Times,* March 7, 1996: A5. The United States has often looked the other way when it comes to militaristic attacks in Cuba by Miami-based Cuban exiles. See *New York Times,* July 12, 1998: 1, 10, 11.

9. Alarcón, 1996: 14.
10. *Constitution of the Republic of Cuba,* 1976: Article 52.
11. *Constitution of the Republic of Cuba,* 1976: Article 12. See *New York Times,* July 13, 1998: A1, A6, A7.
12. Human Rights Watch, 1995: 8. The United States too has periodically restricted the political rights of its citizens. For example, in 1919, in *Schenck v. United States,* speech that presents a "clear and present danger" to the community or the nation was denied constitutional protection by the Supreme Court; the Smith Act of 1940, which was enforced particularly during the McCarthy era in the 1950s, made it a felony to teach or advocate the overthrow of the U.S. government. The act was only repealed in 1977.
13. *For a Free and Democratic Cuba,* n.d.: preface.
14. *For a Free and Democratic Cuba,* n.d.: 3.
15. *New York Times,* May 8, 1995: A12. On Posada Carriles, see *New York Times,* July 12, 1998: 1, 10, 11. Mas Canosa's son, Jorge Mas Santos, charged that The *New York Times* article linking his father to assassination attempts against Castro was "slanderous" and misrepresented Posada Carriles. The newspaper maintained the article was accurate. See also *New York Times,* August 4, 1998: A7.
16. *New York Times,* May 8, 1995: A12.
17. Ibid.
18. Ibid. For a discussion of the Miami/Washington connection that makes use of the terminology of political science see LeoGrande, 1998.
19. *New York Times,* May 8, 1995: A12.
20. *For a Free and Democratic Cuba,* n.d.: 16.
21. Olson and Olson, 1995: 93.
22. Ibid.: 94.
23. See *New York Times,* March 7, 1996: A5; Alarcón, 1996; LeoGrande, 1998; Mead, 1996.
24. Alarcón, 1996: 20.
25. *The NewsHour with Jim Lehrer* (television program): March 20, 1998.
26. *Concilio Cubano,* 1995.
27. Human Rights Watch, 1994b: 2.
28. Ibid.: 6.
29. Ibid.: 7.
30. Comment included in a letter sent to Attorney General Janet Reno, April 26, 1994; it is cited in Ibid.: 8.
31. Personal communication from the Office of Cultural Affairs, Consulate General of France, Miami, June 1996.
32. Cuban American National Foundation, 1996: 15, 10. In truth, there is often little tolerance in Miami; see *New York Times,* July 12, 1998: 1, 10, 11.
33. *New York Times,* April 20, 1998: E3.
34. See De Gámez, 1971.

35. *Naive Art from Cuba*, 1997.
36. Mead, 1998: 45. See Guillermoprieto, 1998b for more on Sánchez Santa Cruz.
37. *Constitution of the Republic of Cuba*, 1976: Articles 125, 126. See also *Human Rights Watch/Americas: Cuba*, October 1994: 13-18.
38. Human Rights Watch, 1995: 25.
39. *New York Times*, May 2, 1998: Editorial. See too *Wall Street Journal*, January 20, 1998: A12, A14.
40. *Universal Declaration of Human Rights*, 1948: Articles 9, 13.
41. *New York Times*, December 28, 1997: obituary.
42. See Human Rights Watch, 1995: 13, and *New York Times*, December 28, 1997: obituary.
43. *New York Times*, April 7, 1998: A11.
44. Human Rights Watch, 1995: 19.
45. Human Rights Watch, 1994a: 14.
46. As cited in Human Rights Watch, 1995: 11.
47. *Constitution of the Republic of Cuba*, 1976: Article 53.
48. Smith, 1987: 195.
49. *Constitution of the Republic of Cuba*, 1976: Article 38d.
50. Camnitzer, 1994: 130.
51. Miller, 1998: 29.
52. Camnitzer, 1994: 133, 258.
53. Miller, 1998: 29.
54. Camnitzer, 1994: 120.
55. De Gámez, 1971: 187.
56. Miller, 1996: 286.
57. Miller, in his book *Trading with the Enemy*, 1996, discusses baseball extensively, using it as a metaphor for viewing Cuban society.
58. *New York Times*, January 2, 1998: A3.
59. *Constitution of the Republic of Cuba*, 1976: Article 38b, 38ch.
60. Ibid.: Article 6.
61. As cited in Rudolph, 1987: 88.
62. Nichols, 1982: 91.
63. Ibid.: 71.
64. See Chapter 7.
65. Smith, 1987: 195.
66. Ibid.: 196.

SEVEN

1. Hofstadter, 1965.
2. Ibid.: 39.
3. *Foreign Relations of the United States 1958-1960: Cuba*, 1991: 483.
4. Ibid.: 490.

5. Lage, 1996: 3.
6. *Foreign Relations of the United States 1958-1960: Cuba,* 1991: 955. See *New York Times,* July 13, 1998: A1, A6, A7, for details on the CIA's long war against Castro.
7. *Foreign Relations of the United States 1958-1960: Cuba,* 1991: 955.
8. Ibid.: 1183. Dispatch from the U.S. Embassy in Cuba to the Department of State, December 16, 1960.
9. Domínguez, 1989: 232-233.
10. See Guevara, 1968, regarding events in Bolivia.
11. *Public Papers of the Presidents of the United States, John F. Kennedy 1961,* 1962: 74.
12. White House statement, February 3, 1962. *Public Papers of the Presidents of the United States, John F. Kennedy 1962,* 1963: 106.
13. Domínguez, 1989: 233.
14. Farber, 1995: 15.
15. Ibid.
16. Mead, 1998: 48.
17. Human Rights Watch, 1995: 2.
18. Farber, 1995: 15.
19. Szulc, 1986: 486-487.
20. Ibid.: 509.
21. Comment made in April 1998. See Fried and Sanders, 1992; Fried, 1997.
22. Oppenheimer, 1993.
23. Quirk, 1993: 814.
24. Cuban American National Foundation, 1996: 17.
25. Mead, 1996: 9-10. Human Rights Watch, 1994b: 8-9. Also see Alarcón, 1996.
26. Mead, 1998: 49.
27. *Constitution of the Republic of Cuba,* 1976: Articles 67 and 68.
28. Mead, 1998: 46.
29. *Constitution of the Republic of Cuba,* 1976: Article 87.
30. Lage, 1996: 10-12.
31. Lage, 1993.
32. *New York Times,* October 12, 1997: 5.
33. Mead, 1998: 49.
34. See Oppenheimer, 1993, for a full and very critical accounting of the sordid affair.
35. *New York Times,* October 12, 1997: 5.
36. Anderson, 1997: 471.
37. Szulc, 1986: 359. Note also Suchlicki, 1997: 234-248.
38. Valdés Vivó, 1978: 114.
39. *New York Times,* February 1, 1998: 3.
40. Espín, 1991: 4-5.
41. Ibid.: 77.
42. *Constitution of the Republic of Cuba,* 1976: Article 92.

43. Ibid.: Article 5.
44. Alarcón, 1997a: 11.
45. Kissinger, 1979: 642.
46. Nixon, 1990: 328.
47. Association of the Bar of the City of New York, 1996.
48. Cohn and Berlin, 1997: S2.
49. *New York Times*, August 27, 1995: A1.
50. Mead, 1998: 49.
51. "A Survey of Cuba," 1996: 12. See Miller and Henthorne, 1997.
52. Sartre, 1961: 159.

BIBLIOGRAPHY

"A Country Frozen in Time." 1995. *Gannett Suburban Newspapers* (May 5): 3B.

"A Survey of Cuba." 1996. *Economist* (April 6): 4-16.

Alarcón, Ricardo. 1996. *Cuba is in a position to demonstrate that the United States is deliberately lying*. Press conference at the meeting of the International Civil Aviation Organization (ICAO). Havana: International Press Center, June 24.

———. 1997a. "Cuba to Return to Batista Days?" *The Human Quest* (May-June): 11.

———. 1997b. Speech delivered to the General Assembly at the fifty-second session of the United Nations. New York: November 5 Press release, Permanent Mission of Cuba to the United Nations.

Albacete, Lorenzo. 1998. "The Poet and the Revolutionary." *New Yorker* (January 26): 36-41.

Ambrose, Stephen E. 1971. *Rise to Globalism: American Foreign Policy Since 1938*. Baltimore: Penguin Books.

Amnesty International. 1984. *Torture in the Eighties*. London: Amnesty International Publications.

Anderson, John Lee. 1997. *Che Guevara: A Revolutionary Life*. New York: Grove Press.

———. 1998. "Havana Journal, The Plague Years." *New Yorker* (January 26): 62-68.

Arat, Zehra F. 1991. *Democracy and Human Rights in Developing Countries*. Boulder: Lynne Rienner Publishers.

Aron, Raymond. 1974. *The Imperial Republic*. Englewood Cliffs: Prentice-Hall Publishers.

Association of the Bar of the City of New York. 1996. Report of the Inter-American Affairs Committee: Legal Validity of the Trade Embargo Against Cuba. New York, March 7.

Avances Medicos De Cuba. 1997. Vol. IV, No. 9.

Barnet, Miguel. 1996. *Biografía de un Cimarron*. Havana: Editorial Academia.

Behar, Ruth. ed. 1996. *Bridges to Cuba / Puentes a Cuba*. Ann Arbor: University of Michigan Press.

Beschloss, Michael. 1997. *Taking Charge: The Johnson White House Tapes 1963-1964*. New York: Simon & Schuster.

Boodhoo, Ken I. 1986. "Violence and Militarization in the Eastern Caribbean: The Case of Grenada." In *Militarization in the Non-Hispanic Caribbean,* pp. 65-89. Edited by Alma H. Young and Dion E. Phillips. Boulder: Lynne Rienner Publishers.

Bulletin of Eastern Caribbean Affairs—Special Issue. 1986. Kingston, Jamaica (January/February).

Castro, Fidel. 1972. "History Will Absolve Me." In *Selected Works of Fidel Castro,* Vol. I pp. 164-221, speech of October 16, 1953. Edited and with an introduction by Rolando E. Bonachea and Nelson P. Valdes. Cambridge: MIT Press.

———. 1998. Speech welcoming Pope John Paul II to Havana, Cuba. Havana, January 21. Press release, Permanent Mission of Cuba to the United Nations.

Camnitzer, Luis. 1994. *New Art of Cuba.* Austin: University of Texas Press. 1994.

Charter of the United Nations. 1945. United Nations, New York: June 26.

Chomsky, Avi and Alfredo Prieto. 1995. "Cuba: The Other Side of the Looking Glass." *Cuba Update* (October): 28-35.

CIA Targets Fidel: Secret 1967 CIA Inspector General's Report on Plots to Assassinate Fidel Castro. 1996. Melbourne: Ocean Press.

CIA World Fact Book. 1996. www.odci.gov/cia/publications/nsolo/factbook/cv.htm.

Cohn, Evelyn F. and Alan D. Berlin. 1997. "European Community Reacts to Helms-Burton." *New York Law Journal* (August 4): S2, S10.

Concilio Cubano. 1995. Official statement. Havana. October 10.

Constitution of the Republic of Cuba. 1976. Havana.

Correo de Cuba. n.d. Vol. I, No. 2.

Cracknell, Basil E. 1973. *Dominica.* Harrisburg: Stackpole Books.

Cuba Economic Report, Summary. 1996. Havana: Ministry of Economy and Planning.

Cuba News. 1998. Miami: Miami Herald Publishing Co., March.

Cuba Update. 1995. (October).

———. 1996. (September).

———. 1997. (Winter).

Cuban American National Foundation. 1996. "The Cuba Paper Series." Paper #14. *Debate Between Jorge Mas Canosa and Ricardo Alarcón.* Miami. September 5.

Cuban Ministry of Public Health. 1996. *Cuba AIDS Statistics.* Havana.

Cuban National Budget. 1996. Havana: Ministry of Finance and Prices.

Dale, Ralph Alan. 1997. "Integrating Natural and Traditional Medicine with Conventional Medicine in Cuba." *Cuba Update* (Winter): 22-26.

Davidson, Basil. 1961. *The African Slave Trade.* Boston: Little Brown & Co.

De Gámez, Tana. 1971. *Alicia Alonso at Home and Abroad.* New York: Citadel Press.

DeMar, Margaretta. 1995. "The Changing Political Economy of the Caribbean." In *The Changing Political Economy of the Third World*, pp. 45-83. Edited by Manochehr Dorraj. Boulder: Lynne Rienner Publishers.

Didion, Joan. 1983. *Salvador.* New York: Washington Square Press.

Disarm Education Fund Cuban Medical Project. 1997 Newsletter. New York.

Domínguez, Jorge I. 1979. "Assessing Human Rights Conditions." In *Enhancing Global Human Rights*, pp.19-116. Edited by Jorge I. Domínguez, Nigel S. Rodley, Bryce Wood, and Richard Falk. New York: McGraw-Hill Book Co.

———. 1982. "Revolutionary Politics: The New Demands for Orderliness." In *Cuba: Internal and International Affairs*, pp.19-70. Edited by Jorge I. Domínguez. Beverly Hills: Sage Publications.

———. 1989. *To Make a World Safe for Revolution: Cuba's Foreign Policy.* Cambridge: Harvard University Press.

Domínguez, Virginia R. and Jorge I. Domínguez. 1981. *The Caribbean: Its Implications for the United States.* New York: The Foreign Policy Association, February.

"Dominica: Seeking Prosperity Through Self-Reliance. An interview with Prime Minister Charles." 1986. *Courier* (November/December): 54-57.

Economic Survey of Latin America and the Caribbean 1983. 1985. Vol. II. Santiago, Chile: United Nations Economic Commission for Latin America and the Caribbean.

Economic Survey of Latin America and the Caribbean 1996-1997. 1997. Santiago, Chile: United Nations Economic Commission for Latin America and the Caribbean.

Eisenberg, Leon. 1997. "The Sleep of Reason Produces Monsters—Human Costs of Economic Sanctions." *New England Journal of Medicine* Vol. 336, No. 17 (April 24).

Eisenhower, Dwight D. 1965. *Waging Peace: 1956-1961.* Garden City: Doubleday & Co.

Erisman, H. Michael, ed. 1984. *The Caribbean Challenge: U.S. Policy in a Volatile Area.* Boulder: Westview Press.

———. 1985. *Cuba's International Relations.* Boulder: Westview Press.

———. 1998. "Cuba and the Caribbean Basin: From Pariah to Partner. Review Essay." *Journal of Interamerican Studies and World Affairs* Vol. 40, No. 1 (Spring): 87-94.

Espín, Vilma. 1991. *Cuban Women Confront the Future.* Melbourne: Ocean Press.

Fagg, John Edwin. 1965. *Cuba, Haiti, and the Dominican Republic.* Englewood Cliffs: Prentice- Hall Publishers.

Falk, Pamela S. 1986. *Cuban Foreign Policy.* Lexington: D. C. Heath and Co.

———. 1995. "Cuban Growth: The Sound of One Hand Clapping." *Wall Street Journal* (July 7) : A11.

Farber, Sam. 1995. "U.S. Policy and the Prospects for Cuban Democracy." *Peace & Democracy* (Spring): 14-16.

"Federalist No. 10." 1961. In *The Federalist Papers*, pp. 16-23. Edited by Roy P. Fairfield. Garden City: Anchor Books.

Feinberg, Richard E. 1981. "Central America: No Easy Answers." *Foreign Affairs* Vol. 59, No. 1.

Feinsilver, Julie M. 1995. "Cuban Biotechnology: The Strategic Success and Commercial Limits of a First World Approach to Development." In *Biotechnology in Latin America*. Edited by N. Patrick Peritore and Anna Galve-Peritore. Wilmington, Delaware: Scholarly Resources, Inc.

"Fidel Castro Attacks 'Track Two' Policy on July 26." 1995. *Cuba Update* (October): 8.

"Fidel Castro Gives Dynamite Six-Minute Speech in Turkey." 1996. *Cuba Update* (September): 17.

For a Free and Democratic Cuba: A Statement of Principles and Objectives. n.d. Miami: The Cuban American National Foundation.

Foreign Relations of the United States 1958-1960: Cuba. 1991. Vol. VI. Washington, D.C.: Department of State.

Frank, Michele and Gail Reed. 1997. *Denial of Food and Medicine: The Impact of the U.S. Embargo on Health & Nutrition in Cuba*. Washington, D.C.: American Association for World Health, March.

Franqui, Carlos. 1980. *Diary of the Cuban Revolution*. New York: Viking Press.

Frei Betto. 1990. *Fidel and Religion*. Melbourne: Ocean Press.

Fried, Albert., ed. 1997. *Communism in America*. New York: Columbia University Press.

———, and Ronald Sanders, eds. 1992. *Socialist Thought*. New York: Columbia University Press.

Furiati, Claudia. 1994. *ZR Rifle: The Plot to Kill Kennedy and Castro*. Melbourne: Ocean Press.

Garfield, Richard and Sarah Santana. 1997. "The Impact of the Economic Crisis and the U.S. Embargo on Health in Cuba." *American Journal of Public Health* (January).

Gellman, Irwin F. 1973. *Roosevelt and Batista: Good Neighbor Diplomacy in Cuba 1933-1945*. Albuquerque: University of New Mexico Press.

Gimbel, Wendy. 1998. *Havana Dreams: A Story of Cuba*. New York: Alfred A. Knopf.

Glissant, Edouard. 1985. *The Ripening*. Translated by Michael Dash. Kingston, Jamaica: Heinemann Educational Books, Ltd.

Gonzalez, Edward. 1982. "U.S. Policy: Objectives and Options." In *Cuba: Internal and International Affairs*, pp.193-221. Edited by Jorge I. Domínguez. Beverly Hills: Sage Publications.

Goodrich, Leland M. 1964. *The United Nations*. New York: Thomas Y. Crowell Co.

Greene, J. Edward. 1984. "The Ideological and Idiosyncratic Aspects of U.S.-Caribbean Relations." In *The Caribbean Challenge: U.S. Policy in a Volatile Region*, pp.33-47. Edited by H. Michael Erisman. Boulder: Westview Press.

Guevara, Che. 1968. *The Diary of Che Guevara*. New York: Bantam Books.

Guillermoprieto, Alma. 1998a. "A Visit to Havana." *New York Review of Books* (March 26): 19- 24.

———. 1998b. "Love and Misery in Cuba." *New York Review of Books* (June 11): 10-14.

Gunn, Gillian. 1993. *Cuba in Transition: Options for U.S. Policy.* New York: Twentieth Century Fund Press.

Halberstam, David. 1973. *The Best and the Brightest.* Greenwich: Fawcett Publications.

Halliday, Fred. 1983. "Cold War in the Caribbean." *New Left Review* No. 141 (September- October): 5-22.

Hearings and Markup Before the Subcommittee on Western Hemisphere Affairs of the Committee on Foreign Affairs. 1983. U.S. House of Representatives, 98th Congress, 1st Session, Part 7: Foreign Assistance Legislation for FY 1984-85. (March 1, 16, April 12, 13).

Hearings Before a Subcommittee of the Committee on Appropriations. 1985. U.S. House of Representatives, 99th Congress, 1st Session, Part 6 (March 28).

Hofstadter, Richard. 1965. *The Paranoid Style in American Politics and Other Essays.* New York: Alfred A. Knopf.

Huberman, Leo and Paul M. Sweezy. 1960. *Cuba: Anatomy of a Revolution.* New York: Monthly Review Press.

Hufbauer, Gary Clyde, Jeffrey J. Schott, and Kimberly Ann Elliott. 1990a. *Economic Sanctions Reconsidered: History and Current Policy.* Washington, D.C.: Institute for International Economics.

———. 1990b. *Economic Sanctions Reconsidered: Supplemental Case Histories.* Washington, D.C.: Institute for International Economics.

Human Rights Watch. 1994a. *Human Rights Watch/Americas: Cuba—Repression, the Exodus of August 1994, and The U.S. Response.* Vol. 6, No. 12 (October).

———. 1994b. *Human Rights Watch/Americas: United States, Dangerous Dialogue Revisited.* Vol. 6, No. 14 (November).

———. 1995. *Human Rights Watch/Americas: Cuba, Improvements Without Reform.* Vol. 7, No. 10 (October).

International Covenant on Economic, Social and Cultural Rights. 1976. United Nations, New York, January 3.

Iyer, Pico. 1996. *Cuba and the Night.* New York: Vintage Books.

John Paul II. 1998. Speech at José Martí International Airport. Havana, January 21.

Kennedy, John F. 1961. *The Strategy of Peace.* New York: Popular Library.

Kincaid, Jamaica. 1988. *A Small Place.* New York: Farrar Strauss Giroux.

Kissinger, Henry. 1979. *White House Years*. Boston: Little Brown & Co.

Klein, Herbert S. 1986. *African Slavery in Latin America and the Caribbean*. New York: Oxford University Press.

Koont, Sinan. 1994. "Cuba: An Island Against All Odds." *Monthly Review* Vol. 46, No. 5 (October): 1-18.

Korn, David A. 1986. *Ethiopia, the United States and the Soviet Union*. Carbondale: Southern Illinois University Press.

Krinsky, Michael and David Golove, eds. 1993. *United States Economic Measures Against Cuba: Proceedings in the United Nations and International Law Issues*. Northampton, Massachusetts: Aletheia Press.

Lage, Carlos. 1993. *Estrategia De La Economía Cubana*. Havana: Editora Politica.

———. 1996. Speech delivered to the General Assembly at the fifty-first session of the United Nations. Permanent Mission of Cuba to the United Nations (November 12): 1-21.

Lazreg, Marnia. 1979. "Human Rights, State and Ideology: An Historical Perspective." In *Human Rights: Cultural and Ideological Perspectives*, pp. 32-43. Edited by Adamantia Pollis and Peter Schwab. New York: Praeger Publishers.

LeoGrande, William M. 1981. "Republic of Cuba." In *Marxist Governments: A World Survey*. Volume 2, pp. 237-260. Edited by Bogdan Szajkowski. New York: St. Martin's Press.

———. 1982. "Foreign Policy: The Limits of Success." In *Cuba: Internal and International Affairs*, pp. 167-192. Edited by Jorge I. Domínguez. Beverly Hills: Sage Publications.

———. 1998. "From Havana to Miami: U.S. Cuba Policy as a Two-Level Game." *Journal of Interamerican Studies and World Affairs* Vol. 40, No. 1 (Spring): 67-86.

León Cotayo, Nicanor. 1991. *Sitiada La Esperanza*. Havana: Editorial Cultura Popular.

Lernoux, Penny. 1991. *Cry of the People: The Struggle for Human Rights in Latin America—The Catholic Church in Conflict with U.S. Policy*. New York: Penguin Books.

Lieuwen, Edwin. 1961. *Arms and Politics in Latin America*. New York: Frederick A. Praeger.

Lipset, Seymour Martin and Aldo Solari, eds. 1967. *Elites in Latin America*. New York: Oxford University Press.

Lowinger, Rosa. 1997. "Old Havana Reborn." *Preservation* (September/October): 41-50.

MacGaffey, Wyatt and Clifford R. Barnett. 1965. *Twentieth Century Cuba*. Garden City: Anchor Books.

Mapping Progress—Cuba. 1998. New York: Women's Environment and Development Organization. March.

Margolis, Paul C. 1994. "Tropical Growth." *Jewish Standard* (December 16): 3, 28.

———. 1996. "Flame of Jewish Life Burns Again in Eastern Cuba." *Jewish Review* (November 15):1, 18.

Martí, José. 1977. *Our America: Writings on Latin America and the Struggle for Cuban Independence.* Edited, with an introduction and notes, by Philip S. Foner. New York: Monthly Review Press.

Matthews, Herbert L. 1970. *Fidel Castro.* New York: Simon & Schuster.

McNamara, Robert S. 1995. *In Retrospect: The Tragedy and Lessons of Vietnam.* New York: Times Books.

Mead, Walter Russell. 1996. "Mutually Assured Stupidity." *New Yorker* (March 11): 9-10.

———. 1998. "Castro's Successor?" *New Yorker* (January 26): 42-49.

Mesa-Lago, Carmelo, ed. 1993. *Cuba After the Cold War.* Pittsburgh: University of Pittsburgh Press.

Miller, Jennifer E. 1998. "A Painter of Cuba." *In These Times* (April 19): 29-30.

Miller, Mark M. and Tony L. Henthorne. 1997. *Investment in the New Cuban Tourist Industry.* Westport: Quorum Books.

Miller, Tom. 1996. *Trading with the Enemy: A Yankee Travels Through Castro's Cuba.* New York: Basic Books.

Mills, C. Wright. 1960. *Listen, Yankee.* New York: Ballantine Books.

Mintz, Sidney W. and Sally Price, eds. 1985. *Caribbean Contours.* Baltimore: Johns Hopkins University Press.

Murray, Mary. 1993. *Cruel & Unusual Punishment: The U.S. Blockade Against Cuba.* Melbourne: Ocean Press.

NACLA, Report on the Americas. 1985. "Mare Nostrum, U.S. Security Policy in the English- Speaking Caribbean." (July/August): 13-48.

Naipaul, V.S., 1974. *The Middle Passage: Impressions of Five Societies—British, French and Dutch—in the West Indies and South America.* London: Andre Deutsch Ltd.

Naive Art from Cuba. 1997. New York: Center for Cuban Studies.

Nash, J. Madeleine. 1996. "Made in Cuba." *Cuba Update* (September): 20-22.

NewsHour with Jim Lehrer, The. 1998. (Television program) March 20.

Nichols, John Spicer. 1982. "The Mass Media: Their Functions in Social Conflict." In *Cuba: Internal and International Affairs,* pp. 71-111. Edited by Jorge I. Domínguez. Beverly Hills: Sage Publications.

Nixon, Richard. 1990. *In the Arena.* New York: Simon & Schuster.

Olson, James S. and Judith E. Olson. 1995. *Cuban Americans.* New York: Twayne Publishers.

"One Thing Cuba Does Right." 1996. *Economist* (September 7): 42.

Oppenheimer, Andres. 1993. *Castro's Final Hour.* New York: Simon & Schuster.

Parsa, T. Z., 1997. "Club Red." *New York* (November 17): 36-43.

Paterson, Thomas G., 1994. *Contesting Castro.* New York: Oxford University Press.

Pattullo, Polly. 1996. *Last Resorts.* London: Cassell.

Peréz-Stable, Marifeli. 1993. *The Cuban Revolution.* New York: Oxford University Press.

Peritore, N. Patrick and Anna Galve-Peritore. 1995. *Biotechnology in Latin America.* Wilmington: Scholarly Resources, Inc.

Permanent Mission of Cuba to the United Nations. 1997. *The U.S. Embargo Is a Deliberate Crime Against the Cuban People's Health.* Press release August 9.

Phillips, Dion E. 1986. "The Increasing Emphasis on Security and Defense in the Eastern Caribbean." In *Militarization in the Non-Hispanic Caribbean,* pp. 42-64. Edited by Alma H. Young and Dion E. Phillips. Boulder: Lynne Rienner Publishers.

Pollis, Adamantia. 1981. "Human Rights, Third World Socialism and Cuba." *World Development* Vol. 9, No. 9/10: 1005-1017.

———. 1982. "Liberal, Socialist, and Third World Perspectives of Human Rights." In *Toward a Human Rights Framework,* pp.1-26. Edited by Peter Schwab and Adamantia Pollis. New York: Praeger Special Studies.

———. 1996. "Cultural Relativism Revisited: Through a State Prism." *Human Rights Quarterly* Vol. 18, No. 2 (May): 315-344.

———. 1998. "Towards a New Universalism: Reconstruction and Dialogue." *Netherlands Quarterly of Human Rights* Vol. 16, No. 1 (March): 5-23.

———, and Peter Schwab, eds. 1979a. *Human Rights: Cultural and Ideological Perspectives.* New York: Praeger Publishers.

———, and Peter Schwab. 1979b. "Human Rights: A Western Construct with Limited Applicability." In *Human Rights: Cultural and Ideological Perspectives,* pp. 1-18. Edited by Adamantia Pollis and Peter Schwab. New York: Praeger Publishers.

Possible Actions to Provoke, Harass or Disrupt Cuba. 1997. Washington, D.C.: Assassination Records Review Board.

Prada, Pedro. 1995. *Island Under Siege: The U.S. Blockade of Cuba.* Melbourne: Ocean Press.

Public Papers of the Presidents of the United States, John F. Kennedy 1961. 1962. Washington, D.C.: United States Government Printing Office.

Public Papers of the Presidents of the United States, John F. Kennedy 1962. 1963. Washington, D.C.: United States Government Printing Office.

Quirk, Robert E. 1993. *Fidel Castro.* New York: W. W. Norton & Co.

Ratner, Michael and Steven M. Smith. 1997. *Che Guevara and the FBI.* Melbourne: Ocean Press.

Reaffirmation of Cuban Dignity and Sovereignty Act. 1996. Havana: National Assembly of People's Power, December 24.

Remirez de Estenoz, Fernando. 1998. *The Future of Cuba: A View from the Inside.* A presentation and discussion at the World Policy Institute—Cuba Education Project, New School for Social Research. New York, April 30.

Richardson, Bonham C. 1983. *Caribbean Migrants: Environment and Human Survival on St. Kitts and Nevis.* Knoxville: University of Tennessee Press.

Robaina, Roberto. 1998. Speech delivered before the United Nations Human Rights Commission. Geneva, March 20. Typescript by the Permanent Mission of Cuba to the United Nations.

Rosset, Peter and Medea Benjamin. 1994. *The Greening of the Revolution: Cuba's Experiment with Organic Agriculture*. Melbourne: Ocean Press.

Rudolph, James D., ed. 1987. *Cuba: A Country Study*. Washington, D.C.: The Department of the Army. Prepared by Foreign Area Studies, The American University.

Ruffin, Patricia. 1982. "Socialist Development and Human Rights in Cuba." In *Toward a Human Rights Framework*, pp. 115-132. Edited by Peter Schwab and Adamantia Pollis. New York: Praeger Special Studies.

Sartre, Jean-Paul. 1961. *Sartre on Cuba*. New York: Ballantine Books.

Scali, John. 1976. "A New Approach to Human Rights and the United Nations." Address at the Shoreham-Americana Hotel, Washington, D.C., delivered March 6. In *Case Studies on Human Rights and Fundamental Freedoms*, pp. 565-571. The Hague: Martinus Nijhoff.

Schlesinger Jr., Arthur M. 1965. *A Thousand Days: John F. Kennedy in the White House*. Boston: Houghton Mifflin Company.

Schwab, Peter. 1985. *Ethiopia: Politics, Economics and Society*. Boulder: Lynne Rienner Publishers.

———. 1995a. "The Embargo: Scrap It." *Miami Herald* (November 28): 17A.

———. 1995b. "Time to Terminate U.S. Embargo On Cuba." *Gannett Suburban Newspapers* (August 23): editorial page.

———. 1997a. "Life is Improving." *Miami Herald* (May 2): 21A.

———. 1997b. "Cuban Health Care and the U.S. Embargo." *Monthly Review* Vol. 49, No. 6 (November): 15-26.

———. 1997c. "*Shabbat* in Havana." *Jewish Currents* (February): 20-21, 34-35.

———, and Adamantia Pollis, eds. 1982. *Toward a Human Rights Framework*. New York: Praeger Special Studies.

Schwelb, Egon. 1964. *Human Rights and the International Community*. Chicago: Quadrangle Books.

Scrinis, Gyorgy. 1995. *Colonizing the Seed: Genetic Engineering and Techno-Industrial Agriculture*. Melbourne: Friends of the Earth.

Segal, Lore. 1964. "Other People's Houses: Sosua." *New Yorker* (March 21): 36-63.

Segre, Roberto, Mario Coyula, and Joseph L. Scarpaci. 1997. *Havana: Two Faces of the Antillean Metropolis*. New York: John Wiley and Sons.

Sembene, Ousmane. 1970. *God's Bits of Wood*. Garden City: Doubleday & Co.

"Should We Change Our Policy Toward Cuba?" 1995. *Critical Issues* (television program) (November 1).

Simons, Geoff. 1996. *Cuba: From Conquistador to Castro*. New York: St. Martin's Press.

Smaldone, William. 1996. "Observations on the Cuban Revolution." *Monthly Review* Vol. 47, No. 11 (April): 20-32.

Smith, Earl E. T. 1962. *The Fourth Floor: An Account of the Castro Communist Revolution.* New York: Random House.

Smith, Robert C. 1996. "Cuba 25." *National Conference of Black Political Scientists Newsletter* (Fall): 8-9.

Smith, Wayne S. 1987. *The Closest of Enemies: A Personal and Diplomatic Account of U.S.- Cuban Relations Since 1957.* New York: W. W. Norton & Co.

———. 1996. "Cuba's Long Reform." *Cuba Update* (September): 14.

Steel, Ronald. 1998. "Lonely At The Top." *New York Times* (March 1): (4)15.

Suchlicki, Jaime. 1997. *Cuba: From Columbus to Castro and Beyond.* London: Brassey's Inc.

Sweig, Julia and Kai Bird, eds. 1997. *Denial of Food and Medicine: The Impact of the U.S. Embargo on Health & Nutrition in Cuba.* Executive Summary. Washington, D.C.: American Association for World Health, March.

Szajkowski, Bogdan, ed. 1981. *Marxist Governments: A World Survey.* Vol. 2. New York: St. Martin's Press. .

Szulc, Tad. 1986. *Fidel: A Critical Portrait.* New York: William Morrow and Company, Inc.

Taft, John. 1989. *American Power.* New York: Harper and Row Publishers.

"This Year in Havana." 1997. *Jewish Week* (May 2): 1, 12.

Traub, James. 1998. "Kofi Annan's Next Test." *New York Times Magazine* (March 29).

Trefousse, H. L., ed. 1965. *The Cold War: A Book of Documents.* New York: Capricorn Books.

United Nations Monthly Bulletin of Statistics. 1997. United Nations, New York: United Nations Department for Economic and Social Information and Policy Analysis, Statistics Department, Vol. LI, No. 10, October.

United Nations Statistical Yearbook 1993. 1995. United Nations, New York.

United Nations Statistical Yearbook 1994. 1996. United Nations, New York.

United Nations Statistical Yearbook for Latin America and the Caribbean 1996. 1997. Santiago, Chile: United Nations Economic Commission for Latin America and the Caribbean, February.

United Nations World Statistics Pocketbook. 1997. United Nations, New York.

Universal Declaration of Human Rights. 1948. United Nations, New York, December 10.

U.S.-Cuba Trade and Economic Council. 1998. New York.

Valdés Vivó, Raúl. 1978. *Ethiopia's Revolution.* New York: International Publishers.

Vallier, Ivan. 1967. "Religious Elites: Differentiations and Developments in Roman Catholicism." In *Elites in Latin America,* pp. 190-232. Edited by Seymour Martin Lipset and Aldo Solari. New York: Oxford University Press.

Vance, Cyrus. 1983. *Hard Choices.* New York: Simon and Schuster.

Walker Evans: Havana 1933. 1989. New York: Pantheon Books.

Wallop, Malcolm. 1997. "Target Castro, Not Cuba's People." *Wall Street Journal* (April 24): editorial page.

Watson, Hilbourne A. 1986. "Imperialism, National Security, and State Power in the Commonwealth Caribbean: Issues in the Development of the Authoritarian State." In *Militarization in the Non-Hispanic Caribbean,* pp.17-41. Edited by Alma H. Young and Dion E. Phillips. Boulder: Lynne Rienner Publishers.

We Remember: A Reflection on the Shoah. 1998. Vatican City.

What You Need to Know About the U.S. Embargo: An Overview of the Cuban Assets Control Regulations. 1996. Title 31, Part 515 of the U.S. Code of Federal Regulations.

Wischnitzer, Mark. 1942. "The Historical Background of the Settlement of Jewish Refugees in Santo Domingo." *Jewish Social Studies* Vol. IV, No. 1 (January): 45-58.

World Bank. 1983. "Dominica Economic Memorandum." Report #4740-DOM. Washington, D.C., October 28.

———. 1985. "Dominica, Priorities and Prospects for Development." Washington, D.C.

World Trade Organization. 1996a. "United States—The Cuban Liberty and Democratic Solidarity Act." (WT/DS38/1) May 13.

———. 1996b. "United States—The Cuban Liberty and Democratic Solidarity Act." (WT/DS38/2) October 8.

———. 1997. "Denunciations of New Actions Against Cuba In The United States Congress—Communication from Cuba." (WT/L/219) June 18.

World's Women 1995: Trends and Statistics, The. 1996. United Nations, New York.

Wright, John T. 1979. "Human Rights in the West: Political Liberties and the Rule of Law." In *Human Rights: Cultural and Ideological Perspectives,* pp. 19-31. Edited by Adamantia Pollis and Peter Schwab. Praeger Publishers.

Young, Alma H. and Dion E. Phillips, eds. 1986. *Militarization in the Non-Hispanic Caribbean.* Boulder: Lynne Rienner Publishers.

Zivs, Samuil. 1980. *Human Rights: Continuing the Discussion.* Moscow: Progress Publishers.

NEWSPAPERS

Barron's
Caribbean Compass
Caribbean Contact
Democrat for St. Kitts
Financial Times
Gannett Suburban Newspapers

Granma
Grenada Today
Grenadian Voice
Jewish Review
Jewish Standard
Jewish Week
Miami Herald
National Catholic Reporter
New Chronicle (Dominica)
New York Times
Wall Street Journal
Washington Post

Index

acts of repudiation, 144, 148, 168
Adams, John, vii, 164
Adams, John Quincy, vii
Africa, 46, 68, 78, 123, 190n1
African slave trade, 123-4
Agenda: Cuba, 142
Agrarian Reform Law, 82-3, 111
Alarcón, Ricardo, 69, 97, 101, 135, 142, 147, 168, 172-5, 177, 180, 182, 185
Albacete, Lorenzo, 128
Albright, Madeleine, 7, 82, 118, 130
Algeria, 68
Alliance for Progress, 32
Alonso, Alicia, 146, 155, 156
Alpha 66, 134, 144
Alternative Criteria, 149
American Association for World Health, 60-1, 62, 73, 76
American Journal of Public Health, 69
American paranoia, 163-4, 169
Angola, 15, 16, 27, 38, 68, 165, 177, 178
Anguilla, 30, 31
Antigua and Barbuda, 20, 22-6, 30, 31, 40, 48, 50, 190n1, 193n42
  and U.S. military bases, 24
Antilles, Greater, 31, 190n1
Antilles, Lesser, 25, 190n1
architecture, 119-20, 121
Arcos Bergnes, Sebastián, 149
Argentina, ix, 74
Aristide, Jean-Bertrand, 49
Arms and Politics in Latin America, 49
Aron, Raymond, 90
art galleries, 154
Arteaga, Cardinal Manuel, 108
Aruba, 25, 193n42
Asia, 66, 78
Association of Caribbean States, 45, 190n1
Association of Independent Journalists, 149
Austin, Hudson, 23

Bahamas, the, 37, 48, 158, 165, 193n42
Baladrón, Carlos (Auxiliary Bishop), 117
Barbados, 20, 22, 24, 30, 31, 37, 40, 43, 44, 45, 47, 48, 50, 190n1, 193n42, 194n64
Barnet, Miguel, 55
Barron's, 173
Basulto, José, 141
Batista, Fulgencio, vii, 2, 55, 56, 63, 71, 107, 120, 195n20
Batistianos, 108, 181
Bay of Pigs invasion, viii, 88, 109, 112, 115, 133, 134, 135, 138, 165
Beatriz Roque, Marta, 148-9
Belize, 37, 193n42
Benjamin, Medea, 80
Bermuda, 25
Bird, Lester, 24
Bird, Vere C., 24, 25
Bishop, Maurice, 20, 23, 35, 106
Blancaneaux Lodge, 37
Blue Ribbon Commission on the Economic Reconstruction of Cuba, 140
BM Group, 97
Bolivia, 100, 165
Bonaire, 25, 193n42
Bonné Carcasses, Félix, 148
Boodhoo, Ken I., 32
Brazil, 5
Bridgetown, 22, 26
Bristol-Myers Squibb, 94
British Virgin Islands, 25, 193n42
Brothers to the Rescue, 97, 135, 139, 141-2, 144, 147
Brzezinski, Zbigniew, 16
Bush, George, 35, 36, 41, 49, 80, 81, 90, 139, 141
Bush, Jeb, 139

Camnitzer, Luis, 153
Canada, 14, 40, 42, 47, 66, 72, 83, 93, 97, 129-30, 131, 149, 183
Cancún, 48
CANF, *see* Cuban American National Foundation
Capri, Hotel, 133
Caribbean Basin, 190n1
Caribbean Basin Initiative, 32-6, 37, 42, 49
Caribbean Community, *see* Caricom
Caribbean Sea, 36, 89, 121
Caribbean, the, viii, 15, 19, 20, 21, 25, 26, 32, 33, 34, 35, 36-7, 41, 68, 107, 187
Caricom, 38, 42, 43, 44, 45, 190n1
Caricom summit meetings, 43, 44, 45, 47, 48
Caridad Abreus, María, 176
Caritas Cubana, 118

Carter, Jimmy, 1, 2, 14, 16, 17, 18, 38, 45, 96
Casa de las Américas, 154
Casi Todo, 155
Castillo de la Real Fuerza, 154
Castries, 27
Castro, Fidel, viii, xi, 7, 9, 11, 17, 18, 39, 40, 56, 57, 59-60, 87, 91, 94, 95, 114-17, 124, 129, 130, 131, 134, 137, 140, 141, 143, 144, 157, 162, 167, 168, 170, 174, 176, 177, 180, 182, 184, 185, 193n55, 194n59
  and agriculture, 88, 95
  assassination attempts against, viii, 114, 133, 134-5, 137, 171
  and the bourgeois, 111-13
  and the Catholic Church, 40, 104-8, 111-15, 117-19, 123, 126, 127
  as charismatic leader, ix, xii, 104, 109, 162
  as communist statesman, x, 166
  and Cuban Jesuits, 112, 119
  defying the United States, x, 77, 88, 91, 162, 169, 170, 171, 173
  and Eastern Caribbean, 36, 193n55, 194n59
  and elections, 81, 109, 149, 161, 165, 186
  as failed theorist, xi
  and food shortages, xi, 39, 40, 57, 79-101, 122
  and Grenada, 43-4, 45, 194n59
  and health care, xi, 63, 76
  impact on his successors, 172, 182, 186, 187-8
  as independent leader, ix, 88, 162, 164
  as Marxist-Leninist, viii, 109
  and opponents, 114, 133-4, 138, 142, 144-5, 146, 148-52, 157-8
  and his place in history, 131, 169-72, 187-8
  and political dissent, 9, 109, 129, 147
  and political prisoners, 129-30, 131
  and Pope John Paul II, xiii, 70, 103-5, 125-31
  as revolutionary, ix, 57, 78, 88, 106, 163-4, 165, 166, 170, 181, 183
  and rhetoric against U.S., x, 84, 88, 91, 173
  and the Soviet Union, viii, xi, 39, 165
  as theorist, xi
  and the Third World, viii, ix, x, 78, 169
  as Third World spokesperson, x, 11-12, 46, 128, 162, 169
  and the United States, x, xi, 7, 17, 53-4, 78, 88, 90, 91, 125, 161-2, 163-4, 169, 170, 171, 172, 182
  U.S. attempts to unseat, viii-ix, 15, 17, 50, 80, 81-2, 86, 97-8, 134-5, 164-5
Castro, Raúl, 94, 95, 127, 160, 177-8, 179-82, 184, 185
Castro's Final Hour, 170
Catedral de la Habana, 119-20
Caterpillar Corp., 94
Catholic Church, Cuban, 103-20, 126, 198n5
  and its constituency, 108, 109, 114, 115
  opposition to Fidel Castro, 111-15
  pre-Castro, 107-8, 115
  post-1959, 106, 108, 111-15, 117-19, 122-4, 130, 131, 167
  and slavery, 123-4
Catholic relief agencies, 118, 130
Cayman Islands, 37
CBI, *see* Caribbean Basin Initiative
CDA, *see* Cuban Democracy Act
CDRs, *see* Committees for the Defense of the Revolution
Center for Cuban Studies, 146
Central America, 15, 21, 32
Central Planning Council, 110
Centro de Ingeniería Genética y Biotecnología, 65, 67, 68
Charles, Eugenia, 22, 23, 25
Chaviano González, Francisco, 149-50
Chile, 48, 165
Chiles, Lawton, 91
China, People's Republic of, 1, 7, 39, 77, 78, 85, 99, 151, 166, 177, 180
Chomsky, Avi, 39
Chrétien, Jean, 14, 129
CIA, 95, 114, 133, 134, 147, 164, 182
Cienfuegos, 14, 120
Cienfuegos, Camilo, 115
CIGB, *see* Centro de Ingeniería Genética y Biotecnología
cinematography, 156
Clinton, Bill, viii, 15, 41, 42, 43, 45, 46, 47, 49, 70, 72, 77, 81, 90, 91, 101, 130, 135, 169, 183-4
CNN, 159
Coard, Bernard, 23
cold war, 15, 16, 17, 19, 28, 38, 41, 50, 107, 169, 178
Colombia, x, 129, 190n1
Columbus, Christopher, 123
Committees for the Defense of the Revolution, 112-13, 148
Commonwealth Caribbean, 29
Compton, John, 25, 27-8
Concilio Cubano, 142-3
Congo, Democratic Republic of, 27, 77, 151
conservatives, xi, 1, 49-50, 82, 110, 143, 164, 177-80, 182
containment theory, 20, 21, 23, 28-9
Continental Grain Corp., 94
Copacabana Hotel, 133
Coppelia Ice Cream Park, 96
Coppola, Francis Ford, 37
Corriente Agramontista, 142, 148
Costa Rica, 33, 193n42
Council on Foreign Relations (U.S.), 49-50
Council of Ministers, 174

Executive Committee, 174
Council of State, 174, 176, 179
Cozumel, 37
criollo elite, 111
Cuba, vii, viii, xii, 14, 16, 17, 19, 25, 38, 42, 105, 123, 125, 129, 138, 148, 149, 151, 167, 169, 170, 171, 174, 179, 180, 181, 182, 184, 187, 188
and baseball, 157-58
and Black/White relations, 111
and the budget, 61, 66, 74, 76
and the Eastern Caribbean, 31, 32, 35, 40, 41, 45, 46, 48, 166
and the economy, xi, 39-41, 42, 44-5, 47, 71, 82-98, 106, 109, 110, 113, 116-17, 118, 149, 160-1, 166, 168, 171, 175, 176, 180-1, 186-7
and education, 44, 46, 62, 153, 158-60
and the embargo, 13, 15, 48, 68, 69, 73, 79-101, 123, 131, 150, 166, 168, 169
and famine, 82, 87, 90, 99, 100-01
and its food crisis, 39-40, 76, 79-101
and food rationing, 84, 85, 86, 96, 122
and foreign trade, 40, 46, 79, 96, 116
and Grenada, 21, 23, 29, 43-5
and housing, 96-7, 110
and human rights, 6, 7, 8, 9, 10-11, 13, 58-60, 129, 168, 181-2
and hunger, 39, 40, 79, 82, 84, 86, 87, 90, 100, 106, 174, 184
and the media, 136, 152, 159-61
and political dissent, 8-9, 116, 117, 129, 133-62, 168, 180, 186
and political prisoners, 17, 117, 125, 127, 129-30, 136-7, 148-52, 161, 166, 168
and political rights, 7, 8, 17, 116, 151, 161, 162, 166, 168
post-Castro, xiii, 175, 177, 179-82, 184, 187
and prostitution, 40, 87, 89
and racial tension, 111, 141
and religion, 40, 103-31, 166
and rural areas, 55-6, 61
and the Soviet Union, viii, 14, 106, 116, 165
and tourism, 31, 46, 48, 87, 89-90, 93, 119-20, 134, 186, 187
and transportation, 39, 48, 86-7
and the United States, 5, 6, 7, 15-17, 20, 23, 24, 27-8, 50, 53-5, 99, 161-2, 165, 166, 171, 172, 176, 180
and the visual and performing arts, 93, 120, 145, 146, 152-6
Cuba and the Night, 88
Cuba Independiente Y Democratica, 142
Cuba, Permanent Mission to the United Nations, 146, 172, 174
Cuba Update, 61, 146
Cuban agriculture, 39, 47, 56, 71, 79, 80, 82-3, 84, 85, 86, 95, 116
nationalization of, 82-3
Cuban American Committee Research and Education Fund, 82
Cuban American National Foundation, xiii, 41, 88, 133, 137-41, 144, 147, 158, 183, 200n3
Cuban-Americans, 41, 45, 47, 70, 81, 82, 88, 137-47, 167, 168, 172, 180
and violence, 134-6, 142-7
Cuban art gallery network, 154
Cuban Assets Control Regulations, 75
Cuban capitalism, *see* Cuban privatization
Cuban Catholics, 112, 113, 115, 117, 118, 120, 124
see also Catholic Church, Cuban
Cuban child care
and day care centers, 10, 62
and infant mortality, 61, 62
and low birth weights, 73, 85
Cuban Civil Current, 148
Cuban Commission for Human Rights and National Conciliation, 147
Cuban Committee for Democracy, 99, 142-3
Cuban Committee for Human Rights in Cuba, 149
Cuban Communist Party, 76, 87, 95, 111, 115, 117, 118, 136, 148, 159, 176, 177, 179, 181
Central Committee, 176, 178
Politburo, 10, 69, 173, 174, 176, 179
Cuban Communist Party Congress, 175, 177
Cuban constitution, 7, 8, 9, 10, 15, 60, 61, 113, 114, 136, 148, 152, 153, 158, 160, 179
Cuban currency, 89, 94
Cuban Democracy Act, 41, 46-7, 50, 54, 70, 80, 81-2, 85, 87, 97, 136, 139, 166, 183
Cuban dissidents, 134, 136, 137, 147-50
Cuban Exodus Relief Fund, 139
Cuban foreign policy, 14-17, 23, 27, 35-6, 38, 40, 43-8, 50-1, 84, 91, 93-4, 100, 104, 106, 130-1, 162, 165-6, 182
Cuban foreign policy professionals, 173-4
Cuban health care, 10, 54-78, 85, 98, 113, 122, 130, 162, 166, 167, 174-5, 184
and antibiotics, 72
and biotechnology, 60, 61, 67-70, 73, 83
and cancer, 61, 63, 68
and doctor-and-nurse teams, 61
and family doctor program, 61
and HIV/AIDS, *see* HIV/AIDS
and mental health clinics, 63-4, 77, 89
and National Immunization Program, 61: diseases: diphtheria, 61; hepatitis-B, 61, 68; meningitis-B, 61; polio, 61; typhoid fever, 61
and optic and peripheral neuropathy, 74

and Parkinson's disease, 65
and pharmacology, 60, 67-70, 73, 130
and polyclinics, 60, 61
and retinitis pigmentosa, 65, 68
and vitiligo, 68
and waterborne diseases, 72
Cuban hospitals, municipal, 56, 60, 62-3, 67, 69
Calixto Garcia, 62
Celia Sánchez Manduley Rehabilitation Center for Asthmatic Children, 63
Hospital Clinic Quirurgico "Hermanos Ameijeiras", 63
National Oncology Institute, 63
Pando Ferrer Opthalmological Hospital, 74
Cuban hospitals, private, 65-7, 69, 83
Center for Placental Histotherapy, 65, 68
Centro Internacional de Retinosis Pigmentaria Camilo Cienfuegos, 65, 66
International Center for Neurological Restoration, 65
Cuban Human Rights Party, 149
Cuban industry, 39, 56, 71, 79, 83, 93, 95, 97, 116
nationalization of, 82-3
Cuban Institute of Cardiovascular Surgery, 68
Cuban Institute of Hematology, 68
Cuban Interests Section, 9
Cuban labor laws, 92-3, 110
Cuban Liberty and Democratic Solidarity Act, *see* Helms-Burton Act
Cuban medical innovations, 60, 65-6, 68-9, 75, 78
Cuban medical personnel, 60-1, 67-8, 69, 76
Cuban military, viii, 15, 38, 93, 176, 177, 178, 180
Cuban Ministry of Economy and Planning, 95
Cuban Ministry of External Relations, 174
Cuban Ministry of Public Health, 61, 64, 66, 69, 74
Cuban Missile Crisis, xi, 14, 84, 165
Cuban music, 145, 146, 147, 155-6
Cuban navy, 90
Cuban prisons, 148-9
Cuban privatization, 92-6, 116, 120, 166, 168, 175, 181
Cuban reformers, 88, 95, 160, 173-7, 178, 180-2, 185
Cuban security services, 148
Cuban socialism, viii, 95, 109, 136, 153, 164, 176, 179, 182, 187
Cuban taxes, 94, 110, 154
Cuban women, x, 10-11, 178-9
and abortion, 10
and contraception and pregnancy, 10, 62, 64, 77, 85
and economic and social rights, 10-11
and employment, 10
and family planning, 10, 62
and health care, 10, 61, 62, 63, 73, 77, 85
and HIV/AIDS, 64, *see also under* HIV/AIDS
and labor, 10
and military service, 10
and mortality, 61
and National Assembly, 10
and Politburo, 10, 179
and students, 158
Cuban Women's Commission on Employment, 10
Cubas, Joe, 158
Curacao, 25, 193n42
Czech Republic, the, 140
Czechoslovakia, 16

David, Ronan, 191n12
de Beauvoir, Simone, ix
del Pozo Marrero, Omar, 130
del Rosario Diego Bello, Caridad, 176
del Toro Argota, Edelberto, 149
Delgado, Isaac, 146
Delgado, Lorenzo F., 100
Democratic Civic Party, 149
Democratic Party (U.S.), 15, 138
Diáz-Balart, Lincoln, 145
Disarm Education Fund Cuban Medical Project, 74
Dole, Robert, 42, 139
Domínguez, Jorge I., 11
Dominica, 20, 22, 23, 24, 25 26, 30, 31, 33, 40, 48, 50, 190n1, 193n42
Dominican Republic, 2, 33, 48, 49, 122, 165, 190n1, 193n42, 194n64
domino theory, 21, 28-9
Drogería Johnson, 71
drug trafficking, 26, 44, 134, 177
Dulles, John Foster, 53
Duran, Alfredo, 99, 143
Dutch colonies, 25, 193n42

Early Detection Program for Breast and Cervical Cancer, 61
East Europe, 71, 84, 105, 106, 116, 120, 153
East Germany, 85
Eastern Caribbean, 19-51, 170
and agricultural crops, 30, 33, 42, 45
and balance of payments, 30
and Caribbean Basin Initiative, 32-6, 37, 42, 49
and drug smuggling, 26, 43, 44, 50
and economic stagnation, 29-32, 33-4, 36, 37, 42, 43, 48
and emigration, 31-2, 50
and population, 30, 31, 32
and U.S. foreign policy, 19-51
and tourism, 23-4, 26, 31, 36-7

Eastern Caribbean Regional Security System, 22, 23, 25, 27, 40, 41, 43, 45, 48, 190n1
Eastern Caribbean war games, 23
Economist, The, 60
Education, 10, 112, 113, 158-60
Eisenhower, Dwight, viii, 15, 53-4, 77, 111, 135, 169
El Salvador, 33, 34, 35, 133-4, 165, 193n42
embargo, the, viii, xi, xii, xiii, 13, 14-18, 39, 41, 46-9, 54, 63, 66, 69, 70-6, 78, 79-101, 104, 106, 111, 115, 116, 117, 119, 125, 126, 129, 130, 131, 134, 144, 156, 167, 169, 173, 182-8; *see also* Cuba, and the embargo
Enders, Thomas O., 20
Erisman, H. Michael, 50
Espín, Vilma, 10, 178-9
Esso Corp., 110
Ethiopia, 15, 17, 38, 68, 95, 165, 177, 178
Europe, 40, 42, 47, 66, 73, 115, 116, 183
European Union, 99, 173, 183, 184
Executive Office (U.S.), 184
Executive Order (U.S.), viii, 14, 130

Farabundo Martí National Liberation Front, 35
Farber, Sam, 166
FBI, 133, 144
"Federalist Paper No. 10," 6
Federation of Cuban Women, 10, 148, 158-9, 178, 179
Federation of University Students, 159
Fidel: A Critical Portrait, 170
Florida, 25, 53, 90-1, 113, 138, 139, 172, 186
  straits of, 82, 97
Florida Marlins, 157
Ford, Gerald, 15
Fort Bragg, 26
France, 22, 23, 24, 25, 28, 36, 58, 191n12
Francisco Rodríguez, René, 154
Frank, Michele, 61-2, 66, 73
Frei Betto, 198n1
French Antilles, 25, 193n42
French Consulate, Miami, 145, 201n31
Fried, Albert, 170
Fulbright, William, viii
Fuster, José, 146

Galvin, John R., 21
García Márquez, Gabriel, x
Gaza Strip, 152
Gema 4, 146
General Agreement on Tarriffs and Trade (GATT), 99
Geneva, 12, 89
Georgia (U.S.), 133
Gingrich, Newt, 42
"Glasnost," 177
Globalization, 128, 183
God's Bits of Wood, 100
Gómez Manzano, René, 148
Good Neighbor Policy, 32
Gorbachev, Mikhail, 177
Gore, Albert Jr., 139
Graduate Institute of Art, 154
Gran Teatro, 155, 156
Granma, 118, 159
Grantley Adams International Airport, 24
Great Britain, 23, 24, 28-9, 30, 36, 58
Greene, Edward J., 25
Grenada, 20, 21, 22, 24, 25, 26, 29, 30, 35, 40, 42, 43-4, 48, 49, 50, 68, 88, 106, 165
  People's Revolutionary Government, 23
  Revolutionary Military Council, 22
Groth, Carl Johan, 13
Grupo Domos, 97
Guadeloupe, 23, 25, 37
Guantanamera, 8, 156
Guántanamo, 24, 120
Guántanamo Bay, vii, 24, 91
Guatemala, 107, 193n42
Guevara, Che, ix, 78, 108, 110, 115, 127, 155, 181
Gunn, Gillian, 39
Gutiérrez Alea, Tomás, 8, 111, 156

Habana Libre Hotel, 84, 96
Haig, Alexander, 170
Haile Mariam, Mengistu, 38
Haiti, 19, 31, 49, 70, 129, 190n1, 193n42
Haitian refugees, 49
Harmony Movement, 149
Havana, 14, 16, 39, 40, 43, 47, 48, 50, 54, 55, 56, 62, 63, 65, 66, 67, 70-1, 85, 86, 87, 91, 96, 103-4, 107-8, 118, 119-20, 121, 122, 123, 125, 127, 128, 129, 130, 135, 144, 153, 154, 155, 156, 160, 162, 172, 174, 176, 182, 186
Havel, Václav, 140
health care, *see* Cuban health care
Helms-Burton Act, 15, 47, 50, 54, 70, 71, 97, 118, 130, 136, 139, 142, 166, 167, 172, 183, 184
Helms, Jesse, 42, 50, 86, 90, 139, 167
Hemingway, Ernest, 133
Hernández, Alberto, 141
Hernández, Juan Manuel, 154
Hernández, Livan, 157-8
Hernández, Orlando, 157-8
Herter, Christian, 164
Hill, John C. Jr., 164
Hilton Hotel, 89
"History Will Absolve Me" speech, 57
HIV/AIDS, 64-5, 68, 73-4
  and AZT, 73
  and blood supply, 65, 74
  and condoms, 73-4
  and Havana Sanatorium, 65
  and interferon, 73
  and National AIDS Prevention and Control Program, 64

and National AIDS Prevention and Management Commission, 64
and National Blood Bank, 65, 74
and National Center for AIDS education, 65
and Pedro Kourí Institute for Tropical Medicine, 65
and prevention, 65, 73
and sanatoriums, 64-5
statistics, 64
and U.S. embargo, 65, 73-4
Ho Chi Minh, 97
Hobbes, Thomas, 2
Hofstadter, Richard, 163-4
Holocaust, the, 115
"Homeland Belongs to All of Us," 148-9
Honduras, 33, 34, 193n42
Huberman, Leo, ix
human rights, 1-18, 50, 57-60, 76-9, 98-100, 101, 103, 113-15, 116, 125, 126-7, 129, 135, 147-8, 149, 151, 152, 161, 162, 171, 174-5, 182, 186
as economic/social rights, 3, 10-11, 76-8, 113, 129, 136, 161, 181, 187
as political/civil rights, 2-3, 11, 98, 113, 114, 129, 150, 161, 180, 187
socialist perception of, 5, 57-60, 113, 114, 126
Third World perception of, 3, 5, 6, 57-60, 126
Western perception of, 2, 5, 6, 11, 57-9, 77, 78, 81, 98, 180
Human Rights Watch, 135, 145, 148, 150

India, 74
Indonesia, 7, 77, 151, 152, 166
Inglaterra Hotel, 89
INRA, 82, 83, 109, 110, 164
Institute for International Economics, 99
Internal Dissidence Network, 148
International Covenant of Economic, Social and Cultural Rights, 77, 99
International Monetary Fund, 72, 116, 131, 166, 187
Iran, 27
Iran-Contra/Angola, 27-8
Iraq, 151
Isle of Pines, 195n20
Israel, 36, 66, 97, 152, 173
Istanbul, 46
Italy, 85, 134
Iyer, Pico, 88

Jamaica, 23, 24, 25, 31, 42, 44, 48, 68, 165, 190n1, 193n42, 194n64
Japan, 74, 101, 173
Jefferson, Thomas, 6
Jewish community, the, 120-3, 124, 144
Shabbat services, 121
see also under synagogues
Jewish Community Center, 121
Jewish Solidarity, 144
John XXIII, Pope, 115
John Paul II, Pope, x, xiii, 70, 71, 103-6, 118, 128, 129-31, 149
and the embargo, 104, 118, 126, 128, 130, 131
visit to Cuba, 103-4, 125-31
Johnson, Lyndon, viii, 49, 54, 98, 111
José Martí International Airport, 103
José Martí National Commission of Human Rights, 149

Kennedy, John F., viii, 2, 32, 54, 114, 134, 165-6
Kennedy, Robert, viii
Kenya, 77
Key West, 53
King Ranch, the, 56
Kissinger, Henry, 15, 182
Korea, North, 99
Kurdish Turks, 151

La Bodeguita del Medio, 133-4
La Charanga Habanera, 146
Lage, Carlos, 88, 95, 164, 174-6
Lane, William, 94
Laos, 107
Latin America, viii, x, 2, 13, 49, 61, 63, 78, 100, 107, 130, 159, 160, 166, 183, 187
Latin film festival, 145
Leeward Islands, 29, 40, 190n1
left, the, ix, x, 20, 153, 165
Lenin, Vladimir, 179
Levinson, Sandra, 146
liberals, ix, xi, 1, 141, 144-7, 160, 177
Liberia, 77, 152
Lincoln Center, Film Society of, 156
LKB Corp., 74
Locke, John, 2
Lomé trade and cooperation accord, 187
López, Kadir ("Kdir"), 155
Lopez-Nussa, Leonel, 154
Los Angeles, 140
Los Muñequitos de Matanzas, 146
Los Van Van, 146
Luis Sierra, Jorge, 176

Madagascar, 156
Madison, James, 6
mafia, the, vii, 147
Malecón, the, 89
riots on, 90-1
Manifest Destiny, vii, 169
Manuel Valenciaga Díaz, Carlos, 176
Marazul Tours, 145
Mariel boat people, 91
Martí, José, 155
Martínez, Regla, 176
Martinique, 22, 23, 25
Marx, Karl, 4, 178
Marxism, xi, 4, 160, 178
and revolution, 14, 111, 114

Marxist-Leninists, viii, 20, 38, 109, 111, 127, 159, 160, 176, 179
Mas Canosa, Jorge, 88, 137-41, 143, 145-6, 170, 183, 200n3, 201n15
Mas Santos, Jorge, 201n15
Matanzas, 123, 157
Matthews, Herbert L., ix
Máximo Gómez Human Rights Front, 149
Maynard, Charles, 26, 33
McCarthy era, 201n12
McFarlane, Robert, 27
McNamara, Robert, 98
Mead, Walter Russell, 168
media, the, x, 159, 174
Medix Corp., 74
Memories of Underdevelopment, 111
Merck Corp., 74
Mexico, 37, 40, 42, 45, 46, 47, 48, 66, 93, 97, 105, 106, 121, 151, 157, 190n1
Mexico City, 48
Miami, 25, 37, 41, 45, 70, 81, 82, 86, 88, 92, 97, 111, 113, 130, 133, 134, 135, 136, 137, 139, 142, 143, 144, 145, 146-7, 149, 150, 159, 161, 162, 172, 180
  Little Havana, 139, 140-1, 143
Miami exiles, xi, 41, 45, 47, 82, 91, 111, 133-4, 135, 137, 138, 139, 141-7, 150, 151, 162, 186
Middle East, 27, 166
Miller, Tom, 86
Mills, C. Wright, ix, 56
Mitchell, James, 20, 25, 26, 44
Mitchell, Keith, 26, 42, 45, 194n59
  and Cuba, 43-4, 45
  and Fidel Castro, 43-4, 194n59
Mobil Oil Corp., 94
Mobutu Sese Seko, 168
Monroe Doctrine, vii, 20, 29, 48
Monroe, James, vii
Montesquieu, Baron de, 2
Montserrat, 31, 193n42
Morocco, 168
Moscow, 14, 20, 106
Mosquera, Gerardo, 153
MPLA, *see* Popular Movement for the Liberation of Angola
Municipal Assemblies of People's Power, 8
Municipios De Cuba En El Exilio, 142
municipios en el exilio, 142

Nacional Hotel, 89, 133
NAFTA, 42
Nassau, 48
"Nation and Immigration" conference, 144
National Agrarian Reform Institute, *see* INRA
National Arts Schools of Cubanacán, 155
National Assembly of People's Power, 10, 69, 173, 174
National Association of Independent Economists of Cuba, 148
National Ballet of Cuba, 96, 146, 155, 156
National Civic Union, 149
National Commission of Independent Unions, 149
National Council for Civil Rights in Cuba, 149, 150
National Institute of Savings and Loans, 110
National Maternal-Child Program, 61
National Museum of Fine Arts, 154
National Opera Company, 96
National Union for Total Independence of Angola, 27
National Union of Writers and Artists, 176
Netherlands, the, 24, 36
New Art of Cuba, 153
New England Journal of Medicine, 54, 74
New Jersey, 41, 81, 138, 140
New York City, 66, 107, 121, 146-7, 156, 172
New York State, 140
New York Times, The, ix, 44, 159
New York Yankees, 158
New Yorker, The, 168
New Zealand, 85
Newsweek, 159
Ngo Dinh Diem, 107
Nicaragua, 19, 20, 21, 23, 35, 165, 177
  and contras, 35
  and sandinistas, 20, 35
Nigeria, x, 7, 123-4, 152
Nixon, Richard, 14, 53, 163, 165, 182
Noriega, Manuel, 35
North American Congress on Latin America, 34
North American Free Trade Association, *see* NAFTA

Obispo, Calle, 71
Ochoa Sanchez, Arnaldo, 177
Operation Mongoose, 114, 134
Oppenheimer, Andres, 170
Organization of Cuban Educators in Exile, 142
Organization of Eastern Caribbean States, 190n1
Ortega, Cardinal Jaime, 118, 131
Ortega, Daniel, 35

paladares, 92
Pan American Land and Oil Royalty Co., 56
Panama, 5, 19, 35, 151, 165, 193n42
  and Canal Zone, 26
Panama Canal, 24
Paradise Island, 37
Patterson, P. J., 42, 44, 193n55
Pattullo, Polly, 89-90
Pentagon, the, 15
Pepsi Cola, 40
Pérez, Fernando, 156
Peru, 77, 151
Petit Martinique, 26
Philippines, the, 5

Pinar del Río, 39, 87
Pius XII, Pope, 115
Placental Histotherapy Center, 65, 68
Platt Amendment, vii
Plaza de la Catedral, 119-20, 131, 154
Plaza of the Revolution, 127
"Poet and the Revolutionary," 128
Point Four Program, 32
Point Salines International Airport, 45, 194n59
Pointe-à-Pitre, 25
Poland, 103, 105, 126
political rights, 136, 180, 181, 182, 185, 186, 187
 violations of, xi, 77, 136: "anti-social acts",136, 148; "clandestine printing",150; "disrespect to the head of state", 150; "enemy propaganda", 130, 148, 149; "fifth columnists", 177; "high dangerousness", 150; "illicit association", 136, 150; "revealing state security secrets", 130, 150; "spreading enemy propaganda," 130, 136, 150
Pollis, Adamantia, 6, 59
Ponjuán, Eduardo, 154
Popular Movement for the Liberation of Angola, 38
Popular Socialist Party, 109
Portal León, Marcos, 176
Posada Carriles, Luis, 138, 200n3, 201n15
preventive detention, 148, 151
Prieto, Abel, 176
Prieto, Alfredo, 39
Profesionales y Empresarios Cubano-Americanos, 144
Project Orbis, 74
Protestantism, 124-5
Puerto Rico, 24, 37, 74, 133, 190n1

Quinto, Pancho, 146

Radio Martí, 88, 138, 147
Reagan, Ronald, 17, 19, 20, 21, 23, 27, 29, 32, 34, 35, 36, 38, 42, 49, 137, 139, 170
Reed, Gail, 62, 66, 73
Remirez de Estenoz, Fernando, 9, 195n33
Réplica magazine, 144
Republic Steel Corp., 56
Republican Party (U.S.), 15, 41, 81, 138, 145
Restano Díaz, Yndamiro, 149
revolutionary boards, 110
revolutionary tribunals, 108
right, the, xi, 25, 34, 144, 153, 163, 167
Riverio Torres, Otto, 176
Robaina, Roberto, 12-13, 88, 135, 174
Roca, Blás, 148
Roca, Vladimiro, 148
Rodríguez Averoff, Raúl, 174
Rodríguez Parrilla, Bruno, 174
Rome, 105, 125
Roosevelt, Eleanor, 77
Roosevelt, Franklin D., 2, 32
Roosevelt Roads, 24
Rosales del Toro, Ulises, 176, 178
Roseau, 25, 191n12
Rosset, Peter, 80
Rousseau, Jean-Jacques, 2
RSS, *see* Eastern Caribbean Regional Security System
Rubottom, Roy R. Jr., 134, 164
Russia, 39
Rwanda, 151

Saenz Montero, Pedro, 176
St. John's, 26
St. Kitts-Nevis, 20, 22, 26, 30, 31, 32, 33, 40, 48, 50, 190n1, 193n42
St. Lucia, 20, 22, 23, 24, 25, 26, 27-8, 30, 31, 40, 45, 48, 50, 190n1, 192n28, 193n42
St. Maarten, 25, 37, 193n42
St. Martin, 193n42
St. Vincent and the Grenadines, 20, 22, 26, 30, 40, 44, 48, 50, 190n1, 193n42
Salas, Roberto, 154
Salazar, Manning, 146
Sanchez, Nestor D., 21
Sánchez Santa Cruz, Elizardo, 147-8
sandinistas, *see* Nicaragua
Santa Damiana, 87
Santana, Fr. Nelson, 112
Santería, 123-4
Santiago de Cuba, 39, 96, 104, 120, 154
Sartre, Jean-Paul, ix, x, 56, 187
Saudi Arabia, 5, 168
Scali, John, 3-5, 7
Schenck v. United States, 201n12
Schlesinger, Arthur M. Jr., ix
Seaga, Edward, 25
Second Naval Guerrilla Group, 134
Sembene, Ousmane, 100
Serbia, 77
Servimed, 66
Sherritt International Corp., 72, 97
Sierra Maestra, ix, 7, 178
Smaldone, William, 67
Smith Act, the, 201n12
Smith, Earl E.T., 56-7
Smith, Robert C., 111
Smith, Wayne S., 16, 96, 139, 160-1
Social Democratic Party, 148
Socialist Thought, 170
Sodano, Cardinal Angelo, 127-8
Sosua, Jewish community of, 122
Soufrière, 23
Soufrière Hill volcano, 31
South Africa, 27, 68, 100
South America, 32, 66, 125, 190n1
Southeast Asia, 107, 170
Soviet bloc, 50, 71, 79, 80, 115-16, 138, 166, 177

Soviet Union, viii, xi, 1, 14, 16, 20, 28, 37, 38, 39, 42, 79, 83, 84, 85, 106, 111, 115-16, 119, 153, 164, 165, 166, 177, 180, 183, 184
Spain, vii, 46, 93, 123-4, 129, 149
Spanish America, 40
"Special Period in the Time of Peace", 39, 41, 71, 84, 95, 116
Special Service Units, 22, 26
Spellman, Cardinal Frances, 107
SSUs, *see* Special Service Units,
Standard Oil Corp., 56, 110
Statute of the International Court of Justice, 6
Steel, Ronald, 99
Strawberry and Chocolate, 156
Suharto, 166
Summit of the Americas, 48, 187
Suriname, 191
Sweden, 74
Sweezy, Paul M., ix
Swiss embassy, 16
Symphony Space Theater, 146
synagogues, Cuban
  Patronato Synagogue, 120-22
  Shevet Achim, 120
  Temple Adath Israel, 120
Szulc, Tad, 170

Television Martí, 138, 147
Texaco, 94
Texas, 27, 140
Third World, the, 5, 6, 38, 46, 57, 60, 67, 77, 78, 97, 98, 101, 107, 126, 162, 170, 171
Tierra del Fuego, 187
Torres, Nelson, 176
Torricelli, Robert, 41, 81, 82, 90, 139
Tortola, 193n42
Toshiba Corp., 74
trade and investment, U.S. business, 93-4, 125, 140, 173, 180-1, 185, 186, 187
Trading with the Enemy Act, the, 70
travel to Cuba, 48, 70-1, 75-6
Trinidad, 154
Trinidad and Tobago, 20, 40, 190n1, 193n42
Trujillo, Rafael, 2
Truman Doctrine, the, 28-9
Truman, Harry, 28-9, 32
Turkey, 46, 120, 151, 166
26th of July Movement, 108-9, 178

underdevelopment, xi, 103-4, 125, 126, 169
UNESCO and Old Havana, 119
Union of Former Political Prisoners, 134
Union of Pioneers of Cuba, 159
Union of Young Communists, 176
UNITA, *see* National Union for Total Independence of Angola
United Fruit Co., 110
United Jewish Appeal-Federation of New York, 122
United Nations, x, 14, 15, 36, 77, 88, 95, 146, 164, 173, 174
  General Assembly, x, 1, 5, 6, 97, 173, 184
  Security Council, 57
  vote against the embargo, 13, 173
United Nations Commission on Human Rights, 12, 13, 77
United Nations Development Program, 72
United Nations Special Rapporteur on Human Rights in Cuba, 13
United Nations Standard Minimum Rules for the Treatment of Prisoners, 148
United States, vii, x, xi, 14, 40, 42, 45, 56, 74, 88, 91, 98, 99, 100, 104, 116, 120, 123, 127, 130, 133-8, 149, 150, 151, 157, 161-2, 163, 166, 169, 171, 173, 176, 181, 183, 185-7
  attempts to negotiate with Cuba, 15-18
  attempts to overthrow Fidel Castro, viii, ix, 81-2, 97, 101, 114, 134-6, 137, 164-5, 167
  and cold war establishment, 1, 17, 101
  and communism, 28-9, 34, 49-51, 53-4
  and Cuban agriculture, 56
  and the Cuban Catholic Church, 104, 107, 119, 126
  and Cuban domestic policy, vii, 50, 56, 80, 171, 182, 185, 186
  and Cuban health care, 53-78
  and Cuban medicine, 54, 65, 69, 70-6, 90
  and Cuban political prisoners, 129
  and the embargo, viii, xii, 7, 13, 14 15, 17, 18, 21, 39, 41, 48, 49, 54-5, 66, 68, 69, 70-6, 77, 79-101, 106, 111, 117, 119, 126, 130-1, 162, 166, 169, 171, 172, 173, 182-8
  and Fidel Castro, xii, 77, 163-6, 171, 172, 182, 183, 184-5
  and the food crisis, 79-101
  and human rights, 3, 6, 8, 11, 12, 13, 58, 69, 76-8, 114, 165, 181
  and hunger in Cuba, 82, 84, 85, 87, 90
  and political dissent, 129, 151, 185-6
  and starving the Cuban people, 80, 82, 84, 87, 166
  and violation of international law, 47, 98, 99, 134, 171, 183, 184
United States Coast Guard, 91, 133
United States Congress, viii, 14, 15, 16, 17, 21, 41, 42, 47, 81, 90, 167, 184
Universal Declaration of Human Rights, 1, 2, 3, 5, 6, 12, 13, 57-8, 76-7, 81, 98-9, 148, 149, 150
University of Havana,40, 148, 160
University Students Federation, 176
Urban Reform Law, 110, 111
Urrutia, Manuel, 109

U.S. blockade, 12, 41, 47, 54, 55, 69, 164, 193n55
U.S. Bureau of Alcohol, Tobacco, and Firearms, 133
U.S. Central Intelligence Agency, *see* CIA
U.S. Commerce Department, 54, 74, 75
U.S. Constitution, 6
U.S.-Cuba Trade and Economic Council, 125
U.S. Customs Agency, 76, 133
U.S. Declaration of Independence, 6
U.S. Department of Justice, 133, 135, 142
U.S. Department of State, 129, 133, 134, 163, 164
U.S. Department of the Treasury, 66, 70, 75, 145
U.S. dollar, 29, 31, 40, 75, 87, 89, 90, 92, 94, 166
U.S. Embassy, Havana, 165, 203n8
U.S. Federal Aviation Administration, 142
U.S. Forces Southern Command, 21, 25
U.S. foreign policy, 19-51, 53-91, 94, 99, 106, 126, 140, 163-6, 171
  and Africa, 14-15, 27-8, 38
  and Eastern Caribbean, 15, 19-51
U.S. General Accounting Office, 138
U.S. House Subcommittee on Military Construction, 21, 24
U.S. imperialism, 5, 7, 8, 90, 136, 169, 172
U.S. intelligence agencies, 16
U.S. Interests Section, 16, 96, 121
U.S. invasion of Grenada, 22, 24, 25, 26, 34, 43, 49
U.S. invasions, 22, 24, 35, 48-9, 172, 191n6
U.S. marines, 26
U.S. Maritime Enforcement Agency, 133
U.S. military bases, 19-21, 22, 24, 25, 48
U.S. Rubber, Co., 56
U.S. sanctions, 66, 165, 182
U.S. subsidiaries, 46-7, 54, 81
U.S. Virgin Islands, 24, 31, 190n1
USA Engage, 94
U.S.S. Iowa, 25
Uzbekistan, 173

Valdés Vivó, Raúl, 95, 178
Vance, Cyrus, 16, 99
Varadero, 89
Vatican City, xiii, 118
Vatican, the, 104, 105, 106, 118, 127, 128, 129, 130, 136
V. C. Bird International Airport, 24
Vedado, 62, 65, 120, 154
Venezuela, 165, 190n1
  Margarita Island, 133, 135
Vietnam, 97-8, 99, 107, 166, 170, 178
Vietnam War, 97-8
Viñales, 87
Virgin Gorda, 193n42
Visual Arts, 145-7, 152-6, 168
  abstract expressionism, 153
  Afro-Cuban art, 153
  ceramics, 146
  folk art, 153
  graphic art, 155
  installation art, 153
  kitsch art, 153
  papier-mâché, 154
  performance art, 153
  photography, 154, 156
  pop art, 86, 155
  representational art, 153
  street art, 86, 154
Voice of America, 138

Wall Street Journal, The, 159
Wang Dan, 151
Washington, ix, 7, 13, 14, 16, 26, 27, 28, 32, 42, 43, 48, 50, 53, 61, 75, 77, 82, 91, 101, 104, 126, 130, 134, 136, 138, 139, 141, 147, 152, 158, 162, 165, 166, 167, 169, 170, 172, 173, 181, 182, 184, 186
West Bank, 152
West Indies, 19, 37, 38, 190n1
  Americanization of, 37-8
  Western dominance, 36-7
  Western tourism, 31, 37-8
Westchester County Hispanic-American Republican Committee, 100
Western Hemisphere, 20, 49, 169
Windward Islands, 29, 40, 190n1
"Within the Revolution everything; outside the Revolution, nothing," 9, 108, 153
World Bank, 72, 116, 166, 187
World Trade Organization, 42, 47, 89, 184
World War II, 28
Wright, John T., 2

Yeltsin, Boris, 140
Yemen, 68
Yoruba, the, 123
Young Communist League, 159, 178
Yukon, the, 187

Zaire, 27, 168
  see also Congo, Democratic Republic of
Zimmer, Richard, 81